D0982230

Chinese Comfort Wome

Chinese Comfort Women

Testimonies from Imperial Japan's
Sex Slaves

Peipei Qiu, with Su Zhiliang
and Chen Lifei

OXFORD
UNIVERSITY PRESS

OXFORD
UNIVERSITY PRESS

Oxford University Press is a department of the
University of Oxford. It furthers the University's objective
of excellence in research, scholarship, and education
by publishing worldwide.

Oxford   New York
Auckland   Cape Town   Dar es Salaam   Hong Kong   Karachi
Kuala Lumpur   Madrid   Melbourne   Mexico City   Nairobi
New Delhi   Shanghai   Taipei   Toronto

With offices in
Argentina   Austria   Brazil   Chile   Czech Republic   France   Greece
Guatemala   Hungary   Italy   Japan   Poland   Portugal   Singapore
South Korea   Switzerland   Thailand   Turkey   Ukraine   Vietnam

Oxford is a registered trade mark of Oxford University Press
in the UK and certain other countries.

Published in the United States of America by
Oxford University Press
198 Madison Avenue, New York, NY 10016

First issued as an Oxford University Press paperback, 2014

Library of Congress Cataloging-in-Publication Data

Qiu, Peipei, 1954–
   Chinese comfort women : testimonies from imperial Japan's sex slaves /
Peipei Qiu, with Su Zhiliang and Chen Lifei.
      pages cm – (Oxford oral history series)
      Includes bibliographical references and index.
      ISBN 978-0-19-937389-5 (pbk.)

   1. Comfort women – China – History. 2. Comfort women – China – Biography.
3. Sino-Japanese War, 1937-1945 – Women – China. 4. Sino-Japanese War, 1937-1945 – Atrocities.
5. Japanese – China – History – 20th century. 6. Soldiers – China – History – 20th century.
7. Women – Crimes against – China – History – 20th century. 8. Abduction – China – History –
20th century. 9. Prostitution – China – History – 20th century. 10. Sex crimes – China –
History – 20th century. I. Su, Zhiliang. II. Chen, Lifei, 1959- III. Title.

DS777.533.W65Q58 2014
940.53'51086949 – dc23   2014002189

1 3 5 7 9 8 6 4 2

Printed in the United States of America
on acid-free paper

For those who suffered in the war

Contents

Figures and Tables

Figures

(All photographs taken by the collaborating researchers of this book.)

Tables

Abbreviations

AWF	Asian Women's Fund
CCP	Chinese Communist Party
CPPCC	Chinese People's Political Consultative Conference
IMTFE	International Military Tribunal for the Far East
NGO	non-governmental organization
NPC	National People's Congress
JWRC	Center for Research and Documentation on Japan's War Responsibility
POWs	prisoners of war
RQHZD	*Riben qinlüe Huabei zuixing dangan: Xingbaoli* [Documented war crimes during Japan's invasion of north China: Sexual violence]
RQHZS	*Riben qinlüe Huabei zuixing shigao* [A history of atrocities: Japan's invasion of northern China]
TXX	*Tietixiade xingfeng xueyu: Rijun qin-Qiong baoxing shilu* [Bloody crimes of the occupation rule: Records of the atrocities committed by the Japanese military in Hainan]
TXXX	*Tietixiade xingfeng xueyu: Rijun qin-Qiong baoxing shilu, Xu* [Sequel to Bloody crimes of the occupation rule: Records of the atrocities committed by the Japanese military in Hainan]
VAWW-NET	Violence against Women in War Network
WAM	Women's Active Museum on War and Peace

Acknowledgments

This book would not have been possible without the assistance and support of many people and institutions, and to them we are deeply indebted. First and foremost, we express our gratitude for and admiration of the twelve Chinese women who courageously came forward and described their experiences in the Japanese military "comfort stations" and their continued suffering after the war: Chen Yabian, Huang Youliang, Lei Guiying, Li Lianchun, Lin Yajin, Lu Xiuzhen, Tan Yuhua, Yin Yulin, Yuan Zhulin, Wan Aihua, Zhou Fenying, and Zhu Qiaomei. Giving us their permission to publish their narratives in English makes a vital page of history accessible to a larger portion of the world.

During our research and writing, numerous people assisted us with field investigations, interviews, and research; although we are immensely grateful to all of them, it is impossible to mention each by name here. From that prodigious list we acknowledge, in particular, the kind assistance of: Cheng Fei, adopted daughter of Yuan Zhulin; Cheng Shaochan of the Research Center for Chinese "Comfort Women"; Chen Houzhi at the Nanmao Farm, Baoting County, Hainan Province; Chen Zuliang, independent researcher in Baoshan City, Yunnan Province; Fu Heji of the Hainan Province People's Consultative Committee Historical Archives; Gao Yulan, daughter of Li Lianchun; Hu Yueling, director of Tianzi Township Cultural Centre, Hainan Province; Jiang Weixun, son of Zhou Fenying; Li Guiming, independent researcher in Yu County, Shanxi Province; Sha Bilu, director of the Baoshan City Longyang District Bureau of Local History and Gazetteer, Yunnan Province; Su Guangming, president of Lingshui County People's Consultative Committee, Hainan Province; Tang Guoqiang, adopted son of Lei Guiying; Tan Maoxiang, son of Tan Yuhua; Wang Anzhang, stepson of Lu Xiuzhen; Zhang Xuefang, daughter-in-law of Li Lianchun; and Zhou Xie, son of Zhu Qiaomei. We also sincerely thank Chen Junying, professor of Japanese at Zhanjiang Normal University; Arimitsu Ken, coordinator of the International Solidarity Council Demanding Settlement of Japan's Past; and Zhu Chunli of the Palace Museum, who kindly sent Japanese materials from their own collections to facilitate the writing of this book. And we thank Yue Zhang, who helped to bring Chinese materials from China to the United States. The East Asian librarians at Columbia University, Dr. Chengzhi Wang, Dr. Sachie Noguchi, and Ms. Ria Koopmans-de Bruijn, have been extremely helpful to our research, and to them we extend our deep appreciation. Lastly, we are also deeply grateful to Ms. Barbara Durniak at Vassar College Library and Ms. Amanda Thornton at the Grants Office for their tireless assistance. We thank our student assistants at the Shanghai Normal University as well as Xuan Liu, Sally DeWind, Maria Ichizawa, and Charlotte Ong at Vassar College. Their help over the years has been extremely valuable. We also acknowledge Vassar College graduates Lesley Richardson's senior thesis research on the "comfort women" redress movement in South Korea and Japan and Leann Peterson's work in translating the first draft of Zhu Qiaomei's account.

This volume is informed by and built on a huge number of studies regarding the "comfort women" issue: to all the authors of the publications listed in the bibliography of this book we are indebted and we offer our thanks. We express heartfelt appreciation to attorney Kang Jian, legal counsel for three of the four Chinese "comfort women'" lawsuits, who spent much time answering our questions and providing consultations. We thank Professor Emeritus Utsumi Aiko of Keisen University and Osaka University of Economics and Law; Professor Emeritus Ishida Yoneko of Okayama University; and Eriko Ikeda, head of the Women's Active Museum on War and Peace, for their invaluable help and advice pertaining to our research on the "comfort women" issue in Japan. We extend our deep thanks to the following individuals, who generously take time out of their busy schedules to read this manuscript at different stages and who provided invaluable comments: to Professor Lizabeth Paravisini-Gebert of Vassar College for her warm support and advice throughout the writing of the book; to Professor Seungsook Moon and Professor Katherine Hite of Vassar College for sharing their expertise on gender politics, social movements, and memory studies and for contributing extremely constructive suggestions; to Professor Jin Jiang of East China Normal University for facilitating this collaborative project and providing constructive suggestions; to Professor Karen L. Thornber of Harvard University for her insightful comments and enthusiastic support; to Dr. Lingling Sun of the Institute of Japanese Studies, Chinese Academy of Social Sciences, for carefully reading and rereading the early draft of the manuscript and for checking the discussion of legal issues concerning Chinese "comfort women's" lawsuits; to Ken Arimitsu, coordinator of the International Solidarity Council Demanding Settlement of Japan's Past, for his consultations and helpful information; to Professor John Joseph Ahern and Professor Bryan W. Van Norden of Vassar College for their insights and encouragement; to Ms. Ning Gu, senior research fellow at the Institute of World History, Chinese Academy of Social Sciences, and Dr. Wei Li, director of the Institute of Japanese Studies, Chinese Academy of Social Sciences, for reading and commenting on the manuscript; to Dr. Susan Jinxia Sun of AkzoNobel, for her unfailing support and incisive comments; and to Professor Fubing Su and Professor Yu Zhou of Vassar College for their particularly stimulating conversations on Chinese "comfort women" and for their helpful suggestions. We also thank Professor Jonathan Chenette, Dean of Faculty of Vassar College, for his suggestion regarding the foreword, and Professor Hiromi Tsuchiya Dollase, Professor Diane Harriford of Vassar College, and Yan Wang of Bridgewater Associates for reading and commenting on parts of the manuscript. The comments and suggestions of the publisher's anonymous readers led to a greatly improved manuscript, and we are deeply grateful.

Our special thanks to Linda Wood, administrative assistant to the Department of Computer Science at Vassar College, for tirelessly checking manuscript drafts and offering warm support throughout the entire writing process. Many thanks also to journalist Fang Yuqiang of Xinmin News for allowing us to take a picture of the 1937 Japanese map, which has the Dayi (Daiichi, in Japanese) "comfort station" in Shanghai clearly marked, and to postdoctoral researcher Wu Junfan at the Shanghai Normal University, who produced an early version of the map of the "comfort station" locations where the twelve women whose stories are related in this volume were enslaved. And we thank Mr. Steven Cavallo; Mr. James Rotundo; and Mr. Jason Kim of Palisades Park, New Jersey, for providing information about the "comfort women" monument in their borough.

The publication of this book owes an immense amount to the professional help of Emily Andrew, senior acquisitions editor; Megan Brand, editor; and Joanne Richardson, copy editor; at UBC Press.

This study was supported by the Emily Abbey Fund and a Class of 2005 gift fund from Vassar College, and the field research was partly funded by Shanghai Normal University. The publication of this book is supported by the Government of Canada (through the Canada Book Fund), the British Columbia Arts Council, and the Susan Turner Fund granted by Vassar College. To these fund donors and institutions we express sincere gratitude.

Last, but not least, we thank our families. Their long-lasting, unconditional support strengthened us as we engaged in research and completed this important project.

Foreword

Liu Mianhuan's parents had several children before she was born but none of them survived, so little Mianhuan, as the only child, was the very life of the family. However, before turning sixteen, Liu Mianhuan was abducted, before her mother's eyes, into the Imperial Japanese Army's stronghold, where she was kept captive and became one of the soldiers' "comfort women." More than half a century later, the traumatic experience was still too painful to speak about. When recounting that horror Liu Mianhuan cried.

I grew up in Yangquan Village, Yu County of the Shanxi Province. My family was not very rich, but we didn't have any financial worries either. We lived a comfortable life before the war started.

In the year I was to turn sixteen, a unit of Japanese troops came and surrounded our village. It was springtime when the tender leaves of willows and elm trees were delicious. The weather was good, so my father went to the fields for farm work after breakfast. My mother and I were sitting at home when we heard a man shout: "Go to a meeting! Go to a meeting!" Later I learned that this man was the Japanese troops' interpreter. The soldiers drove all the villagers to the meeting place where there were haystacks and, after forcing everyone to squat down, they began to pick girls out of the crowd. A Japanese military man who was about thirty years old stopped in front of me and stared at my face. I heard the local collaborators call him "Duizhang" [commanding officer]. The Duizhang said something to the interpreter, who then turned to me, saying: "You look very pretty." They then pulled me out. The soldiers trussed me up tightly and forced me and two other girls to go with them. My mother cried her heart out and tried to stop them, but she was pushed aside. I refused to go and struggled. The soldiers beat me fiercely. Their heavy beating severely injured my left shoulder, and even to this day I still have trouble moving it.

We walked for about three or four hours under the soldiers' guard to the Japanese military stronghold in Jingui Village, where we were confined in cave dwellings. Several military men raped me that day. They hurt me so much, and I was so scared that I wished I could find a hole in the ground to hide myself. From that day on, the Japanese troops raped me every day. Each day at least five or six men would come, and the Duizhang usually came at night. At that time I was not sixteen yet and hadn't had menstruation. The torture made my private parts infected and my entire body swollen. The pain in my lower body was excruciating to the point that I could neither sit nor stand. Since I could not walk, when I needed to go to the latrine I had to crawl on the ground. What a living hell!

The Japanese troops had local people send me a bowl of corn porridge twice a day. They also had the local collaborators guard the door of the cave dwelling where I was detained so that I could not escape. But given my health at the time I wouldn't have been able to run away even if there was no guard. I wanted to die but that would have saddened my parents, so I told myself not to die but to endure.

A person who was my relative lived in Jingui Village. Upon hearing about my detention, he rushed to Yangquan Village to tell my parents. In order to raise money to ransom me my father sold the entire flock of our sheep, which had been my family's source of livelihood, for one hundred silver dollars. He brought the money to the Japanese troops in Jingui Village. My father later told me that he knelt down to kowtow, begging the Japanese officers to let his daughter go home, but the officers wouldn't pay attention to him. Then he begged the interpreter to explain that as soon as my illness was cured he would send me back. By that time I had been confined in the military strong-hold for over forty days and became very sick. Perhaps the Japanese troops concluded that I was too weak to service the soldiers, they eventually took the money and released me.

I could not stop wailing when I saw my father. I could not move, so my father placed me on the back of a donkey and carried me home. Although I returned home the fear of the Japanese soldiers' assault haunted us every day, so my father made a cellar and hid me in it. Sure enough, the Japanese soldiers came again a few months later. I barely escaped the second abduction by hiding in the cellar.

Liu Mianhuan's hometown in Yu County was occupied by the Imperial Japanese Army from 1938 to 1945. Located at the border region between the Japanese occupied area and the bases of the Chinese resistance forces, Yu County was devastated by the occupation army's frequent mop-up operations during the war, and a large number of local women became the victims of the troops' sexual violence. Liu Mianhuan's constant fear of military assault was finally lifted when the war ended, but the trauma and poverty resulting from it continued, causing her pain for the rest of her life. Liu Mianhuan died on 12 April 2012.

Liu Mianhuan was one of many Chinese women forced to become sex slaves for the Imperial Japanese Army during Japan's invasion of China, but for decades the socio-political environment kept them silent, and their sufferings were excluded from the heroic postwar narratives of their nation-state. Only in the past two decades, inspired by the "comfort women" redress movements in South Korea and Japan and supported by Chinese citizens, researchers, and legal specialists, have these Chinese survivors begun to tell their stories. Being nationals of Imperial Japan's major enemy, Chinese "comfort women" were ruthlessly brutalized in the military "comfort facilities," and their stories reveal the most appalling aspects of Imperial Japan's system of military sexual slavery. Yet, until recently, their stories, told only in Chinese, have been largely unknown to the rest of the world.

Since former "comfort women" from different countries broke their silence to tell their stories in the early 1990s, attempts to erase these stories from public memory have never ceased. Recently, two delegations of Japanese officials attempted to remove a small "comfort women" monument from the United States – an incident that drew international attention. The monument, a brass plaque on a block of stone, was dedicated in 2010 at Palisades Park, New Jersey. The dedication reads:

> In memory of the more than 200,000 women and girls who were abducted by the armed forces of the government of imperial Japan, 1930's-1945.
>
> Known as "comfort women," they endured human rights violations that no peoples should leave unrecognized. Let us never forget the horrors of crimes against humanity.

According to its designer, Steven Cavallo, he began his work on "comfort women" in 2008 when he held a solo exhibit that displayed scenes depicting the Holocaust, Japanese internment camps, homeless Vietnam veterans, and "comfort women." People of diverse cultural backgrounds contributed to the erection of the monument, including a Japanese artist. On 6 May 2012, four Japanese Diet members visited Palisades Park and asked the local administration to remove the monument, asserting: "There is no truth (to the claim that) the army organized the abduction."[1] The request was firmly rejected by Mayor James Rotundo and Deputy Mayor Jason Kim, but soon after that a petition was created on the White House's official website, launching a campaign for signatures to ask the Obama administration to "remove the monument and not to support any international harassment related to this issue against the people of Japan."[2] The campaign resulted in over twenty-eight thousand signatures within a month. Reportedly, the massive number of signatures came mostly from Japan, and the petition was advertised in Japan on the websites of Japanese activists and lawmakers, including two Diet members who were part of the delegation that visited New Jersey.[3]

This international controversy concerning the commemoration of "comfort women" underscores the power of memory and the importance of having their stories told. Seventy years after the event, people in Japan and the world are still struggling with what happened to "comfort women" during the Asian War. For many of us who were born after the war, the sufferings of "comfort women" are remote and hard to believe; it often seems to be easier to set them aside or, at the very least, to assign them to the past. However, suffering of such magnitude should not, and cannot, be dismissed. What we choose to recognize and to remember from the past not only affects our present but also shapes our future.

The point of telling the stories of "comfort women" is not to disgrace the people of Japan, any more than the point of commemorating the victims of the Holocaust and the atomic bomb is to disgrace the people of Germany and the United States. Rather, it is to facilitate mutual understanding between Japanese people and their Asian neighbours. Dismissing the sufferings of individual lives in the name of national honour is not only wrong but also dangerous: it is a ploy that nation-states have used, and continue to use, to drag people into war, to deprive them of their basic rights, and to abuse them. To those who genuinely hope to resolve the problems associated with Imperial Japan's wartime "comfort women" and to come to terms with the trauma of the past, it is essential to transcend the posturing of the nation-state and to recognize that the suffering wrought by war is a violation of human life. Only by recognizing the sufferings of "comfort women" can we begin to understand the reality of the wartime "comfort stations" and the nature of the military "comfort women" system. As Diana Lary, Stephen MacKinnon, Timothy Brook, and others show in their studies of the history of China's Resistance War, in order to truly understand what happened in the past, it is necessary to recognize the fact that suffering is history's main subject, not just its byproduct.[4]

It is in the hope of facilitating a fuller understanding of the sufferings of the hundreds of thousands of women whose lives were ravaged by military sexual violence that this book records the stories of Chinese "comfort women" and tells how their agony is remembered by people in Mainland China, one of the major theatres of the Second World War.

Chinese Comfort Women

Introduction

This is the first English-language monograph to record the memories of Chinese women who were detained by the Japanese military at "comfort stations" during Japan's invasion of China.[1] Across Asia, from the early 1930s to 1945, Japanese imperial forces coerced hundreds of thousands of women, to whom they referred as "comfort women," into military "comfort stations" and subjected them to repeated rapes. The term "comfort women" is an English translation of the Japanese euphemism *ianfu*. Given the striking contrast between the dictionary meaning of the word "comfort" and the horrific torture to which these women were subjected in the Japanese military "comfort women" system, "comfort women" and "comfort station" are clearly inappropriate terms. Yet, since the 1990s, these terms, on which decades of international debate, historical research, and legal discourses are mounded, have become widely recognized as referring specifically to the victims and institutions of the Japanese military's system of sexual slavery. For this reason, we use these terms, hereafter, in the interest of readability, omitting the quotation marks.

Information about comfort women appeared sporadically in memoirs, novels, artwork, magazine articles, film, and a few monographs after Japan's defeat,[2] but only with the rise of the comfort women's redress movement in the early 1990s did the issue receive worldwide attention and become a highly politicized international debate.[3] This movement, initiated by South Korean and Japanese scholars and women's groups engaging in feminist and gender issues and internationalized by the support and participation of transnational non-governmental organizations (NGOs), researchers, legal specialists, and an upsurge of media attention, created a public sphere in which comfort station survivors were able to come forward and share their wartime memories.

English Publications of the Survivors' Narratives

In 1991, seventy-four-year-old South Korean survivor Kim Hak-sun (1924-97) stepped forward to testify as a former comfort woman. Since then, an increasing number of comfort station survivors have come forward to speak about their wartime experiences. The survivors' narratives provide first-hand accounts of the reality of the Japanese military comfort stations and are essential to our understanding of the comfort women issue. Over the past two decades researchers in different countries have made tremendous efforts to record and to publish the survivors' personal narratives and to make them available in English for an international community. Among the comfort women's personal stories published in English, two autobiographical books by former comfort women have been widely read: *50 Years of Silence* (1994) by Jan Ruff-O'Herne, a Dutch descendant born in the former Dutch East Indies (now Indonesia), and *Comfort Woman: Slave of Destiny* (1996) by Maria Rosa Henson, a Filipina. Both reveal in compelling detail the anguish of being detained as the sex slaves of Japanese troops during the Asia-Pacific War. Around the same period the accounts of Korean and Filipina victims were published in the mission report of the International Commission of Jurists in *Comfort Women: An Unfinished Ordeal* (1994),[4] just before three influential UN investigative reports characterized the comfort women system as military sexual slavery.[5] The intolerable abuse of comfort women revealed by these investigative reports made a huge impact on the world. In 1995, a collection of nineteen personal stories from former South Korean comfort women, originally published in Korean by the Korean Council for the Women Drafted for Military Sexual Slavery by Japan and the Research Association on the Women Drafted for Military Sexual Slavery by Japan, was translated into English and published in Keith Howard's edited volume, *True Stories of Korean Comfort Women*. The first collection of its kind to be translated into English, this volume offers the collective voices of a group of Korean comfort women who powerfully challenge the official war stories of the nation-states. Since the mid-1990s, more books written in English have offered testimonial accounts by former comfort women, notably Chungmoo Choi's edited volume, *The Comfort Women: Colonialism, War, and Sex* (*positions: east asia cultures critique* 5/1 [special issue]); Dae-sil Kim-Gibson's *Silence Broken: Korean Comfort Women*, a volume accompanying her award-winning documentary film, which includes thirty-six minutes of testimonies from former Korean comfort women; *Comfort Women Speak: Testimony by Sex Slaves of the Japanese Military*, a collection of translated interviews conducted by the Washington Coalition for Comfort Women Issues and edited by Sangmie Choi Schellstede; and *War Crimes on Asian Women: Military Sexual Slavery by Japan during World War II – The Case of the Filipino Comfort Women*, edited by Nelia Sancho and published by Asian Women Human Rights Council.[6] At the same time, excerpts of the survivors' accounts have been included in scholarly monographs and trade books.[7] The comfort women's personal narratives and the scholarly effort to integrate them into international discourse played a vital role in exposing the true nature of the Japanese military comfort women system and the transnational struggle for "memory change."[8] They not only fundamentally subverted the existing social, political, and patriarchal narratives justifying the objectification of women and the link between war and sexual violence but also moved people of the world to care about the comfort women issue and the principle of humanity it involves.

As more and more comfort station survivors' narratives entered the international discourse, the voices of Chinese victims were noticeably lacking. As seen above, the major oral history projects in English have taken testimonial accounts mostly from comfort women who had been drafted from Japan's colonies and the Pacific Islands. Although some scholarly and journalistic works also include excerpts of survivors' personal accounts, few are from Chinese women. This situation seriously impeded a full understanding of this complicated issue.

Key Debates

One of the key debates about the comfort women phenomenon concerns whether the Japanese military forced women into the comfort stations. When South Korean victims first stepped up to testify, the Japanese government denied any Japanese military involvement in forcing women into comfort stations. It held this position until history professor Yoshimi Yoshiaki unearthed Japan's official war documents in 1992. Since then, progressive scholars and legal experts in Japan have played an important role in supporting the comfort women redress movement. In 2007, based on nearly two decades of research, the Center for Research and Documentation on Japan's War Responsibility (JWRC), which is affiliated with most of the Japanese researchers who are working on Japan's war responsibilities, issued the "Appeal on the Issue of Japan's Military Comfort Women." The appeal reiterates, "the former Japanese Army and Navy created the comfort women system to serve their own needs; the military decided when, where, and how 'comfort stations' were to be established and implemented these decisions, providing buildings, setting regulations and fees, and controlling the management of comfort stations; and the military was well aware of the various methods used to bring women to comfort stations and of the circumstances these women were forced to endure." It concludes: "While licensed prostitution in Japan may be called a de facto system of sexual slavery, the Japanese military comfort women system was literal sexual slavery in a far more thorough and overt form."[9]

Outside Japan, scholars, legal specialists, and human rights advocates from different countries have also treated Japan's wartime comfort women system as forced prostitution and military sexual slavery.[10] Until recent years, however, Japanese officials continued to insist that there is no documentary evidence to prove direct government or army involvement in taking females by force to frontline brothels.[11] Outside government circles, conservative writers and neo-nationalist activists argue that comfort women were professional prostitutes working in warzone brothels run by private agencies and that neither the state nor the military forced them to be there.[12]

In discussing sexual violence in armed conflicts, Nicola Henry points out that "the establishment of comfort stations across Asia and the label of 'military prostitutes' had the effect of morally reconstructing the reprehensible act of sexual enslavement into complicit victim participation and collaboration," creating a persistent judicial obstacle to women seeking justice in both domestic and international jurisdictions.[13] Indeed, the diverse ways in which comfort women were recruited, and their varied experiences in the comfort stations, have not only been used by Japanese rightists and conservatives to deny military sexual slavery but have also led some sympathetic scholars to question whether or not the comfort women system can be characterized in this way. In her recent book, C. Sarah Soh, for example, disagrees with the "sweeping characterization offered by progressive Japanese historians, such as 'officially recognized sexual violence' and 'a systematic and comprehensive structure of military sexual slavery.'"[14] Highlighting the diverse ways Korean and Japanese comfort women were recruited and their varied experiences in the comfort stations, she considers it to be "partisan prejudice" to define comfort stations as "rape centers."[15] Soh's book contributes to the ongoing discussion on the subject by locating the comfort women's tragedy not only in the context of Japan's aggressive war but also in the broader social, historical, and cultural contexts that have sustained "gendered structural violence" against women.[16] However, as indicated by its title, it does not discuss the experiences of comfort women drafted from occupied countries,[17] especially China, whereas recent research in China suggests that Chinese women accounted for about half of the estimated total of 400,000 victims of the military comfort women system.[18]

Untold Stories

Chinese comfort women, the majority of whom were abducted and detained by Japanese troops in warzones and occupied areas, suffered extremely brutal treatment coupled with a high mortality rate. In many ways, this was due to the widespread belief among Japanese troops that the vicious treatment of enemy nationals was an expected and acceptable part of the war effort. Many Chinese comfort women died as a direct result of abuse or untreated illness; others were brutally killed as punishment for attempting to escape, as amusement for the Japanese soldiers, or simply to destroy the evidence of crimes committed by the military. Unlike the comfort women drafted from Japan and its colonies, who occasionally figure in Japan's wartime documents, those Chinese comfort women kidnapped randomly by Japanese troops are rarely mentioned. In addition, the Japanese military's deliberate destruction of relevant documents at the end of the Second World War,[19] along with the lack of a thorough investigation on the part of the Chinese government and the International Military Tribunal for the Far East (IMTFE) immediately after the war, also increased the difficulty of current investigations into Chinese comfort women. Since the end of the war, socio-political oppression has kept the few survivors silent. The small number of Chinese women who survived the comfort stations were often regarded by the authorities and citizens of their own country as immoral women who had served the nation's enemy. Some were subjected to criminal investigations and suffered further persecution under various political movements such as the notorious "Cultural Revolution." The strong influence of the Confucian tradition in Chinese society also contributed to the long silence of former comfort women. Confucian social conventions demand that, at all costs, a female remain a virgin until marriage, even if that means risking her life; hence, a survivor of rape was deemed impure and was regarded as a disgrace to her family. Even today, although the socio-political environment has changed tremendously in China and the former comfort women's struggle for redress has evolved (having begun in Korea and Japan) into an international movement, many of the Chinese comfort station survivors are reluctant to admit to having been raped by Japanese troops. Among those who have stepped forward to testify, some are still hesitant to have their stories published.

In postwar China the plight of former comfort women is not the only wartime tale of suffering that, until recently, has remained untold. Diana Lary and Stephen MacKinnon note that, although China's War of Resistance during the first half of the twentieth century was the worst period of warfare in the country's history, and that it resulted in immense destruction and loss of life, in China there is "a reticence verging on denial when it comes to discussing the slaughter," and "Chinese press coverage of Japanese atrocities was consistently low key on both sides of the Taiwan straits."[20] They observed: "The Guomindang (GMD)[Nationalist Party] government on Taiwan has found it difficult to deal with the events that occurred in the process of its own defeat by the Japanese" and "the Communist Party is vulnerable to comparisons: the examination of suffering caused by the Japanese might lead to an examination of the self-inflicted suffering of the Cultural Revolution."[21] Because various socio-political factors combined to keep the victims silent for a long period of time after the Second World War, the comfort women's individual memories were excluded from the nation-state's heroic postwar narrative.

New Research in China

Inspired by the redress movement for comfort women initiated in Korea and Japan, research on the comfort woman issue emerged in China in the early 1990s as a grassroots movement. Since then, independent researchers and activists have carried out investigations. Earlier, most Korean and Japanese researchers, basing their work on documents that had been unearthed and testimonies supplied by comfort station survivors, had estimated that the Japanese military had detained between thirty thousand and 200,000 women during the war.[22] The early estimations, however, do not reflect the large number of Chinese comfort women. Recent findings by Zhiliang Su and Chinese researchers suggest that, from the Japanese army's occupation of the Manchurian area in northeastern China in 1931 to Japan's defeat in 1945, approximately 400,000 women were forced to become military comfort women and that at least half of them were Chinese.[23]

Since the mid-1990s, testimonies by former Chinese comfort women as well as a large number of studies have been published in Chinese; however, beyond a few reports included in Japanese publications, little has been made available to non-Chinese-speaking audiences. The unavailability of information about Chinese comfort women is a serious problem in the current study of the comfort women issue. Because Chinese women comprised one of the largest ethnic groups among comfort women, and because they, as Japan's enemy nationals, received unimaginably brutal treatment in the hierarchically structured military comfort women system, an accurate explication of the scope and nature of that system cannot be achieved without a thorough examination of their experiences.

The Contribution of this Book

Chinese Comfort Women: Testimonies from Imperial Japan's Sex Slaves intends to help fill the aforementioned information gap by providing a set of personal accounts of former Chinese comfort women and by introducing Chinese research findings to the international community. The comfort station survivors' personal narratives and the connection between the proliferation of comfort stations and the progression of Japan's aggressive war in China clearly show the militaristic nature of the comfort women system and the Japanese military's direct involvement in kidnapping, sexually exploiting, and enslaving women. While Japanese military leaders maintained that the purpose of setting up the comfort stations was to prevent the mass rape of local women and the spread of venereal disease among soldiers, the systematic implementation of the comfort facilities for the soldiers' sexual comfort, and the use of hundreds of thousands of women as the means of conveying that comfort, in fact institutionalized mass rape. The twelve women whose experiences are related here were all forced to become military comfort women when Japanese forces occupied their hometowns. These women are from different regions of China, from northern Shanxi Province to southernmost Hainan Island, from metropolitan Shanghai to a mountain village in Yunnan Province, thus indicating the vast scope of victimization. Without doubt, their narratives, corroborated by both regional wartime history and the testimonies of local witnesses, reveal that the comfort women system was a form of military sexual slavery and, as such, a war crime.

The experiences of Chinese comfort women reveal, unquestionably, the Japanese military's use of violence in drafting comfort women. How the women were brought into the comfort stations has been debated since the 1990s. Two important factors have underpinned this long-lasting debate: on one hand, there has been a lack of information about the mass abduction of comfort women in regions occupied by Japanese forces during the war. On the other hand, the Japanese military frequently hid its recruitment methods not only from people in colonized regions but also from people in Japan. In drafting comfort women from Japan and its colonies, Korea and Taiwan, the most common recruitment methods involved false job offers to daughters of poor families and/or the militaristic brainwashing of schoolgirls and young women. The real nature of the "job" was hidden from the victims until they were tricked into entering the comfort stations, at which time they were raped. During the drafting process in these regions, Japanese military personnel often stayed behind the scenes, using brothel proprietors or labour brokers to draft the women. Although such deception was also used in occupied areas, most drafting operations in these regions were much more blatant. The following testimony, given to the IMTFE by John Magee, an American priest of the Episcopal Church who lived in Nanjing between 1912 and 1940, describes how a Chinese girl was abducted and detained as a sex slave by Japanese soldiers in the vicinity of Nanjing.

I took this girl to the hospital at some time in February 1938. I talked to her then at length and then saw her many times after that. She was from the city of Wufu, about sixty miles [about 96.5 km] from Nanjing. Japanese soldiers came to her home – her father was a shop-keeper – accused her brother of being a soldier, and killed him. The girl said her brother was not a soldier. They killed her brother's wife because she resisted rape; they killed her older sister because she resisted rape. In the meantime her old father and mother were kneeling before them, and they killed them, all of these people being killed with a bayonet. The girl fainted. They carried her to some barracks of some kind where they kept her for two months. The first month she was raped repeatedly, daily. They had taken her clothes away from her and locked her in a room. After that she became so diseased, they were afraid of her, and she was sick there for a whole month.[24]

The brutalization of Chinese civilians described in this testimony was widespread during the war,[25] and it is consistent with the cases recorded by Su Zhiliang, director of the Research Center for Chinese "Comfort Women" at Shanghai Normal University. Su records the cases of 102 comfort women who were drafted from Mainland China. Of these, eighty-seven women were kidnapped directly by Japanese troops when their hometowns were occupied; ten were abducted by local Chinese collaborators following the orders of the occupation army; three were first deceived by civilian recruiters with false job offers and then detained in military comfort stations; and two had been prostitutes before the war and were forced to become military comfort women when the Imperial Japanese Army turned their brothels into comfort stations.[26] In order to present an objective view of how Chinese women were forced into comfort stations, this book includes two cases of deception among the twelve survivor narratives. As seen in these two cases (presented in Part 2) and other cases (presented in Part 1), although Japanese military personnel employed deception to round up women in China, this was inevitably accompanied by violence. The vast majority of Chinese comfort women were kidnapped, and, during their abductions, many witnessed the torture or murder of close family members (as John Magee describes above). Japanese military officers both permitted and ordered soldiers to carry out this violence, and they also participated in it directly. Raping and kidnapping became so common that soldiers considered abusing Chinese women to be a sport – one of the few "rewards" of their harsh military life. For example, in his recollection, entitled "Dog," Tomishima Kenji, a former corporal and squad leader in the 59th Division, 54th Brigade, 110th Battalion of the Imperial Japanese Army, related how, on 8 December 1943, his unit made a young girl crawl naked for their entertainment and made a group of local women their "comfort delegation" in a small coastal village near Bohai Bay in China. That day was

Japan's Imperial Edict Day, which celebrated the Emperor's declaration of war against the United States and Great Britain two years earlier.[27]

The experiences of Chinese comfort women highlight the criminal nature of the military comfort stations and the comfort women system instituted as part of Japan's war effort. In assessing the nature of the comfort women system, earlier researchers have classified varying types of military comfort facilities into different categories, according to who operated the facility, length of operation, or "organizational motives."[28] Yoshimi Yoshiaki groups the comfort stations into three categories according to who operated them: (1) those operated by the Japanese military for the exclusive use of military personnel and employees; (2) those run by civilians, but under strict military control, for the exclusive use of military personnel and employees; and (3) those designated by the military as comfort stations that privileged military personnel but that were also open for civilian use.[29] Yuki Tanaka, on the other hand, categorizes the comfort stations in terms of the length of their operation, grouping them as: (1) "permanent" comfort stations established in major cities; (2) "semi-permanent" stations affiliated with large military units; and (3) "temporary" stations created by small troop units in battle zones.[30] Although employing different categorizations, both Yoshimi and Tanaka characterize the comfort women system as military sexual slavery. In her recent book, C. Sarah Soh, intending to "better explain the nature of the comfort system," categorizes the military comfort facilities according to "the motives behind running, supporting, and/or patronizing the facilities."[31] Her three different categories are: (1) the "concessionary" *ianjo* [comfort station] or "commercial houses of assignation and prostitution run by civilian concessionaires to make money"; (2) the "paramilitary" *ianjo* run by the paternalistic military as not-for-profit recreational facilities "to control the troops through regulated access to sex"; and (3) the "criminal" *ianjo* that "came into being primarily as an outcome of sex crimes committed by individual troops against local women."[32] Soh suggests that "the criminal category of comfort stations appears to have emerged primarily during the final years and months of the war" after the attack on Pearl Harbor in December 1941.[33] She contends that definitions of comfort stations and the comfort women system as, for example, rape centres and military sexual slavery "do not offer an accurate view of the comfort system: they simplistically conflate the diverse categories of *ianjo* ... into one."[34]

The complexity of Japanese military comfort facilities does indeed defy any simplistic categorizations, and Soh's attention to the varying motives behind the operation of the comfort stations sheds new light on the intricacy of the phenomenon. Although the organizational motive of her last category, the "criminal" *ianjo,* appears murky, the varying motives of the comfort station operators can certainly be used as a set of criteria to describe different types of comfort stations. However, when this set of criteria is used to assess the overall nature of the military comfort women system, more complete analytical data are required, and the following statistical questions need to be asked: Did the "concessionary" comfort stations comprise a significant number among the Japanese military comfort facilities? Was the organizational motive claimed by the operators of the "paramilitary" comfort stations consistent with their actual effect? Were sexual crimes limited only to the makeshift comfort facilities set up by the individual troops and soldiers in the battlefield? Was there sufficient evidence to support the observation that "criminal" comfort stations emerged primarily during the last years of the war? The experiences of Chinese comfort women are indispensible in answering these questions.

In China, local records indicate that, as early as 1932, when Japanese military authorities implemented the first naval comfort stations in China's major port city, Shanghai, and set up army comfort stations in occupied Manchuria, Japanese troops in northeast China had already kidnapped local women and forced them to become sex slaves. In these cases the soldiers abducted local women, brought them to military barracks, or detained them in civilian homes.[35] The number of these kinds of makeshift comfort stations increased rapidly after the Nanjing Massacre, and, throughout the war, they existed in tandem with officially authorized military comfort stations. The larger Japanese military units commonly set up comfort facilities where the troops were located; however, in addition to this, even a platoon or a squadron would often set up its own comfort facility. Among the twelve Chinese survivors presented in this book, eight were enslaved in this type of improvised comfort facility, which could be a military blockhouse, a barracks, a mountain cave, a small inn seized by the occupation army, a shed made of metal sheets, or the victim's own house. The time of their abduction and enslavement ran from early 1938, immediately after the Nanjing Massacre, to 1944, a year before Japan's surrender. As Zhu Qiaomei relates in the second part of this book, four women in her family were forced to become sex slaves when the Japanese army occupied her hometown on Chongming Island near Shanghai in the spring of 1938. They were not confined to a regular comfort station but, instead, were forced to serve as comfort women in their own homes. Further to this, they were also called to the military blockhouse. This situation was common for Chinese comfort women in occupied areas, but it was uncommon for comfort women drafted from other countries.

The Chinese survivors' narratives also reveal that, while the most brutal crimes often occurred in these impromptu frontline comfort facilities, the sexual abuse and torture of comfort women were common occurrences in the "regulated" comfort stations affiliated with the larger military units or run by civilian proprietors in occupied urban areas. Lei Guiying was nine years old in the year of the Nanjing Massacre (1937) when she witnessed Japanese soldiers raping, kidnapping, and killing local women in the Jiangning District of Nanjing, then China's capital (see Part 2). She was hired to be a housemaid by a Japanese business couple in the Town of Tangshan, but as soon as she turned thirteen and started menstruating, her employers forced her to become a comfort woman in the military brothel they were operating. What Lei Guiying experienced in this civilian-run military brothel is clearly criminal: she was beaten and stabbed with a bayonet by Japanese soldiers (leaving her leg permanently damaged) when she resisted rape and abuse.

Lei Guiying's case is far from isolated. The investigations conducted since 1993 by Su Zhiliang, Chen Lifei, and their research team in twenty-two provinces and cities indicate the vast scope of victimization that occurred at military comfort stations in China. In Shanghai alone 164 former comfort station sites have been located, and this does not include those that are known to have existed but whose exact locations can no longer be concretely verified due to postwar urban development.[36] On the remote southern island of Hainan, researchers found sixty-two former military comfort stations.[37] Chinese comfort women confined in these stations suffered unspeakably cruel conditions. They were given the minimum amount of food necessary to keep them alive and were subjected to continual sexual violence. Those who resisted being raped were beaten or killed, and those who attempted to escape could be punished with anything from torture to decapitation (this could include not only the woman but also her family members).[38]

Confined under these slavish conditions, most Chinese comfort women received no monetary payment; instead, their families were often forced to pay a large sum to the Japanese troops in an attempt to ransom them. The fact that monetary payment was given to some of the comfort women has fueled speculation over whether the comfort stations should be considered commercial brothels and the comfort women professional prostitutes. However, it must be emphasized that, although some comfort women received money when they were recruited and/or were given a percentage of the service fees in the comfort stations, most of them were deprived of their freedom and were continually forced to provide sexual services to the military once they were taken to these stations. Despite a certain disparity in the recruitment and treatment of comfort women, the coercive nature of the comfort system as a whole is undeniable. The Japanese military's explicit discrimination toward the comfort women of different ethnic groups and its especially brutal treatment of the women of enemy countries clearly indicates that the military comfort women system constitutes a war crime: it was implemented for militarist war-related purposes and was made possible precisely because of the context provided by the war. The motives behind the implementation of the military comfort women system, according to military leaders, had to do with preventing the rape of local women and the spread of venereal disease by ensuring that soldiers had regular and regulated access to sex. The effect of the system, however, was quite contrary to its alleged "purpose." As an officially authorized institution it not only failed to prevent rape and the spread of venereal disease but also normalized and fostered massive sexual violence both inside and outside the comfort stations. In addition, the procurement of comfort women entailed kidnapping, human trafficking, and enslavement on an extremely large scale.

The accounts of Chinese comfort women presented in this book expose the multiple social, political, and cultural forces that played a part in their life-long suffering. Indeed, their plight must be considered not only in the context of the war but also in the contexts of history and culture. As Sarah Soh points out, "the abuse and maltreatment of daughters and wives in the patriarchal system, with its long-standing masculinist sexual culture, contributed as much as did the colonial political economy to the ready commodification of these women's sex labor."[39] In order to provide a fuller perspective, this book includes the prewar reminiscences of the twelve survivors (e.g., being sold by one's impoverished parents to another family to be a child-bride or running away from an abusive marriage) as well as postwar descriptions of their being persecuted for having allowed themselves to be defiled and/or for having served the nation's enemy. These individual narratives show that the women's lives are defined by more than their involuntary experiences in the military comfort stations; their hardship before the war and their continued suffering and struggle for justice after the war teach us equally important lessons concerning the fundamentals of (in)humanity. While revealing the many factors that have played a role in the comfort women's prolonged sufferings, these survivor narratives leave no doubt that the military comfort women system amounted to sexual slavery.

Structure

Chinese Comfort Women consists of three parts. Part 1 provides the historical background of the narratives. It traces the establishment of the military comfort women system in Mainland China from the early stage of Japan's aggression in Manchuria and Shanghai (1932) to its rapid expansion after the Nanjing Massacre (1937) to Japan's defeat (1945), revealing the close correlation between the proliferation of the comfort stations and the progression of Japan's war of aggression. In recounting how the War of Resistance (also known as the Second Sino-Japanese War and, in China, as the Anti-Japanese War) and the Japanese military comfort stations are remembered by the Chinese people, Part 1 brings to light aspects of the comfort women system that have not been fully exposed in the existing literature, such as the Imperial Japanese Army's mass abduction of local women, the enlistment of local collaborators to set up comfort facilities, the various types of improvised comfort stations set up by the small military units throughout the battle zones and occupied regions, the ransoms that victims' families were forced to pay to the occupation troops, and the extraordinarily large number of Chinese comfort women. Part 2, which opens with a description of the interview method, presents the narratives of twelve comfort station survivors, grouped by geographical area and told in chronological order. A brief local wartime history precedes each woman's story, with short annotations being provided where needed. The accounts chosen are wide-ranging in terms of geographical location (of both home and comfort station), experience, age at abduction, and length of enslavement. The sexual enslavement and torture described here and in Part 1 are extremely vicious: readers need to be prepared.

Part 3 documents the survivors' postwar lives and the movement to support the former comfort women's redress in China. It shows how, after surviving the brutality of the Japanese occupation and the comfort women system, survivors were then subjected to discrimination, ostracism, and poverty due to the prejudices of their fellow countrypeople and the political exigencies of the time. This section also offers a summary of the major legal debates and events concerning Chinese comfort women's lawsuits and transnational support for the Chinese survivors, particularly from Japanese people. It shows how the suffering and stories of the comfort women, whether Chinese, Korean, Japanese, or another nationality, resonate with women and men all over the world.

Source Materials

The survivors' narratives in Part 2 were recorded in Chinese by Su Zhiliang and Chen Lifei over a ten-year period. The founding members of the Research Center for Chinese "Comfort Women" at Shanghai Normal University, Su Zhiliang and Chen Lifei have, since the early 1990s, played a leading role in the research of comfort women in China and, with the help of local researchers, have documented the life experiences of over one hundred comfort women. The twelve women whose accounts are presented here were selected as representatives of different geographical areas, time periods, and varying methods of procurement. Recognizing that, due to wartime trauma, old age, and poor education, the survivors' remembrances of their horrific experiences over sixty years ago may contain lacunae, Su and Chen made multiple research trips to visit the sites where the women were abducted and enslaved, checked regional historical records, and gathered supporting evidence from local people. While memories do have limitations and inconsistencies, the historical accuracy of the wartime victimization of these women is verifiable, and their narratives, taken together, provide an authentic picture of the reality of Imperial Japanese Military comfort stations.

The Chinese comfort women's narratives presented in Part 2 are translated into English by Peipei Qiu, who also provides the historical context in Part 1 and describes the postwar condition of the survivors' lives in Part 3. The writing of Part 1 and Part 3 is based on a large number of primary sources that, to this point, have only been available in Chinese, and it also draws on a wide range of contemporary scholarship. The historical outline of the Second Sino-Japanese War (1931-45) in Part 1 and Part 2 is based on Chinese, Japanese, and English scholarship, particularly the recent publications that brought together the perspectives of Japanese, Chinese, and Western scholars, such as *China at War: Regions of China, 1937-1945* (Stanford University Press, 2007) and *The Battle for China: Essays on the Military History of the Sino-Japanese War of 1937-1945* (Stanford University Press, 2011). The discussion of the establishment and expansion of the Japanese military comfort women system in Part 1 refers both to wartime documents and to source materials compiled after the war. The Japanese military and official documents made available in Yoshimi Yoshiaki's compiled volume *Jūgun ianfu shiryōshū* (Documents on military comfort women) (Ōtsuki shoten, 1992) and *Seifu chōsa "jūgun ianfu" kankei shiryō shūsei* (Governmental investigations: Documents concerning the military "comfort women"), compiled by Josei no tame no Ajia heiwa kokumin kikin (known as the Asian Women's Fund), 1997-98, provided essential information on the Japanese military structure and its role in the establishment of comfort stations. Chinese research from the past two decades (see below) supplied the physical, documentary, and testimonial evidence of the organized sexual violence of the Japanese imperial forces. In order to provide a more objective and layered description of the proliferation of the Japanese military comfort women system, Part 1 cites both the eyewitness accounts of Chinese civilians and military men published during the war and the diaries and writings of Japanese military men. Reports and diaries of foreign nationals who witnessed the war atrocities in China are used to provide additional observations and details. As well, the existing studies on Japanese military sexual violence and the comfort women system provided immense help to this project in piecing together the historical context.

In describing Chinese comfort women's experiences, Part 1 and Part 3 introduce a large number of historical sources and research findings published in China during the past two decades. Along with the rise of the redress movement in the late 1980s, China saw an outpouring of publications on the atrocities committed by the Japanese imperial forces during the war. These publications, often referred to as *baoxinglu* (reports of atrocities), appeared in television documentaries, films, media reports, online materials, oral histories, novels, memoirs, history books, and so on. Several underlying factors can be observed in this outpouring of *baoxinglu:* the reaction to the neo-nationalist denial of Japan's imperialist violence; the need to preserve the eyewitness memories of the war; the eruption of the long suppressed sufferings of individual victims; the revival of the compilation of regional and local history *(difangzhi)* after the Cultural Revolution; and the inspiration taken from the international redress movement. Amid this outpouring of memories of the war, investigations into Imperial Japan's war atrocities were carried out both nationally and locally, producing large book series and collections as well as monographs and articles. Japanese military sexual slavery, which was largely neglected by the war crimes trials at the close of the Asia-Pacific War, is now given special attention.

Selecting from this staggering body of work, this volume draws on the newly released archival documents concerning Japanese military sexual slavery, such as the interrogation records of captured Japanese military men and their Chinese collaborators. Part I of this book also introduces investigative reports based on field research, historical documents, and eyewitness testimonies, such as those undertaken by the national and local committees of cultural and historical data associated with the Chinese People's Political Consultative Conference (CPPCC),[40] the Chinese Academy of Social Sciences and its provincial academies, university researchers, and local historians. *Qin Hua Rijun baoxing zonglu* (Collection of recorded cases of the atrocities committed by the Japanese forces during Japan's invasion of China), for example, is a collection of reports based on a nationwide investigation conducted from May 1991 to November 1994. The committees of cultural and historical data associated with the CPPCC coordinated the investigation in twenty-six provinces and autonomous administrative regions that had been occupied or invaded by Japanese imperial forces, including Beijing and Tianjin. The collection contains 2,272 investigative reports and eighty-three historical photographs and images, in which Japanese military sexual violence and slavery are exposed in all twenty-six provinces and regions. Another source material introduced in this volume, *Riben qinlüe Huabei zuixing dangan: Xingbaoli* (Documented war crimes during Japan's invasion of north China: Sexual violence), is a special volume in a ten-volume series focusing on Japanese military sexual violence and slavery. It is compiled by China's Central Archive (Zhongyang danganguan), the Second National Archive of Historical Documents (Zhongguo di'er lishi danganguan), and the Hebei Province Academy of Social Sciences. It reproduces the relevant archival documents preserved in the Central Archive, Hebei Province Archive, Beijing City Archive, Tianjin City Archive, Qingdao City Archive, and Shanxi Province Archive, and it also brings together the Chinese survivors' legal testimonies and documentary materials, as well as investigative reports from other Chinese sources.

One of the important features of the current movement to re-examine war atrocities in China is that it started as a grassroots movement and has been carried out by local researchers. *Tietixiade xingfeng xueyu: Rijun qin-Qiong baoxing shilu* (Bloody crimes of the occupation rule: Records of the atrocities committed by the Japanese military in Hainan) and its sequel, both of which are cited in this volume, exemplify such locally initiated research projects. From 1993 to 1995 historians and researchers from all six cities and thirteen counties on Hainan Island engaged in investigating the crimes committed by the Japanese military during its six-year occupation. Located in the South China Sea, Hainan Island was made into a major Japanese military base, and a large number of Japanese troops were stationed there during the war. The investigations reveal that, in addition to killing, burning, looting, torturing, and forcing local people to work on military construction sites, the occupying forces built many comfort stations, of which sixty-two are confirmed. The investigators also found a large group of comfort station survivors. Huang Youliang, Chen Yabian, and Lin Yajin, whose narratives are recorded in Part 2, are among the survivors who came forth to tell their wartime experiences, with the help of local researchers. The investigation produced three volumes with 242 reports of atrocities, including first-hand accounts of the military comfort stations by the survivors and local people who were drafted to work there as labourers.

Beside these concerted investigative projects, in-depth case studies and thematic analyses of the Japanese military comfort women system have been conducted by university researchers and independent scholars, some of whom have written pioneering articles that have been collected in *Taotian zuinie: Erzhan shiqi de Rijun weianfu zhidu* (Monstrous atrocities: The Japanese military comfort women system during the Second World War). As our bibliography shows, the delineation of Chinese comfort women's experiences in *Chinese Comfort Women* is built on a substantial number of Chinese findings. For the readers' reference, Part 1 and Part 3 provide detailed information on all materials used. The cases of Chinese comfort women mentioned in this book all include the victim's identity, the time and location of her victimization, and the source of our information.

In addition to Chinese research findings, Parts 1 and 3 frequently cite Japanese scholarship and research reports, such as those by Yoshimi Yoshiaki, Hayashi Hirofumi, Senda Kakō, Kasahara Tokushi, Hora Tomio, Ishida Yoneko, Uchida Tomoyuki, Tanaka Toshiyuki, Utsumi Aiko, Nishino Rumiko, Kim Il-myon, Kawada Fumiko, Suzuki Yūko, Ueno Chizuko, Ikeda Eriko, Yamashita Akiko, Hirabayashi Hisae, Matsuoka Tamaki, and the researchers at the Center for Research and Documentation on Japan's War Responsibility. These parts also draw on the investigatons of Japanese legal specialists, including those by Totsuka Etsurô, Ōmori Noriko, Onodera Toshitaka, Takagi Ken'ichi, and the lawyers of the Japanese Legal Team for Chinese War Victims' Compensation Claims (Chūgokujin sensō higai baishō seikyū jiken bengodan). Their research not only provides important information on Chinese comfort women but also inspired the writing of this book. In order to facilitate further studies, the postwar lives of Chinese survivors and their struggle for justice is outlined in Part 3. Therein the contemporary scholarship on Japanese war crimes trials and the Allied occupation of Japan, as well as Korean, Japanese, and Western studies of Japan's war responsibilities and the comfort women redress movement, were of enormous help in supplying the intricate historical, political, and legal contexts within which the Chinese comfort women's struggles took place.

Unless otherwise noted, translations of the Chinese and Japanese texts used in this volume are provided by Peipei Qiu. Chinese, Japanese, and Korean names are given according to East Asian practice: family name appears first, followed by given name. Exception is made for those writers who have followed the Western practice of placing their given name first in their own Western language publications. The Pinyin system is used for the transliteration of Chinese terms and proper nouns, except for the names of individuals from Taiwan, for which the Wade-Giles system is used. The modified Hepburn system of Romanization is used for Japanese terms and names. Transliteration of Korean names follows that of the publications from which the names are cited.

When asked why he chose to spend years of his career and much of his personal savings representing Chinese war victims, Japanese attorney Oyama Hiroshi, who led the Japanese Legal Team for Chinese War Victims' Compensation Claims, replied: "I want to be responsible for history. Whether Chinese or Japanese, we all must take responsibility for history."[41] More than sixty years have passed since the end of Japan's war of aggression in Asia and the Pacific region, but the wounds of that war remain in the hearts, minds, and bodies of victimized men and women, and in the collective and individual memories of all nations involved. Healing and reconciliation begin by taking responsibility for history. Until the experiences of the hundreds of thousands of comfort women are properly written into history, our collective memory and understanding of the past is incomplete. This book constitutes a small step toward taking responsibility for that history, and it is dedicated to those who have suffered, to those who continue to suffer, and to those who have cared about them.

PART 1

The War Remembered

1 Japan's Aggressive War and the Military "Comfort Women" System

The Second World War is remembered by most countries in the world as taking place between 1939 and 1945, but for Chinese people the war was much longer. It is known as the Second Sino-Japanese War, the Asia-Pacific War, or (in China) the Resistance War, and it began in 1931, with Japan's occupation of Manchuria.

Japan had pursued expansion on the Asian continent during the late 1880s,[1] and, by the early 1930s, it realized its political and economic encroachment in Manchuria through the operation of the semi-official Japanese corporation known as the South Manchuria Railway Company.[2] On the night of 18 September 1931, a group of Japanese military officers staged an incident involving an explosion on the tracks of the railway owned by the South Manchurian Railway Company near today's Shenyang City in northeastern China and accused Chinese dissident forces of having caused it. Using this incident as a pretext, the Japanese Guandong (Kwantung) Army attacked the cities along the South Manchuria Railway. Two years of careful planning enabled the Guandong Army to rapidly expand its operations, and it quickly overran most of Manchuria.[3] The 18 September incident (also known as the Mukden Incident, or the Manchurian Incident) is generally considered to be the prelude to the Second World War in the Asian theatre. Within a few months Japanese troops occupied the major urban centres of the region, and the Chinese forces led by Zhang Xueliang (Chang Hsueh-liang, 1901-2001) withdrew to south of the Great Wall.[4]

In January 1932, the Japanese army provoked another armed conflict with Chinese forces in Shanghai. This incident was also plotted by the Guandong Army, both to increase its influence in southeastern China and to divert the world's attention while it established the puppet state of Manzhouguo.[5] To distract international attention from Manchuria, the Japanese Special Service organ in Shanghai stirred up anti-Japanese protests in that city, and, as the disturbance escalated, in January 1932 the commander of Japanese naval forces called out the Naval Landing Force, joined by vigilante elements from the local Japanese community, to "maintain order."[6] These forces encountered fierce Chinese resistance, forcing them to call for reinforcements in the form of two army divisions. Intense fighting continued in the following two months. The Chinese 19th Route Army and 5th Army fought on without reinforcements and were eventually forced to withdraw.[7] The League of Nations called for a ceasefire and compelled the Japanese forces to negotiate. The ceasefire agreement established a demilitarized zone and prohibited China from stationing troops on its own land around Shanghai, Suzhou, and Kunshan, while permitting some Japanese Naval Landing units to remain in Shanghai.[8]

Japanese troops' sexual violence against, and enslavement of, Chinese women began soon after the escalation of Japan's aggression in China. The first formal comfort station is known to have been established in Shanghai in 1932, but Japanese forces also kidnapped local women to be their sex slaves in northern China around the same time. As the war progressed, comfort stations appeared wherever troops appeared. A case documented in *Qin-Hua Rijun baoxing zonglu* (Collection of investigative records of the atrocities committed by the Japanese forces during Japan's invasion of China), a nationwide investigation led by the Committee of Cultural and Historical Data of the Chinese People's Political Consultative Conference and published in 1995, records that, in the winter of 1932, a unit of the 16th Brigade, 8th Division, of the Guandong Army occupied the Chaoyang-si area of Beipiao County in northeastern China. The soldiers immediately kidnapped "good-looking" local women and kept them in the military barracks as sex slaves.[9] At the same time, the troops continued to assault women in the nearby villages. Reportedly, over one thousand local women were raped in their own homes; not even pregnant women, young girls, or elderly women were spared.[10] Within the same region, in the autumn of 1935, more than a hundred Japanese soldiers attacked the Dahei-shan area in Beipiao, where the Chinese resistance force was active. Carrying machine-guns, the troops drove the villagers into a large yard, dragged all the women out of the crowd, and raped them in the presence of their family members. Several soldiers ripped off the clothes of a woman who was six months pregnant and tied her on a table in the yard. They took photographs of her while violating her, then cut her abdomen open and plucked the foetus out with a bayonet.[11]

The violence perpetrated by Japanese troops described here is so brutal that it is difficult to comprehend. Yet similar incidents were reported frequently during the war.[12] In searching for explanations of the Japanese military men's atrocious behaviour, scholars have considered various factors, such as battlefield psychology, sexual starvation, and the lack of effective discipline. While all these factors might have played a part in causing the brutality, they cannot fully explain why it was so widespread among Japanese soldiers who, presumably, were not born evil. In analyzing the different atrocities perpetrated by Japanese troops on the bodies of Chinese men and women, Timothy Brook offers the following:

> Men of fighting age were shot or conscripted for labor because they were, or stood in for, the soldiers of the nation. Women of childbearing age were raped or forced into prostitution because they were, or stood in for, the body of the nation. So rape was widely performed as a gesture of conquest, but not simply as a release for male sexual starvation; it was an act of humiliation. Japanese soldiers performed this act on the bodies of Chinese women, but the target of the humiliation was Chinese men: it was proof of their impotence in all ways.[13]

Brook's analysis helps explain not only why atrocious behaviour was so wide-spread among Japanese forces during the war but also why the sufferings of Chinese comfort women were excluded from the heroic narrative of the nation-state after the war. Indeed, the Japanese military men's particularly brutal violence against Chinese women was an act performed for the war and made possible by the war. This "gesture of conquest" was acted out as soon as the imperial army made its first conquests in northeastern China and, as is seen in the following pages, lasted throughout the entire Second Sino-Japanese War.

While soldiers on the battlefields assaulted local Chinese women and made them sex slaves in their barracks in northeastern China,[14] more formal military comfort stations began to emerge in big cities. Evidence shows that Japan's navy first set up military comfort stations in Shanghai during the Shanghai War (the first major battle of the Resistance War) in 1932.[15] Shanghai had been a regular Japanese navy base since the end of the Qing Dynasty, and Japanese brothels appeared in the city as early as the 1880s. By 1882, the number of Japanese prostitutes in Shanghai had already reached eight hundred.[16] For the sake of appearances, the Japanese Foreign Ministry cooperated with the Chinese government's effort to ban prostitution and repatriated nearly six hundred Japanese prostitutes from Shanghai during 1884 and 1885.[17] However, this effort failed to put an end to the Japanese brothels. The number of Japanese prostitutes in Shanghai swelled again, and, in the summer of 1907, licensed Japanese *kashizashiki* (a type of brothel) began to operate in Shang-hai.[18] The *kashizashiki* provided the infrastructure from which the Japanese navy established its first comfort stations in 1932. A document produced by the Japanese Consulate General in Shanghai, "The Current State of the Supervision of the Unlicensed Prostitute in the Concession and the State and

Supervision of Japanese Special Women in Shanghai during 1938," contains a detailed description of the beginning of the military comfort women system. It indicates that the *kashizashiki* run by the Japanese began to operate in Shanghai in July 1907 and employed B-type "entertainers" (prostitutes) in Japan's licensed brothel system. In June 1929, the Shanghai Public Security Bureau ordered the abolition of all licensed Chinese brothels in districts under its jurisdiction and also demanded that Japanese brothels shut down their business in districts under Chinese jurisdiction. At the same time, the Shanghai Branch of the Japanese Women's Association for Rectifying Public Morals *(Fujin kyōfūkai Shanhai shibu)* strongly opposed the licensed prostitution system and petitioned the Japanese Foreign Ministry to address this social concern. Accordingly, that year, the Japanese Consulate General created the "restaurant barmaid" *(ryōtei shakufu)* system as an expeditious way of replacing the abolished licensed brothels. However, with the rapid increase of Japanese military personnel in the region due to the Shanghai Incident in 1932, the navy established comfort facilities (in the form of *kashizashiki*) for the troops, and these continued to operate up until the outbreak of full-scale warfare in 1937. Some of the proprietors temporarily went back to Japan. However, from November 1937 the number of *kashizashiki* in China kept increasing, along with the number of Japanese nationals. By the end of December, there were eleven such *kashizashiki*, of which seven were naval comfort stations, and 191 barmaids (171 Japanese women and twenty Korean women) – seventy-three more than in the preceding year. The four general *kashizashiki* were mostly for overseas Japanese; the seven naval comfort stations were for the exclusive use of navy officers and soldiers. Medical specialists gave the comfort women a physical examination once a week in the presence of an officer from the navy's land battle unit and a police officer from the Consulate General. In addition, there were three hundred temporary comfort women in the army's comfort stations within the jurisdiction of the Japanese Consulate General.[19]

Although the navy's first comfort stations comprised the Japanese brothels that already existed in Shanghai, they were implemented specifically to achieve Japan's military goals as it was accelerating its invasion of China. It has been suggested that, because Japanese forces had suffered a high rate of venereal disease during their Siberian expedition between 1918 and 1922, Japanese military leaders considered facilities for sexual comfort essential to strengthening their troops' morale and preventing the spread of venereal disease.[20] However, far from preventing venereal disease, the comfort women system became a colossal host not only of this but also of sexual violence.

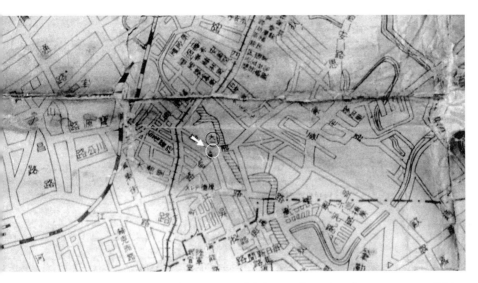

Figure 1 Dayi (or *Daiichi* in Japanese) Saloon indicated with an arrow on a 1937 Japanese map. (Photograph courtesy of Fang Yuqiang)

The comfort stations established in big cities at this time were of consider-able size. Dayi (*Daiichi*, in Japanese) Saloon, one of the first naval comfort stations in Shanghai, occupied several two-story buildings. As is clearly marked on a 1937 Japanese map, it was located on Dong-Baoxing Road, a street ad-jacent to Sichuan-bei Road, where the Japanese navy's land battle units were stationed (see Figure 1). Lu Mingchang, a Dong-Baoxing Road resident who worked as a labourer at Dayi Saloon for fourteen years, recalled that, in the beginning, it contained mainly Japanese comfort women and was open to both Japanese naval officers and overseas Japanese civilians. Later, Korean comfort women were taken into Dayi, and, after the outbreak of full-scale warfare in 1937, it was reserved for the exclusive use of the Japanese navy.[21]

In 1932, the Japanese army followed the navy's example by establishing its own comfort stations in Shanghai. At the time, about thirty thousand Japanese troops were stationed in the Shanghai area, and the number of rapes com-mitted by them became scandalous.[22] On 14 March 1932, Lieutenant-General Okabe Naozaburō, a senior staff officer in the Shanghai Expeditionary Army, wrote about the situation in his diary:

> Lately I have often heard obscene stories about our soldiers roaming around in search of women. These incidents are hard to prevent when the troops are

not engaged in battle. Therefore, we should act proactively by providing proper facilities. We shall consider various measures for meeting the soldiers' sexual needs and shall start to implement them. Lieutenant Colonel Nagami is in charge of this task.[23]

Okabe's measures were also implemented by Okamura Yasuji, deputy chief of staff of the Shanghai Expeditionary Army. Okamura not only authorized the establishment of the facilities following the navy's model but also went a step further and had the governor of Nagasaki Prefecture send a group of women from Japan to China.[24] Evidently, from its inception, the drafting of comfort women was carried out with the knowledge and cooperation of the Japanese military and government. After the outbreak of full-scale warfare, Japanese authorities tightened control over travel from Japan and its colonies to Mainland China. Identification papers issued by the Police Bureau were needed in order to obtain permission to travel.[25] In other words, without the authorization of high-ranking military officers and government officials, this colossal wartime example of human trafficking across borders would not have been possible.

Despite their early connections to the prewar prostitution system, the Japanese military comfort stations differed from the ordinary brothels and the regimental brothels seen in other countries. They differed in that they were initiated by Japanese military authorities for purely war-related purposes and in that most of them were directly supervised and used by the Japanese military. In addition, the vast majority of the women were drafted into the comfort stations by force and were detained for the purpose of continual sexual exploitation. "Notice from the Adjutant to the Chiefs of Staff of the North China Area Army and Central China Expeditionary Force,"[26] issued on 4 March 1938, reveals that, even in Japan, procurement methods "similar to kidnapping" had been used, causing "social problems."[27] To prevent further complaints from the general public, the armies in the field were ordered to take firm control of "recruitment" and to be more careful about whom they chose to carry out this task.[28] However, the army's concern to regulate the methods for recruiting women domestically was mainly to do with protecting its reputation in the eyes of the Japanese people. In occupied areas sexual violence and the kidnapping of local women were commonplace, as is seen in the acts committed by the Japanese unit stationed at Beipiao County. As Japan's military expansion continued from Manchuria into northern China, the abduction of Chinese women to fill the battlefield comfort stations occurred on a much larger, and extremely violent, scale.

After the 1931 incursion into Manchuria, the Guandong Army, toward the end of 1932, advanced north of the Great Wall. By 1933, all areas north of Beiping (now Beijing) fell under Japanese control, and sporadic fighting lasted until total war broke out between the two countries in the summer of 1937. On 7 July 1937, Japanese forces stationed at Lugou-qiao (also known as the Marco Polo Bridge), about fifteen kilometres from Beiping City, conducted nocturnal exercises, during which one soldier lost his way. The commanding officer demanded entrance to the Town of Wanping near Lugao-qiao to search for the missing soldier but was refused.[29] The Lugou Bridge guarded the vital route linking Beiping to the southern area controlled by the Chinese Nationalist forces, and it occupied an important location on the Pinghan (Beiping-Wuhan) Railway. The missing soldier later found his way back to his unit, but the Japanese forces attacked Wanping. Japanese artillery units bombarded Wanping while their infantry and tanks attacked the town as well as the Pinghan Railway Bridge. Chinese troops countered with a fierce defence and retook these strategic posts the following day. Outnumbered by Chinese forces, the Japanese announced that the missing soldier had been found unharmed and asked for a ceasefire and negotiations. However, during the negotiating period, the Japanese army accumulated more troops and, once again, bombarded Wanping. As soon as the negotiations were over, Japanese forces commenced an all-out attack on Beiping, seizing the city and nearby Tianjin within the month.[30]

After the occupation of these two major cities, Japanese ground forces crossed the Yellow River and began their southward advance. On 9 August 1937, the Chinese Peace Preservation Forces guarding Hongqiao Airport exchanged fire with Lieutenant Ōyama Isao, an officer of the Naval Landing Force, and killed him. The Japanese military used this incident as a pretext to bring more warships to Shanghai, and the army ministry ordered the mobilization of 300,000 troops to be sent to that city and to Qingdao.[31] On the morning of 13 August 1937, skirmishes broke out and escalated, and Japanese warships bombarded the Chinese positions in Shanghai.[32] Chinese forces fought back but were defeated after three months of bloody battles.

Immediately after occupying Shanghai and the regions nearby, Japanese forces moved rapidly toward Nanjing, the capital of China at the time. By 10 December they were at the walls of Nanjing.[33] China's Nationalist government leader Jiang Jieshi (Chiang Kai-shek, 1887-1975) ordered Chinese forces to defend to the death the nation's capital. However, discipline broke down and the Chinese Central Army's plan for staged withdrawal from Shanghai crumbled, leaving the defence of Nanjing to warlord troops or new recuits.[34]

Fighting continued over the next three days until the city fell into Japanese hands on 13 December 1937, whereon Japanese troops began the mass slaughter of Chinese civilians and surrendered Chinese military personnel.[35] Exactly how many Chinese civilians and unarmed soldiers were killed during the fall of Nanjing has been debated.[36] According to the IMTFE:

> Estimates made at a later date indicate that the total number of civilians and prisoners of war murdered in Nanking [Nanjing] and its vicinity during the first six weeks of the Japanese occupation was over 200,000.[37] That these estimates are not exaggerated is borne out by the fact that burial societies and other organizations counted more than 155,000 bodies buried. They also reported that most of those were bound with their hands tied behind their backs. These figures do not take into account those persons whose bodies were destroyed by burning, or by throwing them into the Yangtze River, or otherwise disposed of by the Japanese.[38]

The IMTFE judgment describes the ruthlessness of the sexual violence perpetrated by the Japanese soldiers during the Nanjing Massacre, stating that death was frequently a penalty for even the slightest resistance on the part of a rape victim or any members of her family who might have sought to protect her. Throughout the city, young girls and old women were sadistically raped. A large number of women were killed after being raped and their bodies were mutilated. The IMTFE estimates that there were approximately twenty thousand cases of rape within the city during the first month of the occupation.[39] The refugees in a camp at Canton Road sent the following plea for help to the International Committee of the Nanjing Safety Zone:

> There are about 540 refugees crowded in Nos. 83 and 85 on Canton Road. Since 13th inst. up to the 17th those houses have been searched and robbed many, many times a day by Japanese soldiers in groups of three to five. Today the soldiers are looting the places mentioned above continually and all the jewelry, money, watches, and clothes of any sort are taken away. At present every night women of younger ages are forced to go with the soldiers who send motor trucks to take them and release them the next morning. More than 30 women and girls have been raped. The women and children are crying all night. Conditions inside the compound are worse than we can describe. Please give us help.
>
> Yours truly,   All the Refugees
>
> Nanking, 18 December 1937[40]

The actions of the Japanese troops during the Nanjing Massacre outraged the Chinese people and the international community. Considering mass rape to be a potential hindrance to Japan's military advance in China, the Japanese military leaders began to implement comfort stations throughout the frontlines and occupied areas as soon as full-scale warfare began. Okabe Naozaburō, then chief of staff of the North China Area Army, made this clear in his instructions to the commanders of his units. In a memorandum sent out on 27 June 1938, he noted: "According to different sources, the strong anti-Japanese sentiment [among the local Chinese] has been caused by the widespread raping by Japanese troops in many places" and that "the frequent occurrence of rapes in different areas is not merely a matter of criminal law; it is serious treason that damages the occupational order, that obstructs the military actions of our entire army, and that harms our country." He concluded: "Therefore, the acts of individual military personnel must be strictly controlled. At the same time, facilities for sexual comfort must be established immediately to prevent inadvertent violation of the rules due to the lack of such facilities."[41] Okabe's statement shows that the motives behind the establishment of the comfort stations, despite the noble claim of the need to prevent widespread rape, really had nothing to do with protecting local women and everything to do with the implementation of an aggressive war.

Although Japanese military authorities attempted to address the widespread sexual violence, and the military codes stipulated that those who committed rape would be punished,[42] attempts at discipline were ineffective even according to the available Japanese reports. According to the numbers that Oyama Fumio, head of the Legal Affairs Bureau in the Japanese army, submitted to the Tokyo War Crimes Tribunal, twenty-eight military personnel were convicted under the military code of conduct (looting, rape, manslaughter), while 495 were convicted under the domestic criminal law (rape, injuring).[43] These numbers are in striking contrast to the evidence regarding the magnitude of the Japanese military's criminal activity. Since rape was a mere subcategory in the code of conduct, the actual number of sexual crimes that ended in court-martial was extremely small. Thus, it is not an overstatement to say that military commanders virtually condoned raping, looting, killing, and other crimes, Indeed, as Yuma Totani points out, soldiers believed that their superiors tacitly permitted such behaviour, regarding it as the spoils of war − as a reward for their having engaged in prolonged and exhausting battles.[44]

Instead of taking serious measures to punish sexual crimes, Japanese military leaders expanded the comfort station system. Two days before the occupation of Nanjing, the Japanese Central China Area Army ordered the establishment of comfort stations.[45] On 18 December 1937, Major Yamazaki Masao, a staff officer of the 10th Army under the command of the Central China Area Army, indicated in his diary that, when he arrived at Huzhou, a prefecture adjacent to Nanjing, Lieutenant-Colonel Terada had set up a recreation facility and had had the military police round up local women. There were seven women in the facility at the time, but the military police were planning to recruit one hundred.[46] Wartime Chinese records confirm that, around the time of the Nanjing Massacre, the Japanese army had already begun the mass enslavement of Chinese women in comfort facilities. Jiang Gonggu, a Chinese military physician of the Nanjing defence force who remained in the city during the massacre, wrote that, after the fall of Nanjing, the Japanese troops kidnapped and gang-raped women in daylight, even abducting them from the International Safety Zone at Jinling College to be their sex slaves.[47] The same situation was also recorded in the depositions submitted to the IMTFE. The deposition of Mrs. Shui Fang Tsen, the director of dormitories at Jinling College, states that the Japanese soldiers would enter the grounds of the safety zone on the pretext of looking for soldiers when they were in fact looking for girls. According to her, a typical incident occurred on the night of 17 December 1937, when a group of Japanese soldiers forcibly entered the college and carried off eleven young women. Nine of these women made their way back, "horribly raped and abused"; the other two were never heard from again.[48]

In addition to the military's direct abduction of local women, the Japanese army also used local collaborators to gather women. In Nanjing, Qiao Hongnian was one such collaborator, and he helped the Japanese army set up more than one comfort station.[49] Documents preserved in the Nanjing Archives show that, in mid-December 1937, Ōnishi, Head of the Secret Service and staff officer of the Shanghai Expeditionary Army, ordered local collaborators to round up one hundred women for the purpose of establishing comfort stations. Under Qiao's supervision, they took three hundred women from the refugee camp at the Women's College; from among these women, one hundred were selected and presented to Ōnishi. Qiao also helped to prepare two facilities, one at Fuhou-gang and the other at Tieguan-xiang. The comfort stations officially opened on 22 December, with Ōnishi as the head and Qiao Hongnian as his assistant. They were staffed by about two hundred people, including: three ticket clerks (two of whom were Japanese), four bookkeepers, maids, servants, and a large number of comfort women. Thirty attractive young women were assigned to Fuhou-gang for the exclusive use of the military officers, who were charged three yen in military currency per hour and ten yen per night. The rest of the women were sent to Tieguanxiang to service the soldiers, who were charged two yen per hour and had no overnight option.[50] The Japanese army covered the initial operating expenses of the comfort stations; later, they were run on ticket revenue and Ōnishi pocketed the surplus.[51]

Between December 1937 and April 1938, Qiao Hongnian followed the orders of the Japanese army and helped set up three other comfort stations.[52] During the rapid expansion of the comfort women system in China after the Nanjing Massacre, it appears to have been common practice for comfort stations to be directly managed by an army officer who would use Chinese collaborators to draft local women. A similar process was used in smaller cities. According to the recollection of Sugino Shigeru, who served as a member of the Committee on Establishing Military Comfort Stations, on 18 December 1937 a military comfort station was set up shortly after the medical unit of the 3rd Division entered Yangzhou, a city northeast of Nanjing. Sugino and other committee members, accompanied by the local Association for Maintaining Order, rounded up forty-seven Chinese women for the comfort station.[53] Around the same time, two comfort stations were set up in Changzhou east of Nanjing. According to the report of Manba Shitomi, commander of the 2nd Independent Heavy Artillery Siege Battalion: "One [of the comfort stations] was managed by the commissariat and the other by a unit under the direct control of the army headquarters. Each unit was allocated about one hour to use the comfort station on a specified day under the supervision of the commanding officer. Military physicians conducted hygiene checks [of the comfort women] in advance."[54] Clearly, the abduction of Chinese women and their confinement in comfort stations was already very common at the commencement of full-scale warfare between China and Japan.

Parallel to the enslavement of local Chinese women, the Japanese military intensified the trafficking of Korean, Japanese, and Taiwanese women to the Chinese mainland, starting in early 1938. Research suggests that Japan's increased mobilization of women in its colonies and homeland was partly due to security concerns: military leaders worried not only that the abduction of local women might spur more rebellions in the occupied regions but also that Chinese comfort women might pass military information to Chinese forces. The majority of the comfort women shipped to China from overseas were Korean,[55] although a large number of women from Japan and Taiwan were also drafted during this period, and, as the war in the Asia-Pacific theatre progressed, women from other countries were forced to become comfort women as well.[56] Asō Tetsuo, at the time a military physician in the Commissariat Hospital of the Shanghai Expeditionary Army, wrote about the situation in his memoir. On 2 January 1938, Asō examined about one hundred women for sexually transmitted diseases at the Yangjiazhai military comfort station in Shanghai. According to his recollection, about 80 percent of the women were Korean and the rest were Japanese.[57] Unlike the Chinese comfort women, who were primarily kidnapped in the war zones or occupied areas and were rarely mentioned in Japan's official documents, Korean and Japanese comfort women were considered overseas subjects of Imperial Japan, and, for this reason, the Japanese Foreign Ministry occasionally kept records of their numbers. The extant documents of the Japanese consulates in central and eastern China recorded more than one thousand Japanese and Korean comfort women in the cities of Shanghai, Jiujiang, Hangzhou, Zhenjiang, Hankou, Xiamen, Wuhu, and Nanchang between 1938 and 1939.[58] In northern China, the Japanese consulates' records did not list comfort stations as a separate category; consequently, the statistics on comfort women in that area are not available. However, the "Table of Statistics on the Japanese Population by Occupations," compiled by the Japanese Police Department in northern China on 1 July 1939, records that, in the area, there were 8,931 "*geisha*, prostitutes, and barmaids," which, as Yoshimi suggests, must have included a large number of comfort women.[59] As in other regions, in southern China the number of comfort women increased rapidly when fighting spread there. The "Wartime Ten-Day Report," put out by the headquarters of the 21st Army in Guangzhou in April 1939, recorded about 850 comfort women under its direct control and an additional 150 drafted from the hometown of each unit.[60] The report also indicated that these numbers pertain only to areas in which the military police were stationed and that additional comfort stations, such as those established in Sanshui, Jiujiang, Guanyao, Zengcheng, Shilong, and other places, were not included. In fact, on 15 April 1939, the chief of the medical section of the 21st Army reported at his meeting with the Medical Bureau of the Ministry of War that his army imported one comfort woman for every one hundred soldiers, bringing the number of comfort women to between fourteen hundred and sixteen hundred.[61]

These numbers, though incomplete, give us an idea of the rapid increase in the number of Korean, Japanese, and Taiwanese comfort women in China at the time. However, these figures include neither local Chinese comfort women nor small comfort stations under the direct control of particular army units. Field investigations in China since the 1990s reveal that the total number of military comfort facilities and comfort women was much larger

Table 1

"Comfort stations" in Hongkou District, Shanghai, in 1940		
Date	Number of comfort stations	Chinese women detained
May	16	77
July	20	91
August	23	105
September	22	114
October	20	117
November	22	119
December	22	115

than estimates based on Japanese wartime documents suggest. In Shanghai alone the sites of 164 comfort stations have been confirmed, yet evidence indicates that even this number is far too low. The Hongkou and Zhabei districts of Shanghai, for instance, are known to have had a large number of comfort stations. In 1940, an "association of comfort stations" was established in the districts and "Provisional Regulations on Comfort Stations" (Guanli weiansuo linshi guiyue) were issued to enhance their management.[62] However, due to municipal development over the years, some comfort station sites in the area have been difficult to locate and, hence, are excluded from the statistics pertaining to verified comfort stations.[63] During the Japanese occupation, under the auspices of the Shanghai Special City Police Bureau, the Hongkou District Association of Comfort Stations kept records of the number of comfort stations in the district. See Table 1 for the report for 1940.[64]

In addition to the known comfort stations, there seem to have been many comfort facilities under direct military control that were kept secret from the public. A newspaper report in *Dagongbao* on 27 February 1938 reveals that Mr. Lu, a pastor of a small church in Kunshan near Shanghai, happened to see one such military comfort station. In late 1937, after the Battle of Shanghai, Lu went to Shanghai, where he had Japanese acquaintances. A Japanese military officer took him to an "entertainment facility" *(xingle-suo)* located on the Bei-Sichuan Road, Hongkou District. Japanese soldiers stood guard at the entrance of a three-story building that, formerly, had been a bank. When Lu entered with his Japanese friend, he was shocked to see naked Chinese women lying on the floors throughout the building. These women, ranging in age from teenagers to thirty-year-olds, spoke different local dialects. Several Japanese soldiers were walking through the rooms selecting women. These women would be severely beaten by guards if they resisted. Deeply upset, Lu started to leave, but suddenly a young woman stood up and cried for help. Lu recognized this woman as Mrs. Wang, his next-door neighbour. He knew it would be dangerous to show any sympathy toward her, but as a devoted Christian he could not bear to see her beaten by the Japanese soldiers. He begged the Japanese officer who had taken him there to let this young woman go, saying that she was his relative. The Japanese officer believed him and let Lu lead her out. According to Mrs. Wang, she, along with other women, had been kidnapped when the Japanese troops seized Kunshan in mid-November. They had been trucked to Hongkou District in Shanghai and put into this comfort station, where several hundred women were imprisoned and repeatedly raped each day. Some of the women went on a hunger strike and died, but the Japanese military immediately brought in new women to replace them.[65]

This report is in accordance with historical knowledge and the experiences described by other Chinese comfort station survivors. Although it is known that Japanese military comfort facilities were set up in Shanghai beginning in 1932, this particular comfort station and its hundreds of victims are not mentioned in any official Japanese document. If Lu had not seen it by chance and revealed its existence via a newspaper, it would have remained hidden from the world. This comfort station did not exist in isolation. The mass abduction and enslavement of Chinese women occurred in many cities once the war became full-blown, and it was soon happening in all the regions in which Japanese troops were stationed. Mr. Tan, a local resident who fled from Nanjing on 20 May 1938, reported that, by May 1938, less than half a year after the Nanjing Massacre, the Japanese army had established seventeen military comfort stations in that city.[66] At the same time, the troops abducted large numbers of Chinese women and set up comfort stations in the adjacent cities of Nantong, Suzhou, Wuxi, Zhenjiang, Yangzhou, Changzhou, Rugao, Xuzhou, and Hangzhou.[67]

2 The Mass Abduction of Chinese Women

After the occupation of Nanjing, Japan's North China Area Army launched a major offensive from Shandong Province in March 1938, during which Japanese troops encountered strong Chinese resistance and suffered heavy losses in two weeks of close battles at Taierzhuang. In April Japan's Imperial General Headquarters ordered another massive encirclement campaign to destroy China's major field forces. Although the two-month operation captured Xuzhou in Jiangsu Province, the Japanese forces were unable to trap the Chinese armies. Having failed to achieve a settlement by seizing China's capital and being unable to eliminate the Guomindang's (Kuomintang, Nationalist Party) major forces, the Japanese army directed its offensive against strategic points such as Wuhan in central China and Guangzhou in south China. The Japanese military's operations east of Wuhan, along both banks of the Yangtze River and in the mountains to the north, began in the summer of 1938 and eventually involved 300,000 Japanese and 1 million Chinese troops. Around the same time, the Japanese 21st Army directed its offensive against Guangzhou.[1] By late October of 1938, both Wuhan and Guangzhou fell into Japanese hands, and the war spread like fire across China.

The Japanese military's invasion hastened the formation of a united anti-Japanese front in politically divided China. The Nationalist government moved to Chongqing and continued to resist. Although Japanese troops made territorial gains in northern and central China and in the coastal regions, guerrilla fighting, often led by the Communist Party, continued in the occupied areas. At the same time, major Nationalist forces fought to stop the Japanese advance in southwestern China. By 1940 the war had reached an impasse. The frustrated Japanese military deployed *jinmetsu sakusen* (operation destroy all), known as *sanguang* (the three alls – kill all, loot all, burn all) in Chinese, against the resistance forces and civilians in these areas. During this time millions of Chinese civilians were killed,[2] tens of thousands were sent away to perform hard labour,[3] and local Chinese women were abducted to serve as sex slaves as a regular part of military action under Operation Destroy All.

By 1939, the more formal comfort stations were already so much a part of the system that methods of establishing them were being taught at the Japanese military accounting school. Shikanai Nobutaka, a former army accounting officer who studied at the school from April to September 1939, comments in an interview:

> At that time we had to figure out the endurance of the women drafted from local areas *[chōben]* and the rate at which they would wear out. We also had to determine which areas supplied women who would work best and how much "service time" should be allocated to a man from the time he entered the room until he left – how many minutes for commissioned officers, how many minutes for non-commissioned officers, and how many minutes for soldiers. (Laughter) The fees were also decided based on different ranks. Regulations regarding these were called the "Essentials for the Establishment of *Pii* Facilities," which were taught at the army's accounting school.[4]

Pii is a derogatory term that Japanese soldiers used to refer to comfort women.[5] Clearly, the content of the course was all about planning and running comfort facilities. It is worth noting that, when talking about drafting comfort women, Shikanai used a Japanese military term – *chōben* – which literally means "to obtain provisions locally in the battlefield." His use of the term indicates that Chinese women were obtained locally and targeted for service in the military comfort stations. It also shows that these women were not considered to be human beings; rather, they were relegated to the status of military supplies. According to the former commissioned accounting officer of the commissariat of the 11th Army, the Japanese troops generally considered the comfort women nothing more than "public latrines."[6] The officer also indicated that, beginning in the early stages of full-scale warfare, the mid-level leaders of the Imperial Japanese Army employed "getting supplies from the enemy" as a major operational strategy.[7] From 1938 onward, over 1 million Japanese troops were regularly deployed in China.[8] As these troops plundered Chinese resources for army provisions, they designated Chinese women as being among their necessary supplies. *Chōben*, in this context, seems to have been used in a broad sense to refer to the general practice of drafting Chinese women to fill the comfort facilities rather than transporting women from Japan and its colonies. Indeed, the investigations conducted by the Research Center for Chinese "Comfort Women" show that about 60 percent of the military comfort stations in China were set up in rural areas and that they contained an extremely large number of Chinese comfort women who had been drafted from local areas.[9] Women kidnapped from rural areas were sometimes transported to comfort stations in major cities. The Military Entertainment Facility in Shanghai, for example, confined hundreds of women from the northern area of Jiangsu Province and villages near Shanghai.[10] Conversely, women drafted from cities were also transported to stations in remote provinces. According to Jiang Hao's investigation, after occupying Nanjing the Japanese military herded a large number of women into boxcars to take them from the city to other battle zones to function as comfort women for the troops.[11]

Recent research findings in China indicate that, contrary to the common assumption that the recruitment of comfort women was targeted mainly at Japanese and Korean women, from the very beginning of Japan's aggression in China the Japanese military had in fact forced large numbers of Chinese women into military sexual slavery. Historians estimate that the Imperial Japanese Army had approximately 3.2 million regulars during the war and that the majority of them were deployed in Mainland China; at the time of the Pearl Harbor attack, about 70 to 80 percent of Japanese troops were stationed in the Chinese theatre.[12] In order to placate this colossal number of troops, the Japanese imperial forces relied heavily on forcibly drafting local Chinese women in order to set up comfort facilities. After the Japanese bombing of Pearl Harbor in December 1941, when the battle lines extended to Southeast Asia and the Pacific Islands, local women from these areas were also coerced into becoming comfort women. Typically, women drafted from the occupied areas were treated atrociously by the occupation forces.

Although massive numbers of Chinese women were victimized by the comfort women system, until recently, information about Chinese comfort women has been scarce. Previously, based on the information available by the early 1990s, Japanese and Korean researchers held that the total number of comfort women was somewhere between fifty thousand and 200,000 and that 80 to 90 percent of them were Korean.[13] In his research on comfort women, Senda Kakō estimates that the total number of comfort women, from the beginning to the end of the war in the Asia-Pacific theatre, was over 100,000. He cites the soldier-comfort women ratio during the Guandong Army Special Manoeuvre near the border between the Soviet Union and northern China in July 1941 as a reference. Senda reports that Major Hara Zenshirō, a staff officer who was in charge of provisioning the Guandong Army, calculated the troops' needs for sexual services and requested a supply of twenty thousand comfort women from Korea to service 700,000 troops.[14] This request indicated a soldier-comfort women ratio of 35:1. Estimates made by researchers in the 1990s, however, come up with a ratio of 29:1 *(nikuichi)*, which they believe was what was commonly used by Japanese military personnel when drafting comfort women.[15] Kim Il-myon suggests that, if the total number of Japanese soldiers were 3 million, then, according to the 29:1 ratio, the number of comfort women would have been nearly 103,500.[16] Hata Ikuhiko comes up with two estimations: 60,000 based on a 50:1 ratio and 90,000 with a 1.5 replacement rate.[17] Yoshimi Yoshiaki, on the other hand, suggests that, if the replacement rate were 1.5, then the total number of comfort women would have been 3,000,000/29 × 1.5, or 155,172 women. If the replacement rate were 2.0, then the number would have been 3,000,000/29 × 2.0, or 206,897 women.[18] However, due to the limited nature of the information available at the time, these estimates do not adequately reflect the number of Chinese comfort women.

The estimated number, whether 20,000 or 200,000, matters less than the fact that the sexual enslavement of women – whatever the number – is a gross crime. Yet, since numbers help to assess the scope of the victimization, Chinese researchers offered their estimations. Based on the evidence gathered by Chinese researchers since the 1990s, Su Zhiliang suggests that, from 1937 to 1945, the comfort women replacement rate was much higher than was previously thought, approximately 3.5 to 4.0, which brings the estimated total number of comfort women up to either (1) more than 360,000 (3,000,000 Japanese soldiers/29 × 3.5 = 362,068 women) or (2) to more than 400,000 (3,000,000 Japanese soldiers/29 × 4.0 = 413,793 women). In terms of nationalities, he estimates that about 140,000 to 160,000 of the total number of comfort women were Korean and that 20,000 were Japanese, with several thousand being from Taiwan and Southeast Asia and several hundred coming from European countries. The rest were Chinese women, who numbered about 200,000.[19]

It needs to be noted that Su's estimation does not include those women who were sexually violated by the Japanese military but who were not detained as sex slaves for an ongoing period of time. The number of those women, many Chinese researchers believe, is much greater than the number who were taken as comfort women. Journalist Li Xiuping reports that, when she was investigating the Japanese military comfort stations at Yu County, Shanxi Province, in the early 1990s, local people often asked her the same question: "Do you want to know about the women who were detained in the Japanese strongholds or do you also want to know about women who were raped by Japanese soldiers but were not taken away?" When Li told them that she wanted to know about both, the local people would reply: "The latter cases were too many to talk about. You will find it out if you stay in this area a little longer." One example of what Li found out after having spent some time in the area was that, during a single mop-up operation at Yu County, Japanese troops raped over two hundred women in Xinghua Village: only two women managed to escape.[20]

Su Zhiliang's estimation regarding higher replacement rates for comfort women is based on what, over the last two decades, has been revealed about Chinese comfort women's experiences. As the research on Chinese comfort women progressed and the testimonies of former Chinese comfort women became available, the horrifying picture of how they were forced into comfort stations and then tortured began to emerge. Japanese forces used various methods to round up Chinese women. Although it is not possible to obtain statistics on the total number of kidnappings, documented cases suggest shockingly large numbers. For example, during the time of the Nanjing Massacre, the Japanese army abducted tens of thousands of women from Nanjing and the surrounding areas, including over 2,000 women from Suzhou, 3,000 from Wuxi, and 20,000 from Hangzhou.[21] These blatant kidnappings continued throughout the entire war, the youngest abductee's being only nine years old.[22] Local researchers on Hainan Island reported a large-scale abduction that occurred on 24 June 1941 in Lehui County, where four hundred Japanese soldiers burned down the villages of Beian and Dayang, murdered 499 civilians, and took A'niang and dozens of other young women to the military comfort stations at Boao.[23] The brutality Chinese women faced when they were abducted into the military comfort stations was very similar to that faced by Philippine comfort women.[24] Violent abductions were not limited to rural areas or to places where Chinese resistance forces were active. According to the testimony of Mrs. Andrew Levinge, a member of the British Volunteer Aid Detachment at St. Stephens College Hospital in Hong Kong, a group of Japanese military men abducted her and three other female members of the aid detachment when Japanese forces occupied the city. The Japanese troops repeatedly raped Levinge's colleagues; they also detained four Chinese women and sexually assaulted them within the hospital compound.[25]

The alarming scope of victimization may also be seen in the fact that the occupation troops frequently replaced Chinese comfort women in order to satisfy the soldiers' desires for virginity and novelty. Consider the comments of Wu Liansheng, who worked as a janitor at the Zhaojia-yuan Comfort Station in Hainan for nearly two years, from 1942 to 1943. According to Wu, the Zhaojia-yuan Comfort Station opened in February 1942 and regularly kept about twenty to forty-five comfort women. The number of women it victimized, however, was actually much greater than that because Japanese troops frequently moved women from this comfort station to other places, killing those who were too sick or too weak to work. Because their bodies were destroyed and their replacements randomly drafted from local areas, no one knows exactly how many women were enslaved in Zhaojia-yuan Comfort Station from the time it opened until the end of the war in 1945.[26] Similar situations also occurred in large cities. According to a document prepared by the Special Agents Department of the Tianjin Police Bureau on 3 July 1944, a comfort station run by the Japanese Garrison Headquarters in Tianjin drafted comfort women from the city in rotating groups: each group comprised twenty to thirty women who were to be replaced by a new group every three weeks.[27] The document does not mention how long this rotation program lasted or how many comfort stations practised it, but the given replacement rate indicates that this one comfort station would have victimized 370 to 560 Chinese women in a period of one year.[28]

The sexual violence and abduction perpetrated on Chinese women by Japanese troops took particularly brutal forms in areas in which Chinese resistance forces were active. This can be seen in the data documented by a survey entitled "Jin Ji Lu Yu bianqu banian kang-Ri zhanzheng zhong renmin zaoshou sunshi diaocha tongji biao" (Statistics based on the investigations of the civilian damages during the eight-year resistance war against Japanese forces at the Jin Ji Lu Yu border region). It was conducted in January 1946 at the border area of Shanxi, Hebei, Shandong, and Henan provinces, where the resistance forces, led by the Chinese Communist Party, had established their bases in the late 1930s. During the eight years of Japanese invasion of the area, approximately 363,000 women were raped by Japanese troops and 122,000 of them contracted venereal diseases as a result.[29] A report preserved in the Central Archives of China indicates that, during one mop-up operation at the end of 1940, the Imperial Japanese Army raped 4,274 local women at Laizhuo, Hebei Province.[30] A record preserved in Hebei Province Archives, "Ba nian lai Riben Faxisi cuihui Taihang-qu renming de gaishu" (A summary of the damages done by the Japanese fascists to the people in Taihang region over the past eight years), reports that Japanese forces in the region frequently raped and kidnapped local women and regularly detained a large number of them as military sex slaves (see Figure 2).[31] In the Wangxiaoyu stronghold, for instance, soldiers detained over twenty young women who were abducted from the nearby village, including a thirteen-year-old girl whose cries were heard by the local people day and night.[32] He Tianyi, a researcher affiliated

Figure 2 A cave dwelling in Yu County, Shanxi Province used as a "comfort station" by the Japanese troops and the place Wan Aihua was imprisoned in 1943.

with the Hebei Provincial Academy of Social Sciences, reports that, by the end of 1943 in the southern Hebei region alone, the Japanese army had built 1,103 strongholds and that the total number of such strongholds constructed during the war in northern China would, at the least, have exceeded ten thousand. This number, though still incomplete, suggests that the number of Chinese women detained in Japanese military strongholds as sex slaves in northern China alone could have been between 100,000 and 200,000.[33]

The research conducted by Japanese and Korean scholars indicates that larger Japanese military units seemed to have systematically carried out the draft of comfort women rather than relying on apparently random kidnappings. Usually the expeditionary forces would order the rear service staff or adjutants of the army, division, brigade, or regiment to round up women and set up comfort stations. The orders would then be carried out by the commissariat unit, the accounting section, or the military police.[34] Yamada Sadamu, former military police warrant officer and the chief of the military police unit in Baoqing, Hubei Province, wrote in his diary that he was asked by the rear service staff of the 116th Division to draft comfort women after Japanese troops entered Baoqing in the fall of 1944. He assigned the task to a sergeant major, who gathered about a dozen women and turned them over to an adjutant.[35]

The direct involvement of Japanese military officers in establishing comfort stations is also evidenced by their confessions, preserved in Chinese archives. A 1954 interrogation record kept in the Central Archives of China shows that, between 1942 and 1945, under the supervision of Hirose Saburō, senior adjutant of the 59th Division of the Japanese Army, 127 comfort stations were set up at Xintai, Taian, Linqing, Tuxikou, Laiwu, Jinan, Zhangdian, Boshan, Zhoucun, De-xian, and Hedong in Shandong Province. From 1944 to 1945, Hirose Saburō was in charge of the management of the military comfort station named Star Club (Xing julebu in Chinese) in Ji'nan City, Shandong Province, which held about fifty Chinese women between the ages of sixteen and twenty-three.[36] On his capture, Suzuki Hiraku, lieutenant-general and commander of the 117th Division, confessed that, between 1941 and 1942, when he was the commander of the 27th Infantry Regiment, he ordered the establishment of comfort stations in the Hebei area (where his units were stationed) and detained sixty local women. In 1945, when his troops were stationed in the He'nan area, he ordered comfort stations to be set up near the military barracks and abducted another sixty women to be comfort women.[37]

In occupied areas in China, the Japanese military commonly used Chinese collaborators to round up local women. This was often accomplished through the cooperation of the local puppet administrations and the local Association for Maintaining Order (Zhian weichi hui), the latter being a local civilian organization under the supervision of the occupation army. Once the Japanese army had occupied a new territory, it would force each local resident to register for a "good citizen ID card." During this process the military authorities would either pick out young women to send to comfort stations or instruct the local puppet government to do so. Thousands of women were reportedly taken away during the "good citizen ID" registration after the fall of Nanjing to be comfort women for the Japanese military; some were sent to northeastern China to serve the Guandong Army.[38] Smaller military units also forced the local administration to help draft comfort women. It was reported that the Japanese detachment in the Xingyujiang stronghold ordered the nearby village head to send two women to the block-house each night to "sleep" with the soldiers. The villagers strongly resisted this order. The village head, under pressure to comply, asked the members of the puppet village administration to send the women from their own families first; he set the example by sending his own wife. On hearing this, his wife hanged herself.[39] The following order, issued by the Wenshui County Office, Shanxi Province, in 1939, is another documented case. The translation of the document reads as follows:

Order of Wenshui County Office (Chai 1)

The Hejia-xiang Brothel in the county seat was established to protect the county's residents. Since its establishment, good residents in this county have been safe. However, it has been made clear that recently the brothel does not have enough prostitutes in service – only four available excluding those who are ill. The Imperial Army authority has currently ordered that the number [of the women] be increased within three days. Therefore, in addition to the women submitted by the county from the city, all villages of 300 households or more must submit one woman to be a prostitute. The women selected must be around twenty years old, healthy, and good-looking; they must be sent to the county office as soon as possible for examination. Each of the selected women will be given a one-time payment of one silver dollar and provided with the following monthly benefits by the Association for Maintaining Order: twenty-five kilograms of wheat flour, ten cups of millet, two pints of kerosene, and fifty kilograms of coal.[40] In addition, the women may enjoy the gifts from the brothel users. This is an important and urgent matter.[41]

The Hejia-xiang Brothel was a comfort station for the exclusive use of the Imperial Japanese Army. The document produced by the Wenshui County Office shows that the Wenshui County administration had received an order from the imperial army to draft comfort women for the military brothel. In order to justify forcing local women to be prostitutes, the County Office emphasized the importance of the brothel to the safety of local residents. The document indicates that, if civilians failed to follow the military order, the occupation army would take violent action against them. The document also reveals that the brothel was not a commercial institution; rather, the local Association for Maintaining Order was charged with maintaining its operating costs. Evidence of the Japanese army's coercion of local administrations to set up and pay for comfort stations has also been found in Tianjin, Shandong, and other areas in northern China.[42]

When local dignitaries received military orders to draft comfort women, their common excuse for doing so was the safety of local residents. The diary of a military physician affiliated with the 2nd Battalion of the 2nd Independent Mountain Artillery Regiment recorded a case that occurred in a village near Dongshi, Hubei Province, on the bank of the Yangtze River. His diary entry for 11 August 1940 describes how the Chinese women drafted from local families received their medical examination for sexually transmitted diseases:

When it was time for her internal exam, the young woman became increasingly embarrassed and would not take off her pants. The interpreter and the head of the Association for Maintaining Order yelled at her and she finally took them off. When I had her lie down on a bed and began a pelvic exam, she frenziedly scratched at my hands. I saw her crying. Later I was told that she cried for a long time after she left the room.

It was the same with the next girl and I felt I wanted to cry as well. This was probably their first experience with this kind of embarrassing examination and, given the purpose of it, it was no surprise that they felt humiliated. They must have come the whole way crying even as the head of the neighbourhood and the head of the Association for Maintaining Order were trying to convince them that this was for the safety of the village.[43]

Clearly, the young women being examined had been forced by local leaders to be military comfort women. The doctor also wrote in his diary that the battalion commander "consulted with the head of the neighbourhood and the head of the Association for Maintaining Order and asked them to draft women locally," and that "it was not a coercive request at all; everything was left up to their discretion."[44] However, it is plain that local residents in the occupied areas were in no position to refuse any request from the Japanese military.

In fact, reports of coerced collaboration under the Japanese occupation are numerous. Hu Jiaren of Fuli Township, Hainan Island, witnessed one such case. He reported that, in March 1943, a unit of twenty-five Japanese military men occupied Fuli Township, where Hu Jiaren lived. The occupation troops built two military strongholds and demanded that the nearby villages submit two women to be long-term comfort women for the master sergeant and the sergeant first class, and that they submit another five or six women to be short-term comfort women for the soldiers on a daily basis. The occupation army made it clear that, if any village dared to disobey this order, the residents of the entire village would be killed and their houses burned. Consequently, local women Zheng Ading and Zhuo A'niang were turned in to service the sergeants, and the villages in the township took turns submitting five to six women to the Japanese military stronghold each day, as the army demanded.[45]

In a report published in *Guangxi funü* (Guangxi women's journal) in 1941, Wang Bizhen documents another case of the military's coercing local people to submit women to a military comfort station, this time at Tongcheng, Hubei Province. According to this report, the comfort station at Tongcheng detained both women drafted locally and women from Japan, Korea, and Taiwan. The women drafted from Japan and its colonies were assigned to service the military officers, while local Chinese women were assigned to service the soldiers. The report describes the drafting and treatment of the Chinese comfort women as follows:

> Most of the women who are used as the "comforting objects" *[weianpin]* in this comfort station are drafted by force from the local area by the Association for Maintaining Order. These women are allowed to go home after being enslaved in the comfort station for a certain time, but they must have at least five warrantors to guarantee that they would be sent back [to the station].[46] If a released woman is not sent back three days after the due date, all the warrantors and their family members would be buried alive and the members of the Association for Maintaining Order would also be punished.
>
> During the days in service a comfort woman is raped by some sixty soldiers. She is forced to smile when being raped and if she shows the slightest unwillingness she would be ripped naked and whipped ruthlessly, and she would not be permitted to go home for three weeks.[47]

This report was written immediately after Chinese Nationalist forces retook Tongcheng from the Japanese, when intense battles were still occurring in the region. It provides a clear picture of how the Japanese imperial forces blatantly coerced local people into submitting women to military rape centres – a heinous crime made possible due to the absolute power of the Japanese military during the occupation. It is worth noting that the comfort station described in this report was in Hubei, the same province in which the Japanese military physician mentioned above described in his diary his medical examination of Chinese comfort women.

These cases, in which Chinese men were involved in drafting local women for the military comfort facilities, expose the roles the local Chinese played in the implementation of the comfort women system. As seen above, the collaboration between the local men and the occupiers took place under varied conditions.[48] While Qiao Hongnian actively helped to set up the comfort stations and continued to participate in their operations, in other cases local leaders and government officials were clearly coerced by the Japanese military to draft women. Although their actions in forcing women to be military sex slaves cannot be justified by the pressure produced by the occupying power, given the widespread killing and rape carried out by the Japanese forces in the occupied areas, it is obvious that refusal to follow their orders would have put the safety of all local residents at risk. In other words, even though Chinese collaborators were responsible for their part in the crime, the ultimate responsibility lies with the Japanese military.

Besides kidnapping them through the use of armed forces and drafting them through the cooperation of local collaborators, the Japanese military also used deceit to procure Chinese comfort women. The military sent its own agents and/or civilian procurers to recruit young women through false job offers for positions such as maid, nurse, or nanny. Once the women signed up, they were forcibly taken to military comfort stations. The experience of Yuan Zhulin, one of the twelve survivors whose narrative is presented in this book, exemplifies this approach to obtaining comfort women. She was looking for a job in Wuhan in the spring of 1940 when a female procurer told her that cleaning women were wanted in another city, so Yuan and a group of other girls travelled with this woman down the Yangtze River. As soon as they came ashore, Yuan and the other girls were taken to a comfort station by armed Japanese soldiers and held there to be military comfort women. Lei Guiying, another survivor whose experience is detailed in this book, was led to believe that she had been hired by a Japanese couple to be their housemaid. However, when she had just turned thirteen and started menstruating, she was raped and detained in the comfort station run by that couple. In Japan's colony Taiwan, recruitment involved both deception and coercion. According to the research a women's NGO conducted on forty-eight comfort women who were drafted from Taiwan, the majority "were forced to become comfort women after having been recruited on the pretext of joining the youth corps or working as nurses."[49]

Similar to what occurred in Japan and its colonies, in Mainland China deceptive procurement was carried out on a very large scale and was accompanied by extreme violence. Local investigators report that, in the spring of 1942, members of the Japanese military, pretending to be representatives of a Hong Kong company, publicly recruited young women in occupied cities such as Guangzhou and Hong Kong. They rounded up over three hundred young women, many of whom were college and high school students; the youngest were only seventeen years old. These women were then sent to Shilu Comfort Station in Changjiang County, Hainan Island, and detained there by soldiers. Within four years, more than two hundred of these women had been beaten or abused to death.[50] In Hainan, the Japanese army ordered the formation of Battle Field Rear Service Teams. The military told local people that women were needed to do laundry and to clean for Japanese troops as well as to help care for injured soldiers. The Battle Field Rear Service Teams recruited women not only from the local areas but also from large cities such as Shanghai and Guangzhou as well as from other countries, including Korea and the Philippines. Women who were deceived into joining the teams ended up in comfort stations. Some performed hard work for the Japanese troops during the day and serviced them as comfort women at night.[51]

In the occupied territories the Japanese military's deceptive procurement tactics often amounted to nothing more than violent abductions. According to a 6 March 1938 newspaper report in *Shenbao*, Japanese troops in Shanghai drove vehicles around the streets and offered women rides. When women got into the cars, they would be driven to the military camps and forced to be sex slaves. The article reported that three female students took such an "unlicensed taxi" after a movie, when it was raining: "They did not know this was a trap set by the Japanese soldiers. The students were taken by that car to the other side of the Suzhou River and were never seen again."[52]

In big cities such as Shanghai, Nanjing, Wuhan, Guangzhou, and Tianjin, the Japanese army forced a considerable number of Chinese prostitutes to be comfort women. A document entitled "Investigation Record of the Enemy's Atrocities" (Diren zuixing diaochabiao), prepared by the Tianjin Local Court in May 1946, records a case in which the Tianjin Japanese Garrison Headquarters forcibly drafted eighty Chinese prostitutes from Tianjin to be military comfort women. According to the investigation, during April and May 1944, the Tianjin Japanese Garrison Headquarters ordered the Police Bureau of the puppet government of Tianjin to draft 150 prostitutes to service the Japanese troops in Henan Province. A section chief of the Police Bureau then ordered the Tianjin City Entertainment Business Association (Lehu lianhehui or Lehu gonghui) to collect the women. Zhou Qian, the secretary of the association, begged the section chief to consider an exemption, explaining that the prostitutes had to support their families; if they were drafted, their families would lose their means of livelihood. However, the chief scolded him and ordered him to gather the women at the police hospital for a medical examination by the following day. When Zhou informed the members of the association of the order, prostitutes either escaped or hid, and the city's brothels were shut. The Garrison Headquarters and the Police Bureau then sent police to draft prostitutes by force. They rounded up fifty-two licensed prostitutes, but this was less than half of the number wanted by the Japanese military. In order to meet the Japanese demand, the police captured twenty-eight unlicensed prostitutes. All of these women were first delivered to the Japanese Garrison Headquarters and then sent to Henan by train. They were retained by the Japanese troops for more than two months before being released.[53]

According to the recollection of a former Japanese military man, as the war spread through China, female Chinese prisoners of war (POWs) also became victims of the military comfort stations. Taguchi Shinkichi, a former soldier in the 14th Division who was in the northern China battle zone from September 1942 to December 1945, described their situation as follows:

> During the war there was no prison for female POWs at all, so where were they [Chinese female POWs] taken? I heard they were sent to be comfort women. However, those who were suspected of being spies and those who had received training in the Eighth Route Army were not put into ordinary comfort stations for they might escape or get in touch with agents of the Eighth Route Army,[54] which would be very dangerous [to our troops]. Then, where were they sent? They were all sent to the frontlines in northern and central China, to the two or three thousand strongholds where small detachments were stationed. The conditions in these areas were extremely harsh and [Japanese and Korean] comfort women were usually unavailable there. A stronghold was typically enclosed by walls and surrounded by blockhouses. Each blockhouse was garrisoned by a platoon. The female POWs were imprisoned in such strongholds. They were put in rooms made of adobe, separate from the blockhouse, because they were considered dangerous ... Supply of condoms to the frontline detachment was scant, so many of these women who were raped by soldiers without condoms became pregnant. The pregnant women were continually raped as long as they were usable. When they were no longer usable they were then taken out of the strongholds and tied to standing timbers so new soldiers could practice using their bayonets. They were stabbed to death and buried together with their unborn babies. No one knew which soldiers were the babies' fathers. Tens of thousands of Chinese women were buried secretly like this at the thousands of strongholds during the fifteen-year war. I think the number was really uncountable.[55]

Although Taguchi's account is based on hearsay and is difficult to verify, the fact that this kind of information circulated among Japanese soldiers reveals their view of, and attitude toward, Chinese comfort women and POWs. In fact, what Taguchi describes is in accordance with other reports of what happened to pregnant Chinese comfort women and female POWs during the war.[56] The killing of pregnant Chinese comfort women by Japanese soldiers has been reported from other regions,[57] and Wan Aihua's experience, presented in Part 2, recounts how female resistance movement members were tortured by being made into military sex slaves.

Subjected to exceptionally cruel forms of torture in battle zone comfort stations, Chinese comfort women suffered an extremely high death rate. In fact, during Japan's aggressive war, Japanese military officers openly permitted the raping and then the killing of Chinese women. Okamoto Kenzō, a former

Japanese military man who witnessed the Nanjing Massacre, recalled that the higher military officers instructed them to kill rape victims by beating rather than by using a bayonet or gun in order to avoid leaving incriminating evidence.[58] With this kind of authorization, abusing and killing comfort women, particularly women of Japan's enemy nations, became common occurrences. Fu Heji, a researcher on the Committee of Hainan Cultural and Historical Data reports that, on the Sixteenth Day of the Sixth Lunar Month,[59] in 1941, the Japanese army killed fifty Chinese comfort women near the Tayang Bridge at Boao, Hainan, because they had resisted being raped.[60] Researchers in northern China also report that, in the early winter of 1941, Japanese troops raped forty women in Lengquan Village, Pingshan County, Hebei Province, and killed them all by slicing open their abdomens.[61] Although the Japanese military authorities claimed that the purpose of the comfort women system was to prevent rape and the spread of venereal disease, its basic nature was no different than the military officers' instructions to soldiers cited above: both sanctioned murder in order to conceal repeated acts of sexual violence against women.

3 Different Types of Military "Comfort Stations" in China

From the early 1930s to the end of the Second World War, Japanese military comfort stations were established over a vast part of Asia, including Mainland China, Taiwan, Hong Kong, Macau, the Philippines, British Malaya, the Dutch East Indies, Singapore, Thailand, French Indochina, Burma, New Britain Island, New Guinea, Sakhalin Island, Truk Island, and Japan.[1] Practically all the large Japanese military units had formalized or semi-formalized comfort stations attached to them; even small platoon- or squad-size units set up temporary comfort stations. Some well-established comfort stations were in operation for over ten years, while temporary ones existed only for a couple of weeks or days. The majority of these were situated in Mainland China, where the Japanese invasion lasted for fifteen years. Chinese women were drafted into all sorts of comfort stations, with the temporary ones focusing almost exclusively on local Chinese women. These transient frontline comfort stations not only significantly expanded the scope of victimization but also subjected women to exceptionally brutal treatment because they were often situated in extremely harsh surroundings and were completely unregulated.

Since the 1990s, thousands of comfort station sites have been located by researchers in China, from the northeastern border in Heilongjiang to Yunnan and Hainan Island in the south (see Figure 3). If the small temporary comfort stations set up in military strongholds and blockhouses are included in the count, the number of comfort stations in China increases to tens of thousands.[2] In the remote northern province of Heilongjiang, for example, Chinese investigators have confirmed comfort station sites in seventeen cities and towns: Haerbin, Qiqihaer, Mudanjiang, Jiamusi, Dongning, Hutou, Dong'an, Wenchun, Fujin, Sunwu, Acheng, Fuzigou, Boli, Suifenhe, Manzhouli, Jixi, and Mishan. In Dongning County alone the Japanese army set up over forty stations that were staffed by more than one thousand comfort women.[3]

There is no doubt that the implementation of the military comfort women system on such a vast scale could only have been possible with the direct involvement of the Japanese military and the Japanese government. Yet, due

Figure 3 Survivor Huang Youliang (on right) showing the site of Tengqiao "Comfort Station" on Hainan Island, where she was enslaved in 1941 as a "comfort woman."

to Japan's restrictions on access to relevant documentation, information regarding the organization and the operation of these comfort stations continues to be difficult to obtain.[4] Based on the limited number of official Japanese documents uncovered thus far, researchers are able to demonstrate that "the Japanese government and military were fully and systematically involved in planning, establishing, and operating the comfort women system. Japanese officials involved were Home Ministry personnel, including prefectural governors and the police at all ranks; Foreign Ministry officials; and the governors-general of Korea and Taiwan."[5] As Yuki Tanaka outlines, the senior staff officers of the imperial forces gave orders to establish comfort stations, and staff officers of the subordinate units made concrete plans and carried them out. In general, the staff section of each troop was in charge of matters related to comfort women.[6]

The Japanese troops had various names for the comfort stations in China. Besides the commonly used "comfort station," some were given names such as: "The Imperial Military Guest House" (Huangjun zhaodaisuo, Ji'nan City, Shandong Province), "Lotus Corps" (Furong-dui, Zhuxian, Henan Province), "Entertainment Facility" (Xingle-suo, Hongkou District, Shanghai City), "Comfort Camp" (Weian-ying, Shanxi Province), "Soldiers' Paradise"

(Junzhong leyuan, Huangliu Airport, Hainan Island), "Manchurian Military Prostitutes House" (Guandong wuji-guan, Zhenjiang City, Jiangsu Province), "Military Officers' Club" (Junguan julebu, Jiujiang City, Jiangxi Province), "Society of the Friends of the Army" (Junzhiyou-she, Shanghai), "Happy House" (Kuaile-fang, Baoting County, Hainan Island), "Japan-China Friendship House" (Ri-Zhi qinshan-guan, Confucius Temple, Nanjing City), "Comforting Beauty" (Weian li, Hainan Island), "Japan-China House" (Ri-Zhi guan, Anqing City, Anhui), "Military Personnel Club" (Junren julebu, Zhongshan City, Guangdong Province), "Comfort Women Delegation" (Weian-tuan, Deng County, Henan Province), and so on.[7] These names, like the term "comfort station," express the attitude of those establishing them: they were concerned only with the pleasure of the imperial military men and cared nothing for the suffering of the victimized women.

The comfort stations were usually established on expropriated Chinese property. In October 1938, for example, the commissariat headquarters of the Japanese occupation army at Hankou ordered the construction team to secure a location that could accommodate about three hundred comfort women. The construction team searched for suitable buildings and selected an area in Jiqingli in which sixty-eight two-story buildings were clustered together. This place was surrounded by a fence and conveniently located, so it was made into a huge military comfort station.[8] Another example of the large-scale confiscation of civilian properties for the purpose of setting up comfort stations occurred in the Wanchai District in Hong Kong. On 20 February 1942, soon after its occupation of Hong Kong, the Japanese army formed its own military government headed by General Isogai Rensuke. This military government ordered the establishment of comfort stations, with Lieutenant-Governor Hirano Shigeru in charge. A piece of land about eight-hundred metres long on the northern coast of the populous Wanchai District was chosen as one of the locations. The residents were ordered to move out of the area within three days, although many had no place else to go. The military government then sent armed soldiers to force the residents out, giving them no time to collect their belongings. Soon thereafter, a gigantic comfort station opened, with hundreds of rooms that, day and night, were crowded with Japanese troops.[9]

Occasionally, the Japanese forces built comfort stations from scratch, as was the case with the "Yangjiazhai Entertainment Centre" (Yangjiazhai yulesuo). This station became widely known because Asō Tetsuo, a gynecologist and probationary medical officer at the Commissariat Hospital of the Shanghai Expeditionary Army, photographed it and mentioned it in his book.[10] Although known as Yangjiazhai comfort station, this facility was in

Figure 4 Yuan Zhulin revisiting the old temple where the Japanese army kept her in 1940 as a military "comfort woman."

fact not located in Yangjiazhai. Su Zhiliang's 1994 field investigation verified that this comfort station had been located in a small village called Dong-Shenjiazhai about one hundred metres north of Yangjiazhai.[11] Local residents Shi Liuliu, Gu Zhangfu, Shen Fugen, Shen Yuexian, Xu Xiaomei, and Shen Xiaomei recalled that the Japanese army occupied Dong-Shenjiazhai after the Battle of Shanghai broke out in August 1937. Before the Japanese troops came, many houses in the village had been destroyed by Japanese air strikes, and most of the villagers had fled. The Japanese soldiers drove the remaining villagers, those who had been unable to flee, to the western end of the village and created a huge military barracks in the northern end. In the winter of the same year, the soldiers tore down the remains of the destroyed houses on the east side of the village, where they then constructed a dozen wooden houses. Each of the houses had about ten rooms and each room was about ten square metres in size. The troops used these houses as a comfort station, which the local people referred to as "Japanese Brothel" *(Dongyang tangzi)*. When the photograph Asō had taken of the Yanjiazhai comfort station was shown to Shi Liuliu and the other eyewitnesses, they confirmed that the houses in the picture were the same as those they had seen built in

Dong-Shenjiazhai. At the time, the Japanese army also constructed a road from Yangjiazhai to Dong-Shenjiazhai. The Japanese soldiers likely mistook the name "Dong-Shenjiazhai" for "Yangjiazhai."[12]

Thus, the Japanese imperial forces turned different kinds of Chinese properties – including schools, residential houses, public bathing houses, hotels, warehouses, banks, village cottages, cave-houses, and even temples and churches – into comfort stations (see Figure 4). Sometimes they simply used a space in the military blockhouse as a comfort facility, as is described in several cases discussed in this book. The numerous comfort stations in China can be roughly divided into the following four types, according to who set them up and who was responsible for their oversight.[13]

The first type of comfort station was set up and run directly by Japanese military forces. This type includes comfort facilities of varying sizes and forms and can be further divided into (1) formal comfort stations run by large military units, (2) mobile (or temporary) comfort stations used to serve troops during major battles or military operations, and (3) improvised comfort stations set up by small troop units wherever they happened to be stationed. Formal comfort stations established by large military units, such as an army or a division, were often attached to supply bases in big cities and staffed by dozens or even hundreds of comfort women, including both locally drafted Chinese women and women drafted from Japan, Korea, and Taiwan. One example of this type is the "Yangjiazhai Entertainment Centre," where Asō Tetsuo conducted medical examinations on eighty Korean and twenty Japanese women immediately before it opened on 2 January 1938.[14]

Some of the comfort stations run directly by the military operated out of a vehicle, such as a train or carriage, that travelled from place to place. These mobile comfort stations were used in areas where there were not enough comfort women available or where it was difficult to set up a fixed comfort station. Reportedly, the Guandong Army ran comfort trains periodically between 1933 and 1940.[15] Some comfort stations that had fixed locations also periodically transported comfort women to strongholds and blockhouses near the frontlines. The comfort stations in Nada City, Hainan Island, for example, sent about a dozen comfort women to troops stationed in remote areas every month. These comfort women were forced to service about fifty soldiers a day, even during their menstrual period. Many of them contracted venereal diseases or died as a result of torture.[16]

Among the comfort facilities directly run by the Japanese military, the impromptu comfort stations set up by small units made up by far the largest number. These makeshift comfort stations were randomly set up in military barracks and strongholds, local people's homes, temples, or any place convenient to the garrisoned soldiers. The conditions in these comfort stations were unspeakable, and the women confined there were mostly drafted from local areas. The troops sometimes used a military tent or a hastily built shed as a comfort facility. As is seen in the survivors' accounts in this book, some of these stations lacked doors or even walls between the rooms, so curtains were hung to create separate spaces; if a bed were unavailable, the comfort women were raped on the earthen floor. Many of these women were tortured to death, committed suicide, or were killed after being repeatedly raped. According to one of the documented cases, after the Japanese army occupied Fuyang County, Zhejiang Province, on 24 December 1937, the troops set up a comfort station at the City God Temple (Chenghuang-miao) and detained many local women to be their sex slaves. Nine of the women were soon raped to death, and during the Japanese occupation 90 percent of the houses in the town were burned and over twelve hundred residents were killed.[17] A 1939 written report from the chief of the Liyang City Police Bureau states that, after the Japanese army captured Liyang, Jiangsu Province, on 25 February 1938, the soldiers abducted Mrs. Wu, Mrs. Jiang, and other three local women, taking them to their barracks and detaining them, naked, in an empty room, thus making a temporary comfort station. Within a month the women detained there increased to fifty. Many of these women were killed by being forced to endure multiple gang-rapes; those who did not die were drowned in the river.[18]

The second type of comfort station was managed by overseas Japanese, Korean, or Taiwanese brothel proprietors, under the supervision of military authorities, for the exclusive use of military personnel and employees. Military units played an important role in giving permission to open the brothels, providing facilities, overseeing hygienic conditions, and enforcing regulations. The proprietors, closely associated with military officers, collected profits from running these military brothels. This kind of comfort station usually operated in the vicinity of a military barracks. For example, in the autumn of 1940, immediately after the Japanese army occupied Yichang, three brothels run by Japanese and Korean brothel proprietors for military use opened near where the troops were stationed.[19] As is seen in the accounts given by Lei Guiying and Yuan Zhulin (see Part 2), the comfort stations run by civilian proprietors were under tight military control and clearly differed from ordinary brothels.

The third type of comfort station made use of pre-existing "entertainment" facilities approved by military authorities for the use of its personnel. Once

Figure 5 The buildings of Dayi Saloon on Dong-Baoxing Road in Shanghai today.

a facility was designated for the use of military personnel, military authorities would send officers or policemen to inspect and/or oversee the management of the brothel, provide condoms, and send staff to conduct medical examinations of the comfort women. This type of comfort station was open to both Japanese military personnel and civilian users but gave the troops absolute priority. They were mostly found in major cities, such as Shanghai, Wuhan, and Beiping. Dayi Saloon in Shanghai, for example, had been a brothel for overseas Japanese patrons and was owned by a Japanese couple. After 1931, it was designated as a comfort station for use by the Japanese navy. At its peak it occupied three buildings, which still exist today at 125 Dong-Baoxing Road (see Figure 5).

The fourth type of comfort station, also found mostly in cities and towns, was set up by local Chinese administrations or collaborators following orders issued by the Japanese military. As shown previously, after the outbreak of full-scale warfare the Japanese military forces increasingly relied on local Chinese collaborators to set up comfort stations. In Anhui Province, for example, the Japanese army commanded the Association for Maintaining

Order to set up comfort stations as soon as the troops occupied Bangbu in February 1938; 120 local women were abducted and taken to the facilities, which were set up in buildings that had previously been hotels and restaurants.[20] During the same year the occupation army in Fengyang County also charged the local Association for Maintaining Order to set up comfort stations. The Japanese soldiers, assisted by their collaborators, abducted thirty local women to serve as comfort women; even a nun from the local monastery was forcibly taken to the comfort station. Three women committed suicide in their attempt to resist the violence.[21] Some local Chinese collaborators apparently voluntarily helped the Japanese army set up comfort stations, but in many cases their collaboration was actually a result of coercion as the Japanese military threatened to, and often did, kill any local people who refused to provide them with women to be used as sex slaves.

Often, especially in big cities where regimental headquarters were located, comfort stations were divided according to the military rank of the users. The interior facilities and nationalities of comfort women used in stations for officers were quite different from those used for soldiers. The former were often well-furnished and were usually staffed with specially selected Japanese and Korean women. Some comfort stations for the exclusive use of commissioned officers were lavishly decorated,[22] those for soldiers were typically very basic, usually a bed and a table in a small room.

Japanese military forces maintained tight control of each comfort station, whether it was directly run by them or operated by a private proprietor. In different locations comfort stations were supervised and managed by different military officers or sections, but usually they were the responsibility of the rear service staff, management sections of the armies' headquarters in the fields, commissariat officers, the paymaster or adjutants of each regiment or division, or the military police.[23] The 13th Independent Infantry Brigade Chūzan Garrison stationed in Zhongshan, Guangdong Province, for example, established the regulations for the use of comfort stations called "The Soldiers' Clubs." Assignments were delegated as follows:

Clause 3. The unit's adjutant is in charge of supervising, controlling, and advising the management of the soldiers' clubs to ensure their smooth and proper operation.

Clause 4. The medical officer affiliated with the unit is responsible for hygiene facilities in the soldiers' clubs and the implementation of hygiene services. In addition, he is in charge of all hygiene-related matters, including healthcare, food preparation, and schedules of the families, working women, and users of the soldiers' clubs.

Clause 5. The unit's paymaster is responsible for all matters relating to accounting for the soldiers' clubs.[24]

Clearly, besides arranging building facilities and rounding up comfort women, military personnel were also directly involved in comfort station management, overseeing security, regulation, and hygiene. One of the security measures taken by military authorities was the registration of comfort women. According to Yamada Seikichi, the department head of the China Detachment Army Comfort Facilities, when each Japanese comfort woman arrived in Hankou, one of the military officers examined her photograph, a copy of her family registry, her written pledge, her parental consent form, her permit from the police, her identification papers provided by local officials in her home town, and so on. He then filled out a personal examination form describing her personal history and family information and sent a copy of it to the military police.[25] This kind of registration procedure seems to have been conducted for women transported to China from Japan and its colonies but not for Chinese women drafted from occupied areas. As indicated by the accounts of the twelve survivors presented in this book, most Chinese comfort women were deprived of their identity when sent to comfort stations. They were called by a number, an assigned name, or by nothing at all, and they were kept under strict military surveillance – like prisoners. Sentries were stationed at all comfort stations, but Chinese comfort women were under particularly strict guard because they were regarded as enemies of Japan and because their connections with local people increased the possibility of their escape. The Shilu Comfort Station in Hainan, for example, had Japanese soldiers on watch twenty-four hours a day, and comfort women who attempted to escape were either shot to death or severely beaten when captured.[26] According to the eyewitness account of Song Fuhai, who worked as a janitor at the comfort station in the Town of Xinying, Hainan Island, in 1940, a platoon chief named Kawaoka established the following rules for the Chinese comfort women:

- Comfort women are forbidden to go out or escape; any violator and all her family members will be decapitated.
- Comfort women must unconditionally respect and obey the Japanese military personnel.
- Comfort women are under the absolute control of the two supervisors. Those who disobey will be severely punished.

- Comfort women must unconditionally satisfy the needs of the military men of the detachment at any time.[27]

Under such strict control, escape was very difficult if not impossible.

Military authorities provided detailed regulations for the use and operation of comfort stations. Huayue-lou Comfort Station, a three-story wooden building located at 13 Hui'an-xiang, Shangfu Street, Nanjing, was one of the military comfort stations established during the Japanese occupation. According to the recollections of local residents, the station always held about twenty-five comfort women, most of whom were from Yangzhou. These comfort women were assigned numbers and their pictures were hung on the walls in the entrance hall so that the soldiers could indicate their choice.[28] Gu Xiang, who lived at 14 Hui'an-xiang, Shangfu Street, kept a photograph of the comfort station regulations, which were carved on a piece of wood taken from the former comfort station site. The regulations were dated 6 March 1939 and contained the following twelve clauses:

1 The special women in the commissariat comfort station must receive a medical examination conducted by the medical officer from the Military Police Division Commissariat every five days.

2 Those women who are unable to pass the medical examination must receive special medical treatment and are not allowed to resume service without permission.

3 The result of the medical examination of each comfort woman must be recorded and the results must be filed and made available for inspection.

4 The comfort station's schedule is the following:
   Soldiers: 10:00 AM to 6:00 PM
   Officers: 10:00 AM to 9:00 PM

5 The fees for use of the comfort station are the following:
   Soldiers: 1 yen per 30 minutes (50 sen for an additional 30 minutes)
   Commissioned Officers: 3 yen per hour (2 yen for an additional hour)
   High-ranking Officials: 3 yen per hour
   Clerical staff officials: 1.5 yen per 30 minutes (additional charge for an additional 30 minutes)

6 Each client of this designated military comfort station is required to pay the fees, and obtain and use a condom before service, and clean his body in the washroom afterwards.

7 Entry to this designated military comfort station is restricted to the military personnel and the supporting staff of the army. Entry of other people is forbidden.

8　Alcoholic substances may not be brought into this designated military comfort station.
9　Drunken people are not allowed to enter this designated military comfort station.
10　Clients are not allowed to enter any room other than the room that is assigned at the purchase of the ticket.
11　Clients are not allowed to use the comfort woman without using a condom.
12　Those who do not comply with the regulations and those who violate the regulations of the army will be ordered to leave.[29]

The contents of this document are very similar to the "Yangjiazhai Military Comfort Station Regulations" (1938) recorded by Asō Tatsuo,[30] as they are to the "Regulations for the Use of the Soldiers' Clubs" for the 13th Independent Infantry Brigade Chūzan Garrison (1944).[31] Both also prescribed rules regarding hygienic precautions, the schedules and fees for using the comfort station, and the exclusive military use of the facility.

Although comfort station regulations specified the use of condoms,[32] in most cases these regulations were not enforced, particularly at the temporary comfort stations on the frontline, where there was no strict supervision and an insufficient supply of condoms. In some cases, when there were not enough condoms, comfort women and local Chinese labourers were assigned the job of washing and recycling used ones. Some units in the field rebelled against using condoms because they said it was uncomfortable.[33] Even in the best-case scenario, in which servicemen had and used condoms, the rough devices added to the comfort women's pain and caused permanent injury. As a result, venereal disease was widespread among the troops and among comfort women, and pregnancy was common. A child born to a Japanese comfort woman could be taken back to Japan. At the Yangjiazhai comfort station, for example, a Japanese comfort woman reportedly gave birth to a boy; she hired a local village woman to nurse the baby and later sent him to Japan.[34] For a Chinese comfort woman, pregnancy often led to death. Lin Pagong, who, in 1944, worked as a cleaner at a military comfort station called "Happy House" (Kuaile-fang) on Hainan Island, reported that Li Yaqian, a Li ethnic woman of Baoting County, was captured by Japanese soldiers of the Nanlin stronghold. Young and attractive, Li Yaqian was raped by many soldiers each day and soon became pregnant. When the soldiers found that she was pregnant, they dragged her to a hill near Qingxun Village and cut open her abdomen, killing her along with her unborn foetus.[35]

While comfort station regulations called for medical examinations for comfort women and prohibited women with venereal disease from working, medical staff was not always available at frontline comfort stations, and many women were forced to keep working after they had been infected with sexually transmitted diseases as, otherwise, there would not have been enough women to meet the soldiers' demands. In some comfort stations, such as the one in Zhaojiayuan, Hainan Island, comfort women who were too sick to work were killed rather than given medical treatment.[36] Comfort stations located in big cities usually had a washroom or washing area where disinfectant such as a potassium permanganate solution was provided for washing after intercourse, but the hygienic conditions of the stations in small towns and villages were appalling. Those comfort stations often had neither running water nor a sewage system. Since the women were not allowed to go out, they could only wash themselves with water in a small bowl and were forced to use a little container kept in each room when voiding their bowels. The rooms in those comfort stations smelled like a sewer. Even in mid-sized cities like Wuhu, sanitary conditions in the stations were unhealthy. The Fengyi-lou Comfort Station, which opened in January 1938, for example, only allowed the women to bathe three times each month, and each time the comfort women were sent to a public bathhouse they were guarded by armed Japanese soldiers.[37] Under these conditions many healthy women contracted sexually transmitted diseases. In many cities, including Shanghai, the Japanese military forced comfort women to receive an injection of Salvarsan, also known as 606, or Arsphenamine, in the hope of preventing syphilis. Salvarsan is an extremely toxic arsenic-containing substance that is very painful when injected and that often produces serious and sometimes deadly side effects. Many women who received it testified that they suffered from serious side effects, including infertility.[38]

Similarly, while the regulations forbade the drinking of alcohol, drunken violence was frequent in comfort stations. At Huayue-lou Comfort Station, whose regulations are cited above, drunken soldiers often forced their way into the building. Fan Guiying, a local resident who had worked as a tailor for the comfort women at Huayue-lou, recalled how a drunken soldier attempted to get into a room on the second floor. The frightened woman shut the doors to keep him out, but during the struggle the soldier plunged his sword between the doors and cut her arm.[39] Drunken incidents of violence were also recorded in the documents prepared by the headquarters of the military police stationed in central China. For instance, in November 1941 a sergeant went into a military comfort station without buying a ticket and beat a woman who refused to service him. Another recorded incident occurred in February 1942, when a corporal entered a station staffed by Chinese comfort women and went on a rampage with his sword.[40] These incidents came to light because they were flagrant violations of the regulations; however, the violence that occurred on a daily basis behind the doors of comfort stations was never reported. And even in the former cases, punishment was mild; the perpetrators were subject only to strong admonitions or, at most, short detentions.[41]

As is clear from the regulations cited above, the formal large comfort stations usually charged fees, which varied according to the user's military rank. Rates also varied at different stations. In addition, prices were different, depending on whether the service providers were Japanese, Korean, or Chinese comfort women. The following (Table 2) is a sample list of fees charged by comfort stations in different places in China. Japanese yen are the monetary units in the chart.[42]

The established rates of the South Sector Billet Brothel in Manila (c. 1943 or 1944) reflected similar fee differences based on the nationality of the woman; there, for men of all ranks, the hourly fees for services from Chinese comfort women were set at one-half yen less than were the services from Japanese and Korean comfort women.[43] Rather than reflecting any great difference in the services provided in the comfort stations, the different rate for the women of different nationalities reflected Japan's imperialistic policy of treating Japanese nationals different from enemy nationals.

The fees charged by the formal comfort stations created a false image, which led to there being some confusion between comfort women and prostitutes. However, the fees that soldiers paid to comfort stations did not function in the same way as did fees paid to prostitutes. This is because the vast majority of comfort women were coerced and then held captive. In addition, most of the money the soldiers paid went to those who ran the comfort stations, while the comfort women themselves received either nothing or only a very small portion of the payments. Regarding how the military comfort station fees were distributed, the "Regulations for the Operations of Comfort Facilities and Inns" (1943) issued by the Malay army administrative inspector provides some detailed information. According to them, comfort women were to receive 40 to 60 percent of the fees based on the cash advances they received.[44] The rules also indicated that three of every one hundred yen the women received were to be put into savings, and over two-thirds of the money comfort women received was to be applied to the repayment of their cash advances. In addition, the rules specified that, if comfort women became

Table 2

A sample list of fees charged by "comfort stations" in China

Place name	Women			Note
	Japanese	Korean	Chinese	
Concession area in Shanghai	2	1.5	1	2 for Russian, German, and French women
Anqing City, Anhui Province	1.7	1.7	1.5	
Hainan Island, Guangdong Province	Free of charge	Free of charge	Free of charge	
Yi County, Hebei Province	5-8	2.5	2	
Inner Mongolia		2	1.5	
Hankou City, Hubei Province		1.6	0.6	
Border between China and Soviet Union	5	1	0.5	
Guangdong Province	1	0.8	0.5-0.6	

Note: Monetary unit is the Japanese yen.

pregnant or fell ill while working, they must pay 50 percent of the medical treatment expenses. For other illnesses, the women had to pay 100 percent of the expenses.[45]

The offering of cash advances was a common method used by procurers when rounding up comfort women from Japan and its colonies. In order to support their families, women from impoverished families accepted a cash advance of up to fifteen hundred yen before being taken into the military comfort stations. Once in the comfort stations, however, it was not easy for these women to pay off their debt because the costs of clothing, cosmetics, and other daily necessities were often added to their debts. What the regulations issued by the Malay army administrative inspector stipulated was the best-case scenario for comfort women from Japan and its colonies, but even in cases in which comfort women became debt-free, much of their share of any payment for services had to be either put into mandatory savings or contributed to national defence.[46] Those who did manage to save any money suffered huge losses when their old yen were converted into new yen and when inflation soared after the war.[47] It has been reported that Korean comfort women who put their savings into military postal savings accounts were unable to withdraw their money after the war. In addition, women who were paid with military currency lost everything because, after the defeat of Japan, its military currency had no value.[48] Even for the small number of comfort women who reportedly received monetary payment, their experiences still amounted to forced prostitution.[49] According to the account given by Sumita Tomokichi, former engineer of the 6th Regiment, 6th Division, Imperial Japanese Army, published on the website of the conservative organization known as the Association for Advancement of Unbiased View of History (Jiyū shugi shikan kenkyūkai), a Korean comfort woman told Sumita in December 1938 in Hankou, China that her parents had sold her to a Korean dealer for 380 yen and that she had been taken to China to work in the comfort stations run by Koreans: "She said that at the comfort station, each woman had to entertain 25 to 30 men per day, without rest, and very poor food. Many contracted venereal diseases, and there were cases of suicide."[50] Sumita seems to have posted this account online in order to show that comfort women like this Korean woman were prostitutes who worked for money in civilian-run brothels at the frontlines. Ironically, the content of his account reveals vividly the slave-like condition of the forced prostitution of the comfort women system.

The coercive, exploitative nature of the comfort women system is also clear when one examines the experiences of Chinese comfort women in relation to monetary matters. The vast majority of these women were kept in the stations located on frontlines or in rural areas, where there was no regulation or supervision, and the Japanese soldiers did not have to pay for using these improvised facilities. Of the twelve Chinese survivors whose accounts are presented in this book, none received monetary payment from the Japanese military and several said that, in order to earn the necessities of daily life, they had to take on additional work, such as sewing and cleaning, when not servicing Japanese troops. Even in comfort stations in which tickets were sold, Chinese women received little payment. Wang Bizhen's 1941 report of the military comfort station at Tongcheng, Hubei Province, for example, has this to say:

The Japanese soldiers who use the comfort station have to go to the ticket office to purchase a paper slip. There are three types of tickets: first class [Japanese women] is 1.4 yuan; second class [Korean and Taiwanese women] is 0.8 yuan; and third class [Chinese women] is 0.4 yuan. Then they go to find the "comfort object" *(weianpin)* according to the number given on the ticket; they are not allowed to choose from the women as they like, nor are they permitted to stay there longer than the given time. A soldier will be charged an additional amount of the ticket fee for every five minutes passed the given time, and he will have one less opportunity to use the facility.

Although the money the soldiers paid to purchase the comfort station tickets is supposed to be given to the women who serve as the "comfort objects," after many layers of exploitation, very little is left for the women. Moreover, all the medical expenses are charged to the "comfort objects" when they become sick, and the money the women received was not even enough to pay one medical bill. This is how the women suffered under the brutal abuse.[51]

The report of the Tongcheng comfort station describes how women drafted from different countries were brutally exploited in a formal military comfort station. The hierarchical nature of the payment practice described in this report is surprisingly similar to that set forth by the South Sector Billet Brothel in Manila and the Malay army administrative inspector in the "Regulations for the Operations of Comfort Facilities and Inns." It is remarkable that this report, written when the military comfort station system was still in operation, uses the term *weianpin* (comfort object) to characterize all comfort women, regardless of the payment hierarchy created by the comfort station managers, and it clearly distinguishes military comfort stations from commercial brothels.

However, the vast majority of Chinese comfort women confined in improvised comfort facilities did not even receive these paltry service fees. Worse yet, in many cases the families of Chinese comfort women were forced to pay a large amount of money to military comfort stations in their attempts to have the abducted women released. Liu Mianhuan's story, told in the foreword of this book, is one example. Although Liu was successfully ransomed by her parents, the plan would have failed had she not been too sick to service the Japanese soldiers. The parents of a survivor surnamed Li, for example, paid a large ransom but were still unable to obtain her release until such time as she was physically incapable of continuing to service Japanese troops. Japanese soldiers had kidnapped Li from Lizhuang Village when she was fifteen years old. She was raped and beaten daily by a dozen Japanese troops for about five months. Hoping to ransom Li, her parents struggled and eventually managed to borrow about six hundred silver dollars. However, even after accepting all their money, the Japanese troops still held Li captive. In despair, Li's mother committed suicide. Li's father was driven insane by the death of his wife and the capture of his daughter.[52] Testimonies of several other survivors from Yu County and other areas of China recount similar situations.

The extortion, abduction, and abysmal treatment of Chinese comfort women, which was facilitated by the wartime context and the absolute authority of occupation forces, clearly show that the comfort women system was a war crime. Although the sexual violence against women, as has been properly pointed out, has its roots in the patriarchal social structures and "masculinist sexual culture" not only of Japan but also of the countries victimized,[53] the comfort women system directly resulted from, and explicitly benefited, Japan's war of aggression. The wartime experiences of Chinese women recounted in the following pages provide further evidence of the criminal nature of the Japanese military comfort women system.

4 Crimes Fostered by the "Comfort Women" System

The institutionalized sexual violence within the military comfort facilities and the random rapes and sexual assaults committed by Japanese troops in the cities and countryside of occupied regions were closely connected to each other and, indeed, were often combined, forming a spectrum of gender-based war crimes. Chinese women bore the brunt of the sexual violence exhibited by the Japanese military both inside and outside the comfort facilities: the establishment of the numerous comfort stations did not prevent but, rather, fostered sexual violence during the war.

According to Tang Huayuan's investigation, the Japanese 11th Army established military comfort stations at Yueyang County, Hunan Province, in October 1939, but even after that Japanese troops continued raping and assaulting local women in towns and villages. In September 1941, fourteen women who were captured in Jinsha Township (today's Jingzhou Township) resisted being raped and were brutally killed.[1] On 20 September 1941, five Japanese soldiers gang-raped a young girl in Jinsha Township and then forced her sixty-year-old male neighbour, Wu Kuiqing, to have sexual intercourse with her in front of the troops. Indignant, Wu punched the Japanese soldiers; the soldiers then beat Wu to death with heavy sticks and threw his body head first into a manure pit.[2] A month later, the troops went to Ouyang-miao Temple (today's Heyan Village Market, Xinxiang Township) where dozens of women and children had been hiding. The soldiers forced two sixty-year-old women to crawl naked in a courtyard, whipped them until their lower bodies were swollen, and thrust bayonets into their vaginas. The soldiers then raped the other women and forced mothers to have sexual intercourse with their sons, and fathers with their daughters, for the soldiers' entertainment. Those who resisted were executed.[3]

Large-scale sexual violence also occurred in Fengyang County, Anhui Province. Before the Japanese army seized the county seat on 1 February 1938, many local residents had fled, but they returned after 2 February when the occupation authorities guaranteed their safety. However, on 5 February Japanese troops suddenly closed the city gates and began killing residents.

Within five days as many as five thousand civilians were killed and hundreds of houses were burned down. A large number of women, from the ages of eleven to seventy, were raped – not even the pregnant women were spared. One pregnant woman was murdered after being raped; then the rapist-murderer cut open her abdomen and plucked out the foetus with his bayonet. After the mass rape the Japanese army retained a number of the victims to serve as comfort women.[4] After this massacre, on the night of 3 May 1938, soldiers from the Chinese New Fourth Army managed to capture two Chinese traitors and free the detained comfort women.[5] However, the Japanese army retaliated on the following day, killing 124 Chinese civilians who were unable to escape from Fengyang. Saying that the city residents had colluded with "mountain bandits" in the 3 May rescue, Japanese troops rampaged through the Siyanjing and Sanyanjing areas on 8 May, killing eighty civilians and machine-gunning another fifty near the city's west gate. When the soldiers discovered that Chinese civilians had taken refuge in a Roman Catholic church, they set fire to it, killing those inside. The soldiers raped the women caught during the rampage and forced their family members to kneel alongside to watch. If any family member showed the slightest resentment, the raped woman and her entire family were killed. In order to avoid rape and torture, many young women committed suicide by throwing themselves into rivers and wells. In Siyanjing, a well more than thirty metres deep was filled with women's bodies.[6] These mass rapes and murders all occurred in areas with fully operational comfort facilities. This suggests that, rather than preventing violence, as claimed, the comfort women system officially sanctioned sexual violence and fostered criminal behaviour.

Similar vicious crimes were committed by Japanese troops in the comfort facilities, whether the women were confined in urban comfort stations or in remote rural ones. Among the many Chinese women who were abused to death in the comfort stations was one, surnamed Li, who was held in the Wuhuyi Comfort Station in today's Wuyuan Township, Yueyang County, Hunan Province. The Wuhuyi Comfort Station was under the direct control of a battalion of the 11th Army, and the expenses associated with its operation were foisted on local residents.[7] When it opened in October 1939 the station held fourteen comfort women. So far from preventing rape it provided the setting for murder: reportedly, a squad leader and a company commander both desired Li's services as a comfort woman. The squad leader vented his rage on Li. He ripped off her clothes, pushed her to the ground, poured a bucket of cold water through her nose and mouth, stomped repeatedly on her abdomen, and then let a military dog maul her to death.[8]

Comfort women drafted from Japan's colonies were also treated brutally. Local witnesses reported that, when Zhaojian-yuan Comfort Station opened at Nada City, Hainan Island, twenty-one women between the ages of sixteen and eighteen were drafted. Most were from the local area but there were also a few from Taiwan. During the first ten days of the opening of this comfort station, over three thousand Japanese military men visited it. Continually raped, sixteen-year-old Ajiao from Taiwan passed out due to excessive bleeding caused by this form of sexual torture. She was given an injection to stop the bleeding and, only thirty minutes later, was again forced to service the troops.[9]

Surviving daily life in a comfort station meant overcoming all kinds of extreme hardship, including confinement, lack of food and clothing, sexual abuse, torture, surveillance, and the sight of other women dying. The despair of some survivors was so profound that they turned to drug addiction and/or suicide. In Part 2, twelve survivors provide detailed descriptions of the conditions in various comfort stations, but here we offer a brief summary.

Room

A comfort woman was typically confined in a small room not much larger than the size of a bed. A former orderly in the 110th Field Artillery Regiment described what he saw around February 1941 in the comfort station in Shijiazhuang in China. The conditions he describes may be considered typical: "When you opened the door, there was only a small space with a cramped dirt floor. Since the comfort women lived in there, their possessions and furniture were all crowded into the space. A strange smell permeated the narrow rooms."[10] In the temporary comfort stations near frontlines, even beds were often unavailable, so the comfort women were forced to sleep and service the troops on the dirt floor.

Food

Typically, comfort women were barely kept alive in the stations, receiving only minimal food. At the Shimenzi Comfort Station in Heilongjiang Province, for example, the comfort women were given a small amount of sorghum with frozen radishes boiled in salt water in the winter, and sorghum with green onions and salt water in the summer.[11] At the Shilu Comfort Station on Hainan Island, a handful of rice or a few pieces of yam were the daily fare of the comfort women.[12] The women whose interviews appear in this book confirm that they were starved while being forced to service the soldiers. In the more crowded stations, women often had no time to eat between servicing men.

Clothing

Explicit racial discrimination was reflected in what comfort women were forced to wear. According to survivors' testimonies, Japanese comfort women typically wore Japanese robes and were allowed to acquire clothing and cosmetics, although in many cases their cost was added to their debts.[13] Korean comfort women, considered subjects of the Japanese Empire, were often given Japanese robes or uniforms by the military. On important Japanese holidays, they were required to dress up for the entertainment of the soldiers. Although a small number of Chinese comfort women recall that they were forced to wear Japanese robes, most were not given any clothes; instead, they wore only the clothing in which they had been abducted, even after it had turned to rags. Worse yet were the conditions in crowded stations that served a large number of troops: here, the women were forced to remain naked since they were constantly raped.

Medical Conditions

The excessive sexual abuse made many women ill, and sexually transmitted diseases reached epidemic levels in the comfort stations. Whether or not they contracted venereal disease, all twelve survivors (see Part 2) said that, due to sexual abuse, their lower bodies became swollen and extremely painful soon after they were taken into the comfort stations, and none of them received medical treatment. Although military authorities decreed that, in order to control disease, comfort women were to be given medical examinations, this was done mainly to protect the men. Medical examination and treatment were often unavailable at frontline comfort facilities, and many comfort women who were too ill to service the men were left untreated, abandoned, or killed. In 1942, not atypically, three Chinese comfort women who were infected with venereal disease at Zhaojiayuan Comfort Station in Hainan were buried alive within the first month of its operation.[14]

Sexual Slavery and Torture

Comfort women were deprived of their freedom and forced to unconditionally obey the military men's orders. If a comfort woman failed to satisfy military personnel, she was severely punished. Testimonies tell of a comfort woman named Ayan who was stabbed in the leg while a Japanese officer continued to rape her as she lost consciousness,[15] and of a Xinying woman in Zhaojiayuan Comfort Station who, when she refused to meet a soldier's demands, was tied to a brick pillar and had hot pepper powder and salt rubbed onto her genitals.[16] In addition, Japanese troops tortured comfort women for entertainment. One such case is reported as occurring in a comfort station in Longling County, Yunnan Province, where Japanese soldiers poked a long radish into the vagina of a comfort woman named Wang Huandi, causing her death.[17]

Surveillance and Escape

To prevent comfort women from escaping, the stations kept them under strict military surveillance. Chinese women drafted locally were especially closely watched because the Japanese army feared they might have connections with anti-Japanese forces and local people. The regulations of Xinying Comfort Station, Hainan Island, were typical: the comfort women were forbidden to go out, and, if a woman attempted escape, she and her entire family would be decapitated.[18] The army set sentries around the stations, and in many cases the Chinese women were not permitted to leave their rooms even to void their bowels. When they needed to be moved from one place to another, they were always guarded by armed soldiers. Despite the strict surveillance and threat of severe punishment, some Chinese women did risk their lives to escape. Many of them were caught and brutally killed, but a small number of them succeeded with the help of their families and local people. The escapes of Li Lianchun and Huang Youliang are two examples (see Part 2). Their escape stores demonstrate their amazing strength and agency as well as the courage and compassion of the local people who helped them. However, driven by daily physical and mental torture, some comfort women came to rely on drugs to escape their agony, as is seen in Lei Guiying's narrative (Part 2). Given the strict surveillance of the comfort stations, these illegal drugs were most likely supplied by military personnel or station proprietors. Indeed, evidence of such cases is found in existing military documents.[19]

Death and Suicide

Brutal abuse and deliberate killings resulted in an extremely high death rate among Chinese comfort women. Of over three hundred young women drafted by the Japanese army and sent to Shilu Iron Mine Comfort Station on Hainan Island, over two hundred were abused to death in under four years, from 1942 to Japan's surrender in 1945.[20] This death rate was not uncommon. Huang Huirong was drafted by the Japanese army from Guangzhou together with twenty-one women and sent to the comfort station at the Huangliu military airport in Hainan; only four of the women were still alive when the Japanese army surrendered in the winter of 1945.[21] In addition, driven to despair by excessive suffering, many Chinese comfort women committed suicide. Huang Yuxia, for example, was abducted into the Shilu Comfort Station by the

Japanese army a few days after her wedding. Her husband, Liang Xin, went to the comfort station to look for her only to be beaten to death. In extreme grief and despair Huang Yuxia committed suicide.[22] Another case reported from Hainan Island concerns a Li ethnic woman who was confined in the military barracks in Tengqiao City; she was repeatedly gang-raped by Japanese soldiers and committed suicide by biting off her own tongue.[23]

The particularly atrocious manner in which Japanese soldiers treated Chinese comfort women is even recorded in the Japanese army's own wartime documents. As one example, in his report entitled "Special Phenomena in the Battlefields and Policies Regarding Them," prepared in June 1939, First Lieutenant Hayao Torao, a psychiatrist affiliated with the Kōnodai Army Hospital, wrote:

> It has been an extremely widespread idea that the soldiers are free to do anything to enemy women, even things that would never be permitted in the homeland, so when they see Chinese girls they act as if possessed. Therefore, those who have been reported are only the unlucky ones; we don't know exactly how many cases have happened without being reported ...
>
> The military authorities assume that to restrain the soldiers' sexual desires is impossible and set up comfort stations so that the soldiers will not rape Chinese women. However, rapes are committed rather frequently, and the good citizens of China inevitably fear Japanese military men whenever they see them.
>
> Comfort stations have been made official; the commissioned officers were the first to use the stations, and they asked the soldiers to go there as well. Knowing what was going on in the comfort stations, soldiers of conscience laughed scornfully at the military authorities. However, some commissioned officers yelled at those soldiers who would not go to the comfort station, calling them freaks.[24]

Japanese military leaders claimed that comfort stations were primarily established to prevent the occurrence of rape and sexually transmitted diseases among the Japanese forces, but the comfort women system completely failed to achieve these goals. Okamura Yasuji, one of the military commanders who implemented the comfort station plan, admitted: "Even though such units as the 6th Division march with a corps of comfort women, there is no end to the rapes."[25] At the same time, the number of reported cases of venereal disease among the Japanese forces continued to be high: 11,983 new cases were reported in 1942; 12,557 in 1943; and 12,587 in 1944.[26] The real figures would be even larger as there were many unreported cases.

The military comfort women system came to an end with Japan's defeat in 1945, but the brutality became even more extreme toward the end of the war. Japanese troops were expected to kill themselves rather than to surrender to the enemy. Many soldiers forced comfort women from their homeland or colonies to die with them.[27] At the same time, a large number of comfort women were killed in the military's attempt to destroy evidence of the comfort women system. Xu Guojun, a veteran of the Chinese Expeditionary Army, describes the mass murder of Chinese comfort women in Tengchong, a small town located on the border between China and Burma in Yunnan Province:

> We entered the Tengchong County Seat on the morning of September 14, 1944 ... In a military comfort station, seventeen bodies of Chinese comfort women and some babies were lying there; all had been stabbed to death by the Japanese troops. One of the dead women held in her arms a baby, whose body was drenched in blood.[28]

In another report, Pan Shizhi, a newspaper correspondent during the war described how, when the Chinese Expeditionary Army took the last strong-hold in Tengchong on 14 September 1944, the Chinese soldiers found a little girl about ten years old in a dugout. She told the soldiers that Japanese troops had forced her to serve water to the twelve comfort women retained by the unit. These comfort women had been held in a bomb shelter, but one morning a Japanese officer entered with a gun and shot them to death, one after the other. The little girl survived because, having fainted from horror, she was thought to be dead.[29] In the same article, Pan reports that the Expeditionary Army found another murder site, at which over a dozen women's bodies, all with their eyes covered, had been laid out near the city wall.

It is not known how many Chinese comfort women were killed during the war. As we observe in this book, only an extremely small number survived, and the majority of these were ransomed by their family, rescued by local people, or escaped before the war ended. Investigations into the fate of Korean comfort women suggests that 75 to 90 percent of them became war casualties.[30] The casualty rate for Chinese comfort women is likely even higher. During the six years that the Japanese military occupied the Hainan region, for example, it built approximately 360 strongholds on the island and over three hundred comfort stations to service its troops.[31] These comfort stations were generally staffed with ten to twenty comfort women, but the larger ones, such as the Basuogang Comfort Station and the Shilu Iron Mine Comfort Station, each held as many as two to three hundred women.[32] Researchers estimate that, in Hainan alone, over ten thousand women were confined as sex slaves during the occupation;[33] these included women drafted from Mainland China, Korea, Taiwan, Japan, the Philippines, and Singapore, but most were Chinese women drafted locally or from the southern provinces of China. Thus far only forty-two survivors have been found in the region. According to the testimonies of twenty survivors who were available for interviews,[34] eleven of them survived because they escaped from the comfort stations, two were rescued by family members, three were bailed out by local leaders, and only four were freed after the comfort stations were abandoned at the end of the war.[35]

The preceding pages provide an overview of the military comfort women system, from its early stage during Japan's aggression in Manchuria and Shanghai in the early 1930s, to its rapid expansion after the Nanjing Massacre in 1937, to Japan's defeat in 1945. This information shows the close correlation between the proliferation of military comfort stations and the progression of Japan's invasion of China. It also provides a glimpse of the sufferings of the women who were forced into these military facilities. However, as Diana Lary and Stephen MacKinnon observe in their examination of the scars of war that mark Chinese society, the scale of suffering during the Second Sino-Japanese War was so great as to almost defy description and/or analysis.[36] The best way to understand the enormity of the suffering of comfort women and the horror of the military comfort stations is through listening to the life stories of the individual victims. The twelve women who told us about their wartime experiences are among a handful of comfort station survivors found in Mainland China. Their narratives reveal, in detail, the brutalization to which Chinese women were subjected and its long-term impact on their lives.

PART 2

The Survivors' Voices

Figure 6 Locations of the "comfort stations" where the twelve women whose stories are related in this volume were enslaved.

The stories of the twelve comfort station survivors – Lei Guiying, Zhou Fenying, Zhu Qiaomei, Lu Xiuzhen, Yuan Zhulin, Tan Yuhua, Yin Yulin, Wan Aihua, Huang Youliang, Chen Yabian, Lin Yajin, and Li Lianchun – are based on oral interviews conducted by Su Zhiliang and Chen Lifei from 1998 to 2008.[1] At the time this book was written, seven of the twelve women had died.

The interview process was extremely difficult for both the survivors and the interviewers. The nature of the torture to which they were subjected in the comfort stations during the war, coupled with the postwar socio-political climates, made it very painful for the victims to speak of their past. In addition, in the rural areas, where most of the Chinese comfort station survivors lived, traditional attitudes toward chastity remain deeply rooted and contribute significantly to the embarrassment and pain experienced in the telling. In Yunnan Province, for example, although there is concrete evidence of a large number of military comfort stations, few survivors are willing to step forward and relate their experiences. People acquainted with the victims also avoid the subject, fearing damage to their relationship with the victim's family. Li Lianchun, one of the few survivors in Yunnan Province who revealed her experiences as a comfort woman, would not have done so without the support of her children. The psychological trauma and fear of discrimination continue to haunt these survivors, even after breaking their silence. After the war, Yuan Zhulin was exiled from Wuhan City in central China to a remote farm in northeastern Heilongjian Province for seventeen years because it was revealed that she had been a comfort woman for the Japanese military. Even many years later, when she was invited to participate as one of the Chinese plaintiffs in the Women's International War Crimes Tribunal on Japan's Military Sexual Slavery held in Tokyo in December 2000,[2] Yuan Zhulin experienced tremendous anguish the night before her scheduled testimony and said she could not go on stage the next day to recount what the Japanese military had done to her. Chen Lifei sat with her for hours until she finally overcame her pain and fear and gave a powerful speech in the tribunal court. Yet, when a group of legal experts and researchers sought her out at her home in 2001, she would have been unable to go through the account notarization process without professional psychological support to deal with the return of her fear and anguish. In order to minimize the pain of talking about the horrors of the comfort stations, Su and Chen conducted their interviews in locations that were as convenient and as comfortable for the survivors as possible. The interviewers frequently travelled across China to remote villages and walked for hours over rough mountain roads to reach the survivors' homes.

Three groups of basic questions were asked of each survivor concerning her experiences before, during, and after the Japanese invasion:

1   What was the survivor's prewar family and personal background?
2   During the war, how did she become a comfort woman? Were there any witnesses? What did the comfort station look like? How was she treated in the comfort station? How did her comfort station experience end?
3   What is her current marital situation? Does she have any children? What are her relationships with her immediate family members, more distant relatives, and neighbours like? Does she think that she has suffered discrimination or political persecution as a result of her comfort station experience? Has she experienced any psychological aftermath? What is her life like currently?

Out of concern for each survivor's emotional and physical condition, the interviewers refrained from imposing a rigid format and from designating a specific amount of time; instead, they altered the time and direction of the conversation to comply with the needs of each survivor. Therefore, the accounts are uneven in length and format, but all were prompted by the above questions. Some of the survivors were interviewed several times over a long period of time. For example, Su and Chen visited Zhu Qiaomei in her home seven times over the course of five years until her death in 2005. However, due to health concerns, multiple interviews were not possible for every survivor. Su Zhiliang said: "I would not bother these survivors over and over again when I was able to verify the facts of their victimization through one interview, because they told me that each time they talked about their horrible experience, it was as if they were going through the hell again." Su then added: "It's very, very painful. Even I myself could not sleep for days after each interview."

Being sensitive to the condition of the aged survivors, the interviewers carefully verified the accuracy of each woman's oral accounts by such methods as locating the site of the comfort facilities in which she was enslaved, collecting testimonies from other local witnesses, and comparing her accounts with local historical records (see Figure 7). For example, when she was being interviewed, Wan Aihua had trouble remembering some of the details of her abduction due to the trauma it had entailed. However, from the information she provided, such as the plants she saw and the food people were eating at the time, the interviewers were able to approximate the time of year when she had been kidnapped and tortured. After recording her life story, the interviewers drove a long distance to Yangquan Village and found Hou Datu, the owner of the cotton-padded quilt Wan Aihua had used in the comfort station, and obtained his affidavit relating to her torture. With the help of a local volunteer, Zhang Shuangbing, the interviewers also located the cave

Figure 7 The interviewers took a picture of the rock cave where Li Lianchun hid in 1943 after her escape from Songshan "Comfort Station."

in which Wan Aihua was confined and the riverbed where she was first captured. All twelve accounts in this chapter have been verified by such field methods.

The translation makes every effort to be faithful to the survivors' words, which are spare but extremely powerful. In order to enhance the flow and readability of the transcripts, the translation omits the interviewer's questions. The accounts are grouped according to the geographical location of the survivor's confinement and are listed in chronological order: the eastern coastal region in the beginning of full-fledged warfare; the warzones in central and northern China from late 1939 to 1944, where Japanese military expansion reached an impasse; and, finally, the southern Chinese frontlines from 1941 until the end of the war. Before each survivor's account, brief background information is provided to help to situate her experiences within a larger historical context of the war. The testimonies of local witnesses are added to the accounts when there is a lapse in the survivor's recollection, and explanatory notes are provided for terms and events that are unfamiliar to non-Chinese-speaking audiences. Additional information about the postwar experiences of Chinese comfort women is provided in Part 3.

5 Eastern Coastal Region

Lei Guiying

At the age of nine, Lei Guiying witnessed the atrocities the Japanese soldiers committed in her hometown in the Jiangning District of Nanjing around the time of the fall of Nanjing in December 1937. At age thirteen, as soon as she began menstruating, she was forced to become a comfort woman for the Japanese military.

Figure 8 Lei Guiying giving a talk in Shanghai in 2006 to teachers and students from Canada.

I was born in a place called Guantangyan. My father died when I was only seven, so I don't remember his name. My mother's surname was "Li" and her parents lived in Shanghe Village. Guantangyan is located on the bank of a river that runs through Tangshan Town.

In the winter of the year after my father's death, my mother was taken away by a group of people from nearby Ligangtou Village while she was on her way to work. At that time a poor man who could not afford a wedding would snatch a woman to be his wife. At the time I had a five-year-old brother called Little Zaosheng. The men from Ligangtou Village let my mother bring my younger brother with her because he was a boy. I was left behind. My grandparents had already died. My late father had a younger brother in the village, but he was not living with my family. A teenager himself, this uncle was unable to support me, so I had no one to depend on.

Before she was taken away, my mother entrusted me to an old woman who lived in the same village. She gave the old lady some money, hoping she would provide for me. However, the old woman said to me after my mother left: "Girl, I have many children in my house so everyone must fight for food. I don't think you can win the battle to survive here. I will have to send you to another family to be a "child-daughter-in-law."[1] I didn't understand what "child-daughter-in-law" meant when I was given away. I was sent to Wangjiabian Village near Tuqiao Town, and my husband-to-be was much older than I.

When the Japanese army came in 1937, I was about nine years old. I remember that it was the season when the weather was getting cold. Villagers were cleaning up the sweet potato fields and the pond in the village had already frozen over.[2] That day my mother-in-law gave me a hoe and told me to dig out sweet potatoes. As I finished digging and was on my way home, I saw a huge crowd of people running southward. The Japanese troops attacked my hometown. People ran southward because there was a big pond, which they hoped might stop the Japanese from chasing them. The villagers hid themselves in holes deep in the ground. My mother-in-law had two daughters. One was over twenty and the other was turning nineteen. Both of them had bound feet so they could not move quickly.[3] My feet had been bound for a while and then released, so I didn't have their problems. My family members dug two holes that were connected, a smaller one above a larger one. My sisters-in-laws hid in the large hole on the lower level. My mother-in-law hid in the small one above them. They brought a big pot of rice to eat in the holes. My mother-in-law didn't allow me to hide in the holes with them. She said if the Japanese soldiers saw me, the whole family would be killed and I would die too. She gave me some roasted sunflower seeds and soybeans as my food.

Hidden at home I frequently saw the Japanese troops come into the village, where they did a lot of shooting. They shot chickens to eat, but they would not eat the wings, heads, or claws. They also shot cattle. They would keep shooting at an ox until it collapsed on the ground. They only ate the meat on the legs of oxen and threw the other parts away. When they saw us children, some Japanese soldiers took out candies and threw them on the ground. One bold child picked up a candy and ate it. Seeing that, we all followed his example. The Japanese soldiers then grabbed the fourteen- or fifteen-year-old girls. Those who didn't have time to run became their victims. The Japanese soldiers took the girls to those abandoned houses to "sleep."

Tuqiao Town was only five *li* [one *li* is five hundred metres] away from Wangjiabian Village. There used to be many shops and buildings, but they were mostly vacated after the war broke out. My mother-in-law told me to go to the town with some other girls to get goods from the abandoned shops. I was very scared. The goods were quite heavy and I had to climb up high to reach them. I was afraid that I might break my legs in a fall. However, my mother-in-law would have beaten me if I had refused to go. I went to Tuqiao Town quite a few times with other children where I saw that the Japanese troops occupied the good houses in that abandoned town. Several times we ran into the Japanese troops riding on their horses, which scared us to death. The teenage girls would flee desperately. The girls with whom I went to Tuqiao Town were of different ages. The Japanese soldiers would pat our heads and ask how old we were. I was only nine then, but some other girls were around fifteen. The Japanese soldiers would take those fourteen- or fifteen-year-old girls away. This happened several times, but I was very young and at the beginning I didn't know where they were taken or what happened to them, until I saw one of the girls dead. She had been sexually tortured to death by the Japanese soldiers! That day we had gone to an abandoned shop to search for goods. In that abandoned shop we saw many abducted girls, some of whom were already dead. I was extremely frightened. The girls who were still alive were too weak to walk. They were not the girls who had been going to the town with me and I didn't know where they were from. One time I also saw a girl whose belly was bloated. Her father, who wore a pair of straw sandals, was massaging her stomach. Her lower body was covered with blood and bloody pus was dripping onto the floor. We did not dare to go to the town again after seeing these girls.

Three years after I was sent to Wangjiabian as a child-daughter-in-law, my husband-to-be died. At that time I was only ten years old and it was not clear to me whether he was killed by the Japanese or died of illness. I only remember his name – Chen Yu. My mother-in-law was very mean to me and often beat me. My mother-in-law grew silkworms. The silkworms looked like huge caterpillars. When I fed them mulberry leaves they would crawl onto my hands and I would flick them away in fear. When my mother-in-law saw that she would beat me.

One day my mother came to see me. She brought me a pair of flowered shoes made of a quilt cover. I begged my mother to take me with her, but she said: "I cannot. You are a child-daughter-in-law in your husband's family. Besides, I've had a new baby with my current husband." I had no choice but to stay. I fell ill. My mother-in-law told me to spread some straw on the ground outside of the house and lie out there under the sun. A nice grandpa who had relatives in Ligangtou Village was sympathetic when he saw me unable to eat or drink. [This old man was not Lei Guiying's grandfather. It is a Chinese custom to use a kinship term to refer to an older person in order to show one's respect, even though the person is not a blood relative.] He made soup to feed me and persuaded my father-in-law to obtain treatment for my illness. Thanks to this nice old man, I was taken to a doctor and given medicine. I recovered gradually and then I begged that kind grandpa to bring me to my mother. He quietly led me out of the village to Ligangtou, where I was reunited with my mother. My mother had given birth to a little boy with her new husband. This little brother of mine was very cute. I carried him around and played with him, but he was a little too heavy for me to carry. One day when I was holding him up he fell over my shoulders. My mother's mother-in-law grabbed my hair and beat me. My mother cried. She said to me: "Sorry, I cannot let you stay any longer. I will find you another home where you can be their child-daughter-in-law." Thus, my reunion with my mother lasted for less than ten days and I became a child-daughter-in-law again. I was twelve that year [1941].

My father-in-law in this new family owned a dye house in Sihou Village not far from Ligangtou. My husband dyed cloth and I helped him heat the dye pot. Cloth was dyed in the pot and then taken out to dry. My husband went to collect cloth in the town. He also herded cattle and cut hay. I worked hard to help with various jobs, yet my mother-in-law often yelled at me and beat me.

Life in this household was unbearable, so I escaped not long after I was married into the family. With a bowl and a pair of chopsticks I begged, going from village to village. The weather was very cold. I came across a nice old couple, who asked me if I was hungry and gave me crispy rice crust. I heard the grandpa talking about going to Tangshan, so I asked him to take me with him.

Having neither job nor home, I wandered the streets of Tangshan begging. An old woman said to me: "Girl, I know a place where you can have meals to eat. You just have to do some work." She told me the place was called Gaotaipo. It was owned by a Japanese couple named Shanben. ["Shanben" is the Chinese pronunciation of the two characters used to write the Japanese surname "Yamamoto."] I didn't know that place was, in fact, a military brothel until much later. I had no idea that it was a comfort station, nor did I know what a comfort station was at that time.

[Lei Guiying stopped recounting her story and told the interviewers that, besides the Gaotaipo comfort station, there was another comfort station in Tangshan. It was referred to as "Dai Li's Mansion" (Dai Li lou) or "Big Mansion" (Da lou). The remains of the Gaotaipo comfort station have been removed and a new building has been constructed on the site.]

At Shanben's house I worked as a nanny and maid. There were two children in the family. One was a boy named Hatsurō, who was about six years old; the other was a little girl named Nobu-chan. [The children's names are recorded as Lei Guiying pronounced them.] Their mother appeared to be kind. She gave me money to take the children out to shows, which she called *katsudō*. I didn't understand any Japanese at first. Once Mrs. Shanben wanted me to buy *nankin mame,* but I had no clue what she was talking about. She then went in and brought out a bag to show me. It turned out *nankin mame* were peanuts.

Mr. Shanben was a businessman. Mrs. Shanben was often not home, but I didn't know exactly what she was doing. It seemed that she worked at a shop local people called "Tianfu Devil's" selling groceries. Every now and then Mr. Shanben would take a military vehicle to Shanghai to buy goods like sugar or soy sauce and then sell them to the Japanese troops. Mr. Shanben had a card that enabled him to enter the military compound freely.

The Shanbens' house, which I later figured out was a military brothel, was near a highway. There was a kitchen next to the entrance and a large storage room on the east side. Next to the kitchen was a small storage room where I slept. They put the things they bought from Shanghai in the small storage room. There was a centre hall with two side rooms. Next to them there was a huge room with a wide bed. Thirteen girls lived there. They were all Chinese but wore Japanese robes. The older girls at Gaotaipo were about seventeen or eighteen, and some of the younger ones fifteen or sixteen. I often saw Japanese men come and take one or two of the girls into the bedroom with them. The robes these girls wore had wide sleeves and a sash. They wore flowers in their hair. None of them could speak Japanese. When the Japanese soldiers came, they called the girls *gu'niang*. [This is a Chinese word meaning "maiden."]

I turned thirteen in 1942 and I began menstruating that year. Mrs. Shanben smiled at me. "Congratulations!" she said, "You are a grownup now." I remember that it was a summer day and a lot of Japanese troops came to the Shanbens' house. I saw them picking out good-looking girls and mumbling something. Mrs. Shanben told me to change into a Japanese robe that had a bumpy sash at the back and to go to that large room. Before I could figure out what was going on, I was pushed over to the Japanese soldiers. I was frightened. A Japanese soldier pulled me over, ripped off my clothes, and threw me on the wide bed. I resisted with all my strength. My wrist was injured during the fight and the wound left a scar that is still visible now. The Japanese soldier pressed my belly with both of his knees and hit my head with the hilt of his sword while crushing me under his body. He raped me.

On weekdays not many Japanese soldiers came to the comfort station, so I continued working as a nanny in the house. Many Japanese troops came on weekend evenings. Sometimes five or six came in a group. They also came during the day, but they didn't spend the night there. When I first went to Gaotaipo, there were always many girls and a lot of Japanese soldiers; usually ten or more of them would come together. Later the number of Japanese troops decreased to five or six at a time. I could tell that some of them were officers because I saw the guard stand and salute. Each officer wore leather boots and a long sword and threw his weight about. The soldiers each carried a rifle with a bayonet.

The large room containing the wide bed was about twenty-five square metres and had a cement floor. The bed built against the walls was lower than my knees and covered with straw mats. The Japanese soldiers took off their shoes before getting on the bed rather than at the entrance of the room. The wide bed ran from wall to wall without any separators; when the Japanese troops came, curtains were hung on metal wires to divide it into a small space for each girl. A row of stands for bowls stood against the wall on the opposite side of the room. There was also a small dining table. Meals were brought into the room and the girls were not allowed to go out.

The Japanese soldiers used rubber condoms. I had seen condoms before when I was cleaning the house, but I didn't know what they were then. We were told to wash our lower bodies after each time a Japanese soldier came. There was a greenish substance in the wash water. Mr. Shanben distributed towels, toilet paper, and Japanese robes to the girls. The robe had a bumpy sash at the back. We had nothing else besides these things.

At Gaotaipo Comfort Station the girls were given three meals a day – usually rice with soy sauce, and on some rare occasions there was canned fish – but often not enough to eat. Because I worked as the nanny in the house, I was allowed to go to the kitchen. Sympathetic kitchen workers sometimes gave me food, which I shared secretly with the other girls. Unable to leave the room, the girls stayed on the wide bed every day and played cards. Occasionally the Japanese military men gave finery to the girls they liked, but I didn't see any of the girls receive any monetary payment. I saw some of the older girls playing with the gifts, but I never received anything from the Japanese troops because I was too young.

Most of the girls learned to smoke cigarettes in the comfort station and some smoked opium. I had no idea where or how the girls obtained the opium. The girls smoked stealthily in the latrine. Later I picked up the bad habit, too, and it took me a long time to quit smoking opium.

When I was forced to move into that big room, there were only four girls, including me. Life there was hell. Once I saw a group of Japanese soldiers rape a girl continuously. When they left we saw that her belly had already swelled up. The older girls massaged her lower abdomen; then blood and fluid gushed all over the floor. One day I saw the Japanese soldiers burning a dead girl's body on a pile of firewood; the girl had been tortured to death in the station. Many years later my husband told me that, when he had worked as a forest ranger, he had also seen Japanese troops burning the bodies of girls by pouring kerosene on them. The flames leapt up very high.

I suffered horrible torture in the comfort station. One day a Japanese soldier came in the afternoon. He put his two legs on my abdomen, which hurt me badly and made me bleed. I resisted as hard as I could, trying to push him off my body. The Japanese soldier then beat me and stabbed my leg with his bayonet. I used all my strength to crawl toward the door. Several people saw me and one young man who was a distant relative of mine saved me from being killed, but the bayonet stabbing crippled me.

I realized that, sooner or later, I would be tortured to death by the Japanese troops at Gaotaipo; I was determined to escape. I worked as the nanny in the house, so I knew the way out. When my wounded leg recovered and I was able to walk, I made up my mind to run away.

I did so in the early morning one day toward the end of 1943. The weather was very cold. I sneaked out the back door of Gaotaipo Comfort Station when the rest of the people were still sound asleep. Running for my life, I dared not look back. I ran all the way to my mother's house in Ligangtou Village. After a period in hiding, I settled down in the village.

After the liberation my life changed. I worked hard and became the leader of the local women's work team. At seventeen I married a man of the Tang family, but I was unable to bear a child. We adopted an abandoned boy who was very sick and almost dead. I held him in my arms and felt very sorry for him, so I brought him home from the local police station.

I haven't been to Gaotaipo again since my escape. For about half a year I was raped by the Japanese troops there; I never want to see that place again. When I escaped from Gaotaipo, I brought a few things with me, including a Japanese lunchbox and some Japanese clothing. I didn't keep them because they made me angry and upset when I looked at them. Now I only have this left. I saw the girls in the comfort station use it. I thought it must be useful medically, so I took it with me. But I didn't know what it was.

[Lei Guiying showed the interviewers a small bottle with dark powder in it. A test conducted later indicated that the powder was potassium permanganate, which must have been put in wash water for hygienic purposes in the comfort station.]

Now my adopted son has grown old and I have great-grandchildren. I don't have many years left to live. The anguish of my torture in the past is pent-up in my heart and is stifling me. My son said to me: "You didn't do anything wrong. You were forced to become a comfort woman. You should not let this page of history be buried in silence." I think he is right. I must tell the truth, and I want justice.

Since the redress movement began in the 1990s, support for the Chinese survivors increased in China. When Lei Guiying suffered a stroke and was brought to the emergency room in the Jiangsu Province Traditional Chinese Medicine Hospital on 22 April 2007, people from all walks of life came to visit her; flower and fruits baskets piled up in front of her room. Young people from northern China who had never met Lei Guiying also came to visit her and made donations to pay for her medical treatment. Lei Guiying fell into a coma that evening: she never woke up. On 26 April 2007, Lei Guiying died at the age of seventy-nine. She was laid to rest in the Tangshan Christian Church cemetery.

(Interviewed by Chen Ketao in May 2006; interviewed by Su Zhiliang and Chen Lifei in July 2006)

Zhou Fenying

After the fall of Nanjing, Japanese forces advanced into the adjacent areas. In March 1938, the Japanese army occupied Rugao, a small county about 280 kilometres east of Nanjing. Japanese soldiers raped women indiscriminately, including young girls of eight or nine and seventy-year-old women. At the same time, the troops established comfort stations both inside and outside Rugao city limits.[4] Zhou Fenying was kidnapped and taken to one of the military comfort stations in the area during this period.

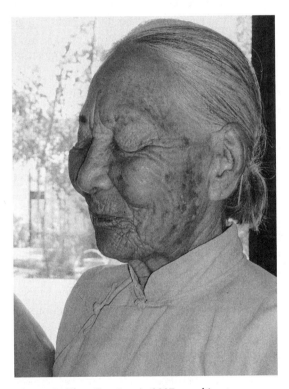

Figure 9   Zhou Fenying, in 2007, speaking to interviewers of her wartime experiences.

My parents were natives of Wenchi Village, a small village across from Yangjiayuan Village, where I live now. My father's name was Zhou Fusheng. My mother didn't have a formal name. People called her the "Sixth Girl." My parents owned no land, so the family depended on my father working as a farmhand for others. I was born in the Lunar Fifth Month [1917]. My parents already had four sons when I was born, and the family was often starving. Seeing no way to provide for another child, my parents thought I might be able to survive if they could give me away. However, it was not easy to find a family to take me. In rural places at that time boys were wanted because they were seen as able to do the farm work when they grew up. Girls were unwanted and were called "money-losing goods" since they would serve another family when they were married and their parents had to spend a fortune to pay for the dowry. One day, in despair, my parents placed me on the roadside in the early morning, hoping that someone would see me and take me home. However, an old woman in the neighbourhood recognized me and brought me back to them. Holding me tightly, my parents cried their hearts out.

When I turned five I was sold to the Ni family in nearby Yangjiayuan Village to be a "child-daughter-in-law," as was commonly done at the time. [A child-daughter-in-law would be treated as an adopted child first and then become the wife of their son when she reached adulthood.] I was so young that I no longer remember anything else about my family of birth except the nicknames of my older brothers.

My father-in-law was called Ni Er and the villagers called my mother-in-law Ni Er's. They had two sons: the older son was called Ni Jincheng, and the younger one Ni Gui. I was Ni Jincheng's child-bride-to-be. Ni Jincheng was ten at the time, five years older than I. My mother-in-law was a capable and tough woman. My father-in-law rarely stayed home. He had an affair with another woman and had a child with her. My mother-in-law raised her two sons mostly by herself and the family was very poor. Jincheng and I weren't married until 1936, when he was twenty-four and I was nineteen. People said that I was an exceptionally pretty girl for I was fair-skinned and of slight build. [During the interview trip, local people told the interviewers that Zhou Fenying had been a famous beauty in the area. She was already ninety and had lost her eyesight at the time of the interview, but she still dressed neatly, wearing a straw hat that protected her face from the sunlight.] Jincheng and I grew up together and we loved each other very much. He protected me as if he were an older brother. We "separated out" from my in-laws' house after we were married. I said "separated out," but we didn't really have our own house to move to. We just added a small room to my in-laws' straw-thatched cottage and built our own cooking stove. This little thatched addition with mud walls became our bridal chamber.

The Japanese army occupied Rugao about two years after we were married. [Rugao is located in the Changjiang River Delta. Yangjiayuan Village, where Zhou Fenying lived, is in the Town of Baipu, Rugao City.] I clearly remember the day when the Japanese troops came into our village. It was in the spring of 1938 and that day was my cousin Wu Qun's birthday. She was about my age and also good-looking. My husband was away from home working in the fields. We heard that the Japanese troops accompanied by local traitors had come to kidnap girls. All the women in the village ran desperately trying to escape. My cousin and I ran for our lives. We crossed a little river and hid ourselves behind a millstone in a villager's courtyard, but the Japanese troops chased after us and found us. Later we learned that the Japanese troops had been looking for good-looking girls to put in their comfort station. Because my cousin and I were known for our good looks, we had been targeted. The Japanese soldiers tied our feet with ropes so that we could not run away. Then they had us loaded into a wheelbarrow, one on each side, where they tied us tightly with more ropes. They forced some villagers to push the wheelbarrow to the Town of Baipu. The ropes and the jolting of the wheelbarrow hurt our bodies like hell all the way.

At Baipu we were unloaded at Zhongxing Hotel. The owner of the hotel had fled before the Japanese army came, and the Japanese troops made the hotel their comfort station. We were scared to death and couldn't even cry. When I looked around, I saw about twenty girls were already there. The barracks held about fifty Japanese troops, who kidnapped dozens of young women from nearby villages to be their comfort women. Each of the girls in the comfort station was given a number. The number was printed in red on a piece of white cloth, which was about three *cun* long and two *cun* [1 *cun* equals ⅓ decimetre] wide. People said that the numbers were given based on the looks of the girls; I was made number one.

We were not allowed to step out of the station. There were two or three elderly women from the Town of Baipu who cleaned, delivered food and water and so on. There was also an old woman, a Chinese, who supervised the women and collected fees. This old woman gave us a yuan or so every month to buy daily necessities, but this money was far from enough. Because we were only given two coarse meals a day we were always hungry. I had to save that money and ask people to buy me some food when I was starving. At mealtimes we were taken to a large room with six or eight big tables, each of which seated eight people. Each of us had a small room with a bed, a small table, and a little stool. There was also a basin in my room. All the women had to share towels and one big tub of water for bathing. I wore my own clothes all the time I was in the station, and, as time went on, I had to ask my in-laws to send me a change of clothing.

I was extremely frightened when I was forced to service the Japanese troops. I had heard that Japanese soldiers would stab every Chinese man and rape every Chinese woman they found. On the first day I could not stop crying and my mind fell into a trance, so one of the cleaning women stayed in my room with me until a Japanese soldier came in. The soldier became very angry when he saw me crying. He pushed his bayonet against my chest, snarling in a low voice. I thought he was going to kill me and I almost passed out. The Japanese soldier then raped me.

The Japanese troops came to the station about every seven days, and we were made to do other jobs when the soldiers didn't come. Many of the soldiers had two or three stripes on their epaulettes, so I guessed they were officers. They paid the old woman with military money to buy tickets before coming to pick girls. Quite a few of them would pick me, and some came to my room regularly. I cried every day, hoping that my husband could free me from this place. However, the place was closely guarded by the soldiers and there was no way for him to rescue me.

The Japanese officers made me follow their orders. If I obeyed they sometimes gave me a small gift, but if I showed even the slightest unhappiness they would yell at me. I was forced to do whatever they told me to. I remember that a Japanese person wearing white clothing came to check our bodies, including our private places. I didn't understand what he was doing at the time, but I was very scared and my whole body shook when he checked me. The Japanese doctor also came to check me when I fell sick in the comfort station. The old woman gave us some small rubber caps and told us to put one on the soldier's penis when he arrived.

I was kept in the comfort station for about three months. In the seventh month that year [1938], Mr. Yang, a clerk who was working in the puppet town government, helped free me. People said that Mr. Yang had had an interest in me because of my good looks, so he paid a ransom and used his connections to get me released. Mr. Yang wanted me to be his concubine, but I refused. I told him that I had a husband and I wanted to go home.

When I was released my mother-in-law did not want me to return home. She could not take the widespread gossip in the village, where people were saying that I had been defiled by the Japanese troops. However, my husband, Jincheng, accepted me. He said, "Fenying was kidnapped by the Japanese troops, but this was not her fault." He brought me home despite what the villagers and my mother-in-law said. Still, he was deeply humiliated because they looked down on me. I could sense that his heart was filled with anger and hatred toward the Japanese troops. At the time Chinese forces were enlisting soldiers to fight the Japanese army in our area. Jincheng wanted to join the Chinese army, but I didn't want him to leave. I said to him: "If you really want to go, take me with you. I'll go anywhere you go." I then followed him everywhere. The Chinese enlisters came to our town several times, but Jincheng was unable to join the army because of me. However, he was determined to seek revenge. One morning when I woke up I found he was gone.

That was at the end of the year [1940], the Lunar Eleventh Month. I knew he went to fight against the Japanese forces. Jincheng never returned home. Years later the local government informed me that Jincheng had joined the First Regiment of the New Fourth Army (Xinsijun).[5] He was killed in a battle at Guxi in Taixing County in 1941.

A kind man in the village, Mr. Jiang, often helped me with heavy work after my husband left home. He was thirteen years older than I and was not married due to the lack of money. In 1943 he proposed to me. We were married that year and had a son a year later. We named our son Jiang Weixun.

After the establishment of the People's Republic of China, my first husband, Ni Jincheng, was granted military honours. When my second husband died, I told my son and grandchildren about my painful past. I also told them that I had married twice and how my first husband joined the resistance forces and fought to his death against the Japanese troops. I wanted them to remember who had committed the atrocities against me and the Chinese people.

I now live with my son, my grandson, my grandson's wife, and my great-granddaughter. In 2007, my son read in a newspaper article that comfort station survivor Lei Guiying had died. [This is the same Lei Guiying whose narrative is presented earlier.] He also learned that the Japanese high court had just rejected two cases filed by former Chinese labourers and comfort women. I cried when my son told me that. I respected Lei Guiying, who had the courage to reveal her experiences to the world and to testify on behalf of all the comfort women. The Japanese government refuses to take responsibility for the crimes Japanese soldiers committed against Chinese women during the war, but I can be one of the witnesses. I let my son send letters to people telling of my experience in the comfort station. [Jiang Weixun sent the letters to Rugao City Women's Federation, the Association for Research on the Nanjing Massacre, and the Jiangsu Province Academy of Social Sciences.] My son told me that the right-wing activists in Japan want to cover up the crimes committed by the Japanese military, but we cannot let them have their way. Although Lei Guiying died, I will continue her efforts.

One year after she revealed her experience in the Japanese military comfort station to the public, Zhou Fenying died on 6 July 2008 at her home in Yangjiayuan Village, Rugao County.

(Interviewed by Su Zhiliang and Chen Lifei in October 2007)

Zhu Qiaomei

On 18 March 1938, three months after the Nanjing Massacre, Japanese forces landed on Chongming Island, which is located at the mouth of the Yangtze River near Shanghai. The island, from a military perspective, was an important geographical position. Two Japanese warships and five combat planes covered the landing and the occupation forces stationed in each of the four major towns on the island. One month later, three hundred additional Japanese troops from Shanghai and Ningbo were assembled on Chongming. Wang Jingwei's puppet government also sent security troops to the area from Shanghai.[6] Although, after the outbreak of war on the Pacific front in 1942, some troops were dispatched to the battlefronts at Burma, Singapore, and elsewhere, a large number of troops remained on Chongming Island until Japan's surrender in 1945. Many local women were assaulted and abducted into the military comfort stations during the Japanese occupation. Zhu Qiaomei and Lu Xiuzhen were both forced to serve as Japanese military comfort women on Chongming Island.[7]

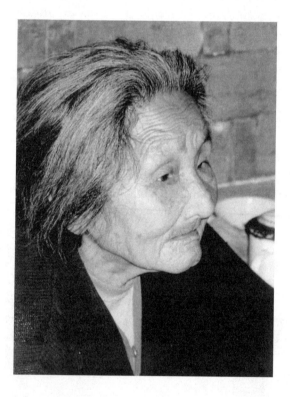

Figure 10   Zhu Qiaomei at the 2001 notarization of her wartime experiences.

My name is Zhu Qiaomei. Because my husband's last name was Zhou, I was also called Zhou Qiaomei, or Zhou Aqiao ["Aqiao" is her nickname.] I was born in Ximen of Xiaokunshan in Songjiang County, Shanghai, in the Year of the Dog and am now ninety-one years old.

In my youth I was a bookbinder working at Commercial Press in Shanghai; I married Zhou Shouwen in 1928. In 1932, the Japanese forces bombed the Commercial Press building so I lost my job and fled to Chongming with my husband. From that time on we never left Chongming. We settled in Miaozhen Town and opened a little restaurant named "House of Eternal Prosperity" (Yongxing guan). Our restaurant was not big and mainly served cold dishes and light refreshments, but the business was good. My husband and I had a very good relationship, so we lived a quiet and sweet life. In July 1933, I gave birth to my second son, Zhou Xie.

In the spring of 1938 the Japanese army occupied Chongming and Japanese troops built a blockhouse at Miaozhen, where one company of Japanese soldiers was stationed. The remains of that building were torn down a few years ago. Japanese troops constantly came out to assault the village people. We didn't have anywhere to run to, so we stayed in our little restaurant. One day, several Japanese soldiers dashed into our restaurant, wearing yellowish uniforms and holding long rifles. They forced all of the customers to leave and raped me in a locked room. At that time I was two or three months pregnant with my third son, Zhou Xin.

The Japanese unit,[8] whose name I think was "Songjing Company" ["Songjing" is written in two characters, which are read as "Matsui" in Japanese], lived in a two- or three-story building.[9] I remember that people called the unit head "Senge," and the head of a squadron "Heilian" [These names are hard to reconcile because they do not seem to be the pronunciations of the characters used in common Japanese names; the local people may have pronounced the names incorrectly], and there was an interpreter. They searched high and low for good-looking women to "comfort" the Japanese officers. In order to meet the desires of the Japanese officers, they forced seven townswomen to form a "comfort woman group." These "Seven Sisters" were Zhou Haimei (Sister Mei), Lu Fenglang (Sister Feng), Yang Qijie (Sister Qi), Zhou Dalang (Sister Da), Jin Yu (Sister Yu), Guo Yaying (Sister Ying), and me (people called me Sister Qiao). We became those Japanese troops' sex slaves. They declared us set aside for special service to the military officers. The ordinary soldiers, who were not allowed to touch us, assaulted the other girls of the town.

The seven of us remained in our own homes. The interpreter would give us service assignments or call us to the blockhouse. Sometimes the Japanese military officers also forced their way into our homes to rape us. If we didn't let them, they would smash things in our houses or shops and would take out their bayonets and threatened to kill us. "Die! Die!" they yelled. The horrors were beyond human imagination.

When I was first abducted by Japanese troops I was already pregnant, but the Japanese officers raped me despite the baby in my belly. And merely two months after I birthed the child I was again subjected to frequent rapes. I had a lot of breast milk at the time, so the officers Senge and Heilian would suck my breast milk dry every time before raping me. Afraid of being killed, I had no choice but to put up with these atrocities. The Japanese troops designated a special room in their blockhouse for raping us. In the room there was only a bathtub and a bed. When we were taken in, first we had to bathe and then the Japanese military men would rape us on the little bed next to the tub. Other than that the troops never took any hygienic measures. We were almost tortured to death; no form of remuneration was ever mentioned.

This kind of torture continued until 1939. Every week I was assaulted by the Japanese troops at least five times, sometimes even more. It has been so many years now that I can't remember the details very clearly, but I remember there were times I was taken in there and kept for an entire day and night before I was released. Let me tell you something I didn't want to say before: among the "Seven Sisters" I mentioned earlier, Sister Mei was my mother-in-law who was already over fifty years old at the time. Those Japanese troops really sinned! Sister Feng was my mother-in-law's younger sister who was about forty years old, and Sister Da also was a relative – a distant cousin of mine. Four in just one family suffered these atrocities; what a miserable fate!

Seeing how I was tormented by the Japanese military, my husband Zhou Shouwen chose to fight and joined the local anti-Japanese guerrilla force. But later he was seized by the Japanese troops and beaten to death. After the liberation, we found only one surviving witness who knew how he had died; this didn't conform to government regulations, which, required at least two witnesses, so my husband didn't earn a title of honour. How regrettable!

I was finally freed in 1939 when the Japanese troops withdrew from Miaozhen. By that time I had already developed serious venereal disease and other diseases. Today I still suffer from constant headaches, renal disorder, as well as incurable mental trauma. I am not able to free myself from mental stress, even though I never did anything of which I should feel ashamed. One thing I feel extremely bitter about is that my husband was beaten to death by the Japanese soldiers. Since his death I have been living in widowhood and have never remarried. For a long time I didn't want to talk about what the Japanese army had done to me: it was utterly unspeakable. Now, I have only my second son Zhou Xie and my third son Zhou Xin. I live with Zhou Xie. He is my legal representative for my lawsuit against the Japanese government. The Japanese troops were so evil; I am fighting to regain my dignity and honour. Guo Yaying, whom we called Sister Ying and who had lived next door to our little restaurant, had also opened a restaurant. I am a witness to Sister Ying's torture. I demand a formal apology and compensation from the Japanese government.

After the death of Zhu Qiaomei's husband, their restaurant was destroyed and Zhu Qiaomei's family became destitute, living for decades in an old, tattered shed. On 20 February 2005, Zhu Qiaomei succumbed to illness in her home at the age of ninety-five. The Research Center for Chinese "Comfort Women" sponsored the placement of a gravestone to commemorate her life.

(Interviewed by Su Zhiliang and Chen Lifei in May 2000, September 2000, February 2001, and March 2001)

Lu Xiuzhen

During their occupation of Chongming Island the Japanese forces set up a comfort station called Hui'an-suo in the Town of Miaozhen. The station, whose buildings no longer exist, was established on the property of local Chinese residents. There was no highway connecting the Town of Miaozhen and the village where Lu Xiuzhen had lived, so the villagers did not expect the Japanese soldiers to traverse the difficult paths to their homes and, therefore, did not hide. Lu Xiuzhen and other women were thus easily kidnapped by Japanese troops and taken to the comfort station.[10]

Figure 11 Lu Xiuzhen, in 2000, giving a talk at the International Symposium on Chinese "Comfort Women" at Shanghai Normal University.

I was born in the Year of the Horse [1917], in a village north of the Miaozhen River on Chongming Island. Both of my parents were poor peasants and had no means of supporting me, so they gave me to the Zhu family to be their adopted daughter. However, my adoptive parents changed their minds later and wanted to make me their oldest son's child-bride. I appreciated being their daughter but didn't want to be their child-daughter-in-law, so I refused and even attempted to run away. Because of this situation, I remained unmarried when I turned twenty-one. [At that time it was a common practice in rural China for females to marry at a very young age, often around or before eighteen. Twenty-one was considered rather old for marriage.] That year [1938] the Japanese army occupied Chongming Island. I heard that the Japanese troops had vacations. Their officers had a week-long vacation, while the soldiers had three days. On their vacation days the military men would come to the villages from where they were stationed. They looted chickens, grain, or anything they could find and shot oxen and pigs to eat. Worse even than that, the Japanese soldiers kidnapped the girls and women they could find. Women in the village were frightened to death, running for their lives as fast as they could when they saw the Japanese soldiers. Those who did not flee fast enough were captured. I was one of the girls captured by Interpreter Jin and the Japanese soldiers. My mother heard about my capture and went to beg the Japanese soldiers to release me. She kneeled in front of them, holding me tightly so that they could not drag me away. The Japanese soldiers then raised their rifles and yelled fiercely at my mother, "Let her go with us or we will burn your house to ashes!" Chinese people suffered hellishly when the Japanese army invaded our country. Japanese soldiers could kill us at will with their guns, so my mother had no way to save me. Those Japanese troops were not human; they were no different from beasts.

The day I was kidnapped was an extremely cold day in the Second Lunar Month, when the Chinese New Year was just over. I was taken to the military compound in the Town of Miaozhen, Chongming County. The building was a two-storey house in which were confined over a dozen local young women. I was unfamiliar with most of them. I only knew one girl, whom we called XX the Beggar, and another one named XXX. [The names are omitted to protect the victims' privacy.]

I was assigned to a room on the lower floor of the building. Each of us girls had a very small room in which there was a bed and nothing else. The building was very close to the military barracks. It was guarded by soldiers, but we were allowed to walk around the facility and do things such as washing clothes. The platoon chief ordered soldiers to watch us and not to let us go too far, and we were not allowed to enter the barracks.

Shortly after I was taken into the comfort station I was raped by many soldiers. My lower body hurt so much that I could neither walk nor even sit. The platoon chief came frequently. He was about thirty years old and wore a sword. He came every two or three days, usually during the day, and sometimes brought canned food with him. I noticed that the Japanese troops stationed at Chongming often ate canned food. Perhaps they feared being poisoned by the Chinese people; they would not eat any dish made by Chinese cooks before testing it by having a Chinese person eat it first. Occasionally the soldiers gave us a little of the food they brought over, but they never gave us any money. Needless to say, I never dared to ask for money.

As time passed, the platoon chief seemed to have said something to the soldiers and prohibited them from entering my room; so only the platoon chief himself frequented my room. The soldiers resented me very much since they were not allowed to touch me. When the chief was not around, they would retaliate by throwing my clothes up on top of the roof and so on. With no extra changes I had to wear the same clothes all the time and wash them at night. When the platoon chief found out about what the soldiers had done to me, he scolded them. The soldiers stopped bullying me after that, while the platoon chief kept me to service only himself, abusing me viciously.

The big house had a cook who made the meals, which usually consisted of rice and a bowl of vegetables. Sometimes the vegetables were served in small dishes placed in a large box. Labourers in the house were all Chinese. One of the workers was a traitor named Xu Qigou, who supervised the comfort women. His wife worked as the cook, did laundry, and also served meals to the Japanese soldiers. This woman was very mean; she often yelled at us and gave us only a very small amount of food. We were always starving.

The Japanese soldiers did not wear condoms when they raped the women in the station. Occasionally a doctor, who was a Chinese person, gave us physical examinations. I remember the doctor came two or three times and he stuck something into our lower body to check it. I don't remember if we were given any medicine.

I was kept in the comfort station until one morning in the Fifth Lunar Month that year [1938] when I escaped from that place. It was when the fields turned golden yellow and the villagers were harvesting wheat. I had planned to escape for a long time. That day, when I saw the Japanese soldiers off guard, I sneaked out. I made sure that nobody noticed me then ran without stopping. There was a highway near the comfort station and I knew my hometown was on the south side of it, but I didn't dare to go back there. Fearing that the Japanese soldiers might come after me by the highway, I didn't go that way but instead ran along small paths. I ran for a long while without a specific destination until it occurred to me that I had a relative who treated me like a daughter in Shanghai, so I decided to go there.

The trip to Shanghai was hard, but I managed to get a free boat ride across the Yangtze River and to find my relative. She sympathized with me and let me stay at her place. She also sent a message to my family saying that I was with her. I didn't return home until a person from my hometown came to tell us that the Japanese troops had been relocated.

Because I had been raped by the enemy, people in my village gossiped about me, saying that I slept with Japanese soldiers. I was unable to find a prospective husband until I was thirty-three years old, when someone introduced me to Mr. Wang, a custodian at Huaihai Middle School in Shanghai. He was looking for a woman to help care for his family after his wife died, leaving him with two young children. I married him, but I was unable to bear children. People in my village believed that a person defiled by Japanese soldiers would bring bad luck and could not produce anything good. They said I could not even grow things well in the fields. I lack education and have no knowledge of medicine, so it's hard for me to tell if my infertility was due to the damage caused by the Japanese soldiers.

I am so embarrassed talking about these things. These things are so hard to talk about, but my stepson and daughter-in-law have been very supportive and they encourage me to tell the truth and seek justice. I am very old now and I cannot stomach the atrocities done to me any more. I cannot walk, my head is dizzy all the time, and my memory is failing me. I hate the Japanese troops who destroyed my reputation and my life. Japanese troops invaded our country and committed the crimes that caused my misery; whether they admit it or not, that fact cannot be altered. Some Japanese people do not admit the bad things Japanese troops did in the past, but other survivors and I are still alive and we can provide evidence. We will fight to the end!

On 14 February 2001, Shanghai Jing'an District Notary, Shanghai Tianhong Law Firm, and the Research Center for Chinese "Comfort Women" notarized the testimonies of Lu Xiuzhen, Zhu Qiaomei, and Guo Yaying regarding their experiences as Japanese military comfort women. A year later, Lu Xiuzhen died on 24 November 2002. Chen Lifei and Zhang Tingting, from the Research Centre for Chinese "Comfort Women," attended her funeral, and the research centre sponsored the placement of her tombstone.

(Interviewed by Su Zhiliang and Chen Lifei in March and May 2000, and February 2001)

6 Warzones in Central and Northern China

Yuan Zhulin

When the Japanese forces attacked Nanjing the Chinese Nationalist leaders shifted their headquarters to Wuhan, Hubei Province, then the most populous city in central China as well as a transportation centre. Japanese forces launched major air strikes on Wuhan in April 1938,[1] and this was followed by a massive campaign in the summer of the same year. Chinese forces committed a large number of units to protect Wuhan. Bloody battles, which involved 300,000 Japanese and 1 million Chinese troops, lasted for months in the region and resulted in heavy casualties on both sides. The defence eventually fell to Japanese troops at the end of October 1938.[2] The Japanese army continued to press westward and southward after the occupation of Wuhan, but it was unable to completely control Hubei and the nearby provinces. The war in the Chinese theatre was deadlocked. During the seven years of fighting in the region the Japanese military established a full-blown comfort women system in the occupied areas of Hubei. Yuan Zhulin was one of the many Chinese women enslaved in Japanese military comfort stations there.

Figure 12 Yuan Zhulin, in 1998, attending a public hearing in Toronto on the atrocities committed by the Japanese military during the Asia-Pacific War.

I was born in Wuhan City, Hubei Province, in 1922, on the Sixteenth day of the Fifth Lunar Month. My father, Yuan Shengjie, and my mother, Zhang Xiangzi, had three daughters. They were very poor and didn't have the money to send me to school. Unable to support us three girls, my parents sent my two sisters and me to other families, one after the other, to be child-daughters-in-law. My family fell apart and I never saw my sisters again. I married Wang Guodong, a chauffeur, at the age of fifteen. We were not rich, but we loved each other and lived a comfortable life.

However, our peaceful life didn't last very long. In June 1938, the year after we were married, the Japanese armies launched attacks on Wuhan City. My husband was at work in the faraway area controlled by Chinese forces. I had no place to escape to and stayed home. Not long after my husband left, my mother-in-law began to treat me like an outcast. She thought I was an extra burden on the family and, since her son might never be able to return, she forced me to leave the family and remarry. I felt very humiliated, yet I had no choice but to marry a man named Liu Wanghai. The following year I gave birth to a girl named Rongxian. She was the only child I birthed. [Yuan Zhulin didn't want to talk about her only daughter at the interview. Later the interviewers found out that the child had died of neglect while Yuan was held as a comfort woman.] Liu Wanghai didn't have a stable job; in order to help support the family, I worked as a maid, although frequently I could not find a job in the turmoil and economic depression during the Japanese invasion.

In the spring of 1940, a local woman named Zhang Xiuying came to recruit workers. She said that cleaning women were wanted at hotels in the other cities in Hubei Province. I had never met Zhang before, but since it was very difficult to find a job at the time, several other young girls and I signed up. I was eighteen years old then and good-looking, so I stood out among the other girls.

I didn't know until much later that Zhang Xiuying was a despicable woman. Her Japanese husband could speak some Chinese; following orders issued by the Japanese army, he was rounding up Chinese women to set up a comfort station. I still remember how he looked; he was a man of medium height who often wore Western-style suits rather than a military uniform. He had dark skin and bug-eyes, and people called him "Goldfish Eyes." He was about forty years old.

I left my second husband, Liu Wanghai, and my daughter behind and travelled aboard a ship down the Yangtze River. In the beginning I was quite happy to have found a job, and I thought it could bring me a better future after the initial hardship. The ship arrived at Ezhou in about a day. As soon as we went ashore, we were taken to a temple by Japanese soldiers. As a matter of fact, the Japanese army had already turned the temple into a comfort station. A Japanese soldier was standing guard at the entrance. I was frightened by the devilish-looking soldiers and didn't want to enter. By now the girls and I realized that something was not right, so we all wanted to go home. I cried "This is not a hotel. I want to go home." But the Japanese soldiers forced us inside with their bayonets.

As soon as we entered the station the proprietor ordered us to take off all our clothes for an examination. We refused, but Zhang Xiuying's husband had his men beat us with leather whips. Zhang Xiuying yelled at me maliciously: "You are the wife of a guerrilla! You'd better follow the instructions!" [Zhang was likely referring to Yuan Zhulin's first husband, who worked in the area under the control of the Nationalist Party (Guomindang), which led the fighting against Japanese forces.] The physical examination was over very quickly since none of us was a prostitute and no one had a venereal disease. After the examination, the proprietor gave each girl a Japanese name. I was named Masako. Each of us was assigned a room of about seven or eight square metres that had only a bed and a spittoon.

The following morning I saw a wooden sign hung on the door of my room with "Masako" written on it. There were also similar plaques hung at the entrance of the comfort station. That morning a lot of Japanese soldiers were swarming outside of the temple gate. Soon a long line formed at the door of each room. I ... [sobbing] was raped by ten big Japanese soldiers. I became so weak by the end of the day that I was unable to sit up. The lower part of my body felt as if it had been sliced with knives.

From that day onward, I became a sex slave to Japanese soldiers. I heard that each Japanese soldier had to buy a ticket to enter the comfort station, but I never saw how much they paid. I certainly never received a penny from them. The proprietor hired a Chinese man to cook us three meals a day, but the food was very bad and the amount was very small. We girls who suffered numerous rapes every day needed to wash our bodies, but there was only a wooden bucket in the kitchen for us to take turns using. There were dozens of comfort women at the station, so the bath water was unbearably dirty by the end of each day.

Each Japanese soldier usually spent about thirty minutes in a room. We couldn't get any rest even at night because the military officers often spent a couple of hours, sometimes the whole night, at the station. The proprietor didn't allow us a break even during our menstrual periods; he continued to let the Japanese soldiers come in one after another. He made us take some white pills and told us that there would be no pain if we took them. We didn't know what the pills were. I threw them away like the other girls. The Japanese army required the soldiers to use condoms at the comfort station, but since many of them knew that I was new and probably didn't have syphilis, they would not use a condom when they came to my room. Soon I became pregnant. When the proprietor found out that we weren't taking the pills, he made everyone take them while he watched.³

Life became even more miserable after I became pregnant. I realized I would die sooner or later as a result of the abuse by the Japanese soldiers, but I didn't want to die. My parents were still alive and they needed me to take care of them. I secretly talked to another Hubei girl whom the Japanese troops called "Rumiko," and we planned to escape. However, we were caught as soon as we ran out. A Japanese soldier held my hair and violently hit my head against the wall. Blood immediately gushed out. The beating left me with incurable headaches; I still suffer from them to this day. [Yuan Zhuling had a miscarriage and because of that she was unable to bear a child for the rest of her life.]

From the first days when I was imprisoned in the comfort station, a Japanese military officer named Fujimura took a fancy to me. He was probably the head officer of the Japanese army stationed in Ezhou. At the beginning he bought tickets to visit the comfort station, as the other Japanese soldiers did, but after a while he requested instead that the proprietor send me to the place where he lived. Compared with the conditions in the comfort station, life conditions at Fujimura's house were better, but I was still the officer's slave with no freedom. After a while Fujimura lost interest in me. At that time a lower-ranking officer named Nishiyama seemed to be rather sympathetic toward me, and he asked Fujimura to give me to him. I was then taken to where Nishiyama's troops were stationed. This was quite an unusual experience, which, to this day, makes me believe that Nishiyama was a kind person.

Around 1941, I obtained Nishiyama's permission to return home to visit my parents, only to find that my father had already died. My father had worked as a labourer. Because he was a small man and very old, he was frequently fired and had difficulty finding another job. He starved to death. I went to look for Liu Wanghai, but couldn't find him either. I had no place to go, so I returned to Ezhou, where Nishiyama was.

The Chinese War of Resistance against Japan ended in August 1945. Nishiyama asked me to go with him, either to Japan or to Shihuiyao, a place that was then under the control of the New Fourth Army.⁴ I did not go with him because I wanted to find my mother. [Yuan Zhulin stopped talking at this point and heaved a deep sigh.] Nishiyama was a good man. He served in the Japanese army, but he didn't take advantage of his position to extort money. The shirt he wore was torn and ragged. He told me that he had once made a hole in a ship that was carrying supplies to the Japanese army and sank it. And when he saw Japanese troops electrocuting Chinese people who sold salt illegally, he felt sympathetic and he gave packages of salt to the Chinese people. [The Japanese military imposed strict control over the market during the war. Free purchase of salt was prohibited in some occupied areas.] Nishiyama left alone and I haven't heard from him since.

[Yuan didn't know whether Nishiyama had returned to Japan or had gone to Shihuiyao. She inquired about his whereabouts over the years with no results. Later, however, during the political turmoil in China, Yuan's relationship with the Japanese man brought her more hardship.]

After the Japanese surrender, I found my mother and went to live with her in her hometown, a small mountain village in the vicinity of Wuhan. We worked as day labourers to support ourselves. In 1946, I adopted a girl who was only a little over two months old. I named her Cheng Fei.

I returned to Wuhan after the Liberation in 1949 and lived at Number 2 Jixiangli. One day I saw Zhang Xiuying, the woman who had tricked me and the other girls into the living hell. Zhang was running a shop with an old man at the time. I immediately reported her to the local policeman in charge of household registration. I still remember that policeman's last name – Luo. But Officer Luo said: "Forget it. Those things are hard to investigate." His words chilled my heart as if it were doused with ice water. Zhang Xiuying has probably died by now.

Although deep in my heart, memories of my horrific past have always haunted me and caused me sleepless nights, my life with my mother was relatively peaceful. But, one day at a meeting called "Tell Your Sufferings in the Old Society and the Happiness in the New" *(yi ku si tian)* my naïve mother talked about my miseries when I was forced by the Japanese army to be a military comfort woman. This caused us big trouble. Children in the neighbourhood chased me, shouting: "A whore working for the Japanese! A whore working for the Japanese!"

In 1958, the Neighbourhood Committee officials accused me of having been a prostitute working for the Japanese,[5] and they ordered me to go to the remote northern province of Heilongjiang. I refused to go. The head of the Neighbourhood Committee then deceived me by saying that they needed my residence booklet and food purchase card for a routine check. They took these documents and revoked them. The policemen in charge of household registration then ordered me to reform through hard labour in the country-side. We were forced to move to Heilongjiang. My house was confiscated.

We spent the following seventeen years in Mishan [in Heilongjiang Province, northeast China] doing farm work, such as planting corn and harvesting soybeans. The weather was very cold there and we didn't have any firewood with which to warm ourselves. Each month we only got six *jin* [1 *jin* equals 0.5 kilograms] of soybean dregs to eat. [Soybean dregs are the solids left after the oil is extracted from soybeans, which are normally used to feed horses and cows, etc.] My adopted daughter was so hungry that she would grab dirt and eat it. We suffered all kinds of hardship. Luckily there was a section chief named Wang Wanlou who felt very sorry for how we suffered, so he helped us obtain permission to return to Wuhan. That was in 1975. I will be forever grateful for his kindness.

Today I am receiving 120 yuan [about fifteen dollars at the time] in monthly support from the government. My adopted daughter gives me 150 yuan every month, but she is retired, as am I. My health has long been destroyed. Because of the beatings by the Japanese soldiers, I have headaches every day that cause me difficulties sleeping. Even after taking many sleeping pills, I still cannot sleep more than two hours. For the remainder of the night, I sit in pain waiting for daybreak.

[At the end of the interview, Yuan Zhulin cried.]

My life was destroyed by the Japanese military. My first husband and I would never have been parted if there hadn't been the Japanese invasion. I have nightmares every night. In the nightmares I see myself suffering in that horrible place, suffering miseries beyond human imagination.

I am now seventy-nine years old. I don't have many years left. The Japanese government must pay compensation for our sufferings. I don't have time to wait any longer.

Yuan Zhulin moved to Zhanjiang City, Guangdong Province, to live with her adopted daughter in January 2006; she could no longer live alone due to old age and poor health. Two months later she suffered a stroke and died in hospital at the age of eighty-four. Chen Lifei and Yao Fei, from the Research Centre for Chinese "Comfort Women," attended the ceremony at which her ashes were laid to rest.

(Interviewed by Su Zhiliang in 1998 and 2001)

Tan Yuhua

Between 29 September and 6 October 1939 Japanese forces suffered a major defeat in Hunan Province south of Hubei.[6] Chinese Nationalist soldiers fought fiercely to stop the advance of the Japanese army and, from 1939 to 1944, engaged in four major battles to defend the provincial capital, Changsha. In order to control Hunan, the Imperial Japanese Army deployed ten divisions with about 250,000 to 280,000 soldiers to the battle in 1944.[7] During approximately five years of fighting in the area Japanese troops established a large number of comfort stations. Tan Yuhua's hometown in Yiyang County, Hunan Province, was occupied by the 40th Division of the Japanese army in June 1944, a few days before the City of Changsha fell to the Japanese.

Figure 13 Tan Yuhua, in 2008, in front of her home.

My original name was Yao Chunxiu. I was born in the Seventeenth Year of the Republic of China [1928] in Yaojiawan, Shilang Township, Yiyang County, Hunan Province [today's Yaojiawan Group, Gaoping Village, Town of Oujiangcha, Heshan District, Yiyang City]. My father, Yao Meisheng, was a villager, but he was unable to do farm work due to his disabled legs, so he made a living as a craftsman, making bamboo items. My mother did not have a formal name; people called her "Yao's wife."

I was the only girl in the family, so my parents let me attend school for fun with my cousins. I attended a private village school for a few years. I still remember that our teacher was Mr. Yuan; he later stopped teaching after the Japanese troops occupied our area. I learned how to read *Zeng guang xian wen*[8] and *You xue qiong lin,*[9] but I've forgotten most of the characters I learned.

The Japanese troops came to my hometown in the Thirty-Third Year of the Republic of China [1944], when I was sixteen. Local people all fled. That day I was having my supper when I heard the neighing of horses and braying of donkeys at the riverside. I saw the Japanese troops crossing the Dazha River, marching in our direction, and creating an air of terror. We were frightened and ran away, but my father was unable to run with us because his legs hurt. My mother, uncle, cousin, and I ran without stopping until we reached the Fumen Mountains sixty *li* [thirty kilometres] away, where there were no Japanese soldiers around. We stayed at my aunt's house for about half a year. During the Japanese occupation local people always helped each other, kindly providing food and lodging to others who had fled from Japanese attack.

I remember that, when we ran away, we were still wearing over-jackets, and it was already around the Eighth Lunar Month when we returned home. We heard that the township formed an Association for Maintaining Order run by local people, so we thought that order had been restored and that it would be safe to return home. People who had stayed in the area told me the Japanese troops had burned houses and randomly opened fire in Zhuliang-qiao.[10] They set fire to houses one after another. Many houses had thatched roofs at that time so they were easily burned down.

My family had a tile-roofed house so it was not burned. Our house was across the road from Zhuliang-qiao, where the Japanese soldiers often fired their guns. We placed a large table in the central room and covered it with a cotton-padded quilt. When we heard the gunfire we would hide under the table watching the soldiers passing by my house.

The Japanese soldiers were stationed in Zhuliang-qiao and also on Shizi-shan Mountain about one *li* away from Zhuliang-qiao. On top of the mountain the Japanese troops built a lookout tower, which was constructed of wooden boards mounted to three big camphor trees. A guard standing on the tower could keep watch over the entire town of Zhuliang-qiao. The Japanese soldiers made a tunnel, and they went back and forth through it to Zhuliang-qiao.

One day I saw the Japanese soldiers capture a villager named Qiu Siyi, tie him to a wooden frame, and let an army dog maul him to death. The Japanese army dog was huge; it looked like a wolf. I also saw a woman captured by the soldiers, but I didn't know her name. She had attempted to escape but failed; the Japanese soldiers buried her alive. Another girl who was also buried alive looked very young, like a teenager. A soldier shovelled dirt onto her body; he stopped in the middle of his task and laughed until she died. I didn't know the girl's name.

My cousin was married right after we returned to our village in the Eighth Lunar Month, and soon after that I was married, too. Fearing the chaos of the war, our parents urged us to get married as soon as possible. However, fewer than twenty days after my wedding, I was kidnapped by Japanese troops. It was in the Ninth Lunar Month when the weather was not yet very cold. I was so frightened at the time that I cannot clearly remember what happened. I don't know the exact date and time, but I remember that I was wearing a single-layer coat. The Japanese troops came from the other side of the river, not from Zhuliang-qiao, so we didn't notice them approaching the town and were unable to run away in time.

The Japanese soldiers caught my crippled father first. They made him kneel down, and a soldier threatened to kill him with a long curved sword. I couldn't help crying out, so the Japanese soldiers found and caught me. The soldiers also captured two other girls, Yao Bailian and Yao Cuilian, both of whom were my cousins and schoolmates; both were older than I. One of my aunts died during that attack. The soldiers arrested my father to force him to work for them, but my father was unable to perform hard labour due to his disability so the Japanese soldiers killed him. I lost my father forever.

The other girls and I were taken to "Jade Star House" (Cuixing-lou) in the Town of Zhuliang-qiao. Dozens of women were already in the house when I was taken in. We were locked together at first and then sent to separate rooms. For two days I was unable to eat anything; I was too frightened.

Zhuliang-qiao used to have a lot of shops: grocers, cloth shops, drapers' shops, and so on. The shop owners all escaped when the Japanese troops came, abandoning everything to run for their lives. The Japanese soldiers occupied those empty houses and confined the abducted women in them. Jade Star House used to be a house of entertainment that looked like a hotel, but it had in fact been a brothel. When the Japanese army came, they occupied this and the other shops in the neighbourhood. This house had two stories and was a wooden building; its walls were made of two layers of wooden boards. I was locked in a room on the lower level where there were two or three rooms altogether. They forced me to have sexual intercourse with a Japanese military man. I was so young at the time but was brutally raped. The Japanese man spoke a lot, but I didn't understand what he was saying, and I didn't want to listen either. He beat me if I did not follow his orders.

The room in which I was confined was very small and had no furniture except for a bed. The Japanese military man came to my room every night and left in the morning. He sometimes came during the day as well, bringing several Japanese officers with him; they talked about something I didn't understand. No other Japanese soldiers came to my room. I guess I was assigned to this military officer. I don't remember his face, but I remember that he was neither tall nor particularly fat and was always wearing a military uniform.

A Japanese soldier hit the soft spot on my side with his gun when the troops abducted me. The internal injury it caused became increasingly painful, although there was no scar on my skin. I still suffer from the sharp pain in my side today; it radiates through my entire lower back. At the time no doctor examined me, and they didn't give me any medication either.

I was kept by the Japanese troops for about a month. Only a small number of officers who seemed to be of high rank in the army came to the Jade Star House. Women in the house didn't know their names and called them *taijun*.[11] Many Japanese soldiers were stationed in the stronghold on Shizi-shan Mountain, and those soldiers carried rifles. Our meals were prepared in the military cookhouse in the stronghold and sent down from Shizi-shan Mountain. We ate with the soldiers.

We were not allowed to go out. An armed guard always stood at the entrance of the house watching the women. He would catch and beat anyone who attempted to escape. I was completely listless at this time, unable to think or speak properly. The only thing in my mind was going home, but there was no way for me to leave the house. I saw some other women in the house and chatted with one who washed dishes there. She was as listless as I. We knew we would end up dying if we remained there, and we wanted so badly to get out of the place and return home, but we neither dared to talk about this nor did we dare to cry out loud. We could only keep our sorrow deep in our hearts; the only thing we could do was sigh and quietly shed tears together. We lived in constant anxiety, worrying about what would happen to us the next day. We missed home so much, but we dared not run away. I heard that one woman was captured after an attempted escape and was buried alive. We had no freedom and no way to break out.

I was finally bailed out by Yao Jufeng, head of the local Association for Maintaining Order. He was a relative of my mother's, so my parents begged him to help obtain my release. Yao Jufeng obtained the Japanese officer's permission to let me return home briefly by telling them that there was an emergency in my family and that he would send me back to the comfort station afterwards. The officer gave me a small towel when I left the Jade Star House. He had never given me any money, and the towel was the only thing I received from him.

[Tan Yuhua hid at her relative's house after she left the comfort station and didn't go back. Yao Jufeng's wife was arrested as a punishment for Yao's helping Tan escape.]

Soon after I got out of the Jade Star House the Japanese troops arrested Yao Jufeng's wife; perhaps they found out that Yao Jufeng had deceived them. Yao's wife, named Jiang Yulan, was a tall woman. The Japanese soldiers ripped off her clothes and dragged her naked body over the snowy ground. The weather was very cold and she was dragged through the snow. Her skin was badly blistered from the dragging, and the bloody blisters on her body became infected and didn't heal for a long time. That was in the winter of the Thirty Third Year of the Republic of China [1944], when the Eleventh Lunar Month was already over. I didn't dare to stay at home so I hid in my relative's house and only went back home occasionally. Luckily, the Japanese soldiers didn't capture me; since I didn't stay at home I didn't know if they had come to look for me or not. I couldn't return home until all the Japanese troops left my hometown after Japan's surrender.

I was married twice. My first husband was named Gao Fengsheng, and I had a son with him when I was twenty years old. My son was named Gao Qiaoliang; he died in 1998 of an illness. After my first husband died I married Tan Guifu in 1965 in Yiyang and moved to Mulun Village, Xinkang District, Wangcheng County, Changsha City. My second husband was one year younger than I; he died in 1978 at the age of fifty-two. Tan Guifu's ex-wife was also named Chunxiu, so he wanted me to change my name from Yao Chunxiu to Tan Yuhua, using his family name.

Even today I often have nightmares in which I relive the torture of the Japanese troops and wake up crying. In the nightmares I remain extremely frightened, seeing the Japanese soldiers marching towards me as I run desperately in fear, crying. Looking back, after that experience, I hate the

Japanese troops! I feel so helpless in my old age. If I had the resources I would sue them and demand that they restore my dignity. I hate the Japanese troops so much that I don't know what I might do if I saw them in front of me.

The Research Center for Chinese "Comfort Women" invited Tan Yuhua to come to Shanghai in July 2008 to talk about her wartime experience to history teachers from Canada and the United States. Her health has been rapidly declining in recent years.

(Interviewed by Su Zhiliang in 2001 and by Chen Lifei in 2008, with the assistance of Yin Chuming)

Yin Yulin

The Japanese army entered Shanxi Province in northern China in September 1937 soon after the beginning of full-fledged warfare and occupied the provincial capital Taiyuan on 9 November.[12] From 1937 to 1944, the Imperial Japanese Army operated a series of "mop-up" campaigns to wipe out the resistance activities led by the Chinese Communist Party in Shanxi and the nearby provinces. Japanese soldiers' sexual violence escalated during these operations; they frequently killed women who dared to resist rape and kidnapped a large number of local women, taking them to randomly placed comfort facilities.[13] A 1938 newspaper article reported that, after the Japanese army left the Yuanqu County Seat, the resistance forces found the blood-soaked clothing of over sixty Chinese women in the Japanese-occupied county hall.[14] In August 1940, the communist forces launched a large-scale campaign called the Hundred Regiments Offensive, which significantly damaged Japan's strategic position in the area.[15] The Japanese military retaliated with genocidal operations against the resistance forces and local civilians.[16] Yu County, lying at the border between the Japanese-occupied area and the resistance bases, was within the region of fierce fighting. Yin Yuling was one of the women abducted by the Japanese troops stationed near her village in Yu County during this period.

Figure 14 Yin Yulin, in 2001, praying in her cave dwelling.

I grew up in Wuer-zhuang Village, Xiyan Town, Yu County. My parents were poor peasants and I had an older brother and two older sisters. I was born in the Year of the Snake. At fifteen I was married to a man named Yang Yudong of Hou-Hedong Village. Yang Yudong was sixteen years older than I and had been married before. He was an ugly-looking man, but his family was quite rich. Life was comfortable in the family. I gave birth to a boy when I was nineteen, but the boy became ill and died at one year of age.

In the Tenth Lunar Month of that year [1941], when the weather was cold and we were wearing cotton-padded jackets, Japanese soldiers dashed into Hou-Hedong Village. I remember the time because that was the day my husband died. He died of typhoid before my son reached age one. When the Japanese soldiers saw the coffin and heard that my husband had died of typhoid, they feared being infected and left. However, later the soldiers came again after the coffin was carried away. I was in deep grief for my husband at the time and too weak to resist them. The Japanese soldiers easily caught and raped me.

After that initial time, the Japanese soldiers stationed in the blockhouse on top of nearby Mount Yangma came to my house frequently and raped me. Every time my parents heard my screams they rushed over to protect me, but each time they were dragged out to the yard and beaten by the Japanese soldiers. Several times they were beaten until blood covered their faces, and I saw blood gushing out of their mouths. This situation lasted for a long time. Every day two or three Japanese soldiers came down the mountain to rape me at my home, which left me constantly terrified. I remember, among the Japanese troops who came, there was a tall man who had a heavy mustache. He might have been an officer because he always put on an air of grandeur. He often arrived in civilian clothes, and each time he came, the other soldiers would not show up. Another one, who must have been an officer as well, often wore a black top and brownish-yellow trousers; he often came without his gun. Frightened of the rapes while having no place to hide, my body was always trembling with fear. What a horror!

The Japanese soldiers never used any contraceptive devices when they raped me. They would order me to bathe before they raped me. You could never imagine how evil these soldiers were: afterwards they would wash their lower bodies in our cooking bowl! Water in the area was extremely precious; there was no running water or well so I had to carry water from a faraway place. However, the Japanese soldiers didn't care at all when they used my water. I always felt my body was very dirty after I was raped, so each time after being raped I would scoop water from the container and wash myself repeatedly. Since there was no man in the house who could help me carry water, I had to save every drop of available water and sometimes even had to reuse the washing water.

The Japanese soldiers also took me by force to their stronghold on Mount Yangma, where they raped me. The first time they took me to the block-house it was an evening, before I had my supper. I was taken up the mountain by the head of the village's Self Guard Corps, traitor Liu Erdan. He forced me to mount a donkey and guarded me. Once we reached the mountain path I had to dismount and walk on foot. Walking on the mountain road was excruciating on my feet, especially as they had been previously bound.

When we arrived at the stronghold on the mountain, the Japanese soldiers forced me into a small blockhouse. It was already dark outside and it was even darker inside the blockhouse. On a heated brick bed there was something whitish, perhaps it was a cotton-padded mattress. The Japanese soldiers ripped off my clothes and an officer held a candle to examine my body. He looked at my lower body very carefully, perhaps checking to see if I had venereal disease, but at that time I didn't know what he was doing and I was very frightened. I thought I was going to die! I remember that man's face clearly. It was a dark face, full of hair, and his two eyes were glowing like a wolf's! The candle drippings fell on my body one by one and scalded my skin, but I dared not cry. My body shook with each drop of hot wax and I kept shaking out of fear. I didn't dare look at the officer; I only stared at the dripping candle, hoping it would all be over soon.

The officer began to rape me after that. He rose from the bed and returned repeatedly, torturing me almost the entire night. I was shaking in the dark the whole time, and ever since then I have suffered from incurable trembling. Each time when I am nervous my body begins to shake uncontrollably. Look at my hands. They are trembling now. I cannot talk about that horrible experience. Whenever I speak of it, I become nervous and feel tremendous pain in my heart.

The following day I was taken back to the village by Liu Erdan before dawn. A few days later I was again taken to the blockhouse. This time a Japanese soldier and Liu Erdan conducted me there together. They forced me to walk and kept yelling at me for being too slow. I was taken into that small block-house again. This time a crowd of Japanese soldiers gang-raped me. I hurt so much that I didn't even have the strength to cry. The soldiers finally let me leave before daybreak. This was repeated again and again; I don't remember how many times I was taken to the mountaintop. After the torture in the blockhouse at night, during the day the Japanese soldiers would come to my home to assault me, wearing wooden sandals. They told a Chinese collaborator to threaten me and to say, "Don't even think of running away, or your head will be off your shoulders!"

This situation lasted for two full years until I turned twenty-one. By that time I had become very sick. I suffered from constant dizziness and body aches as well as from a menstrual disorder. My sister was also raped by the Japanese soldiers. She was carried to the blockhouse and held there for a long period of time. We often bemoaned our fate, wondering, "Why us?" In order to escape the horrible situation I tried to remarry, but everyone knew that I had been raped by Japanese soldiers, and no man in the region wanted to marry me. Knowing that it was impossible to find a man in Yu County who would marry me, I married a man named Yang Erquan in distant Zhengjia-zhai Village in Quyang County and finally escaped the misery.

My second husband was the same age as I. He was a shepherd, a very honest person. His family was poor but I did not mind; he did not look down on me either. Indeed, he was a really nice person. We helped each other in our poor life. The torture of the Japanese soldiers damaged my health. In order to cure my uterine damage my husband took on several hard jobs simultaneously for many years to earn money for my treatments. He peddled goods and also cleaned cesspools to earn some millet, and then he sold the millet to make some money. He encouraged me, saying, "You will get better." I wanted to repay him for his kindness and to be able to have children with him, so I did my part, too, and sought treatment. I was so happy when I finally became pregnant and gave birth to a son at age thirty-three. Later, I gave birth to a girl.

China won the Resistance War, and the Japanese troops fled back home in 1945. However, my misery did not disappear with them. Although I was able to bear children, my uterine damage was never completely cured. It has bothered me for more than fifty years. Sometimes it is better, sometimes worse, with a filthy reddish discharge. My husband worked too hard and damaged his own health as a result. He died in 1991. I was deeply saddened.

My sister has suffered even more than I have. She was not able to have children because of the torture, so she was abandoned by her husband and she had to remarry twice. At this time both my sister and I still suffer from severe uterine damage. Our lower bodies hurt constantly, which makes every movement very difficult. My health has been declining in recent years. The lower back pain that has bothered me for years has become worse, as has the trembling in my hands and legs. I am also suffering from acute psychological problems, such as intense fear and nightmares in which I relive those past experiences. I am trembling right now as I recall the past horror. These unspeakable things are really hard to talk about, but I can no longer keep silent. If I don't speak out, people will not know how evil those Japanese troops were.

I am now living with my son and daughter-in-law. After I die they will continue to fight for justice. Generation after generation we must continue fighting those who deny the Japanese troops' atrocities, until they admit them!

In 2001, the Shanghai TV Station and the Research Center for Chinese "Comfort Women" jointly produced a documentary entitled The Last Survivors (Zuihou de xingcunzhe), *which records Yin Yulin's life story. On 6 October 2012, Yin Yulin died in her cave dwelling after the life-long suffering.*

(Interviewed by Su Zhiliang and Chen Lifei in 2000 and 2001)

Wan Aihua

After the Hundred Regiments Offensive the Japanese army increased the number of its strongholds to twenty-two in Yu County,[17] and it continued waging fierce campaigns to wipe out the resistance, while the Chinese forces continued fighting back and mobilizing local villagers. Wan Aihua, who participated in the resistance movement, was captured by the Japanese troops during these mop-up operations.

Figure 15 Wan Aihua, in 2000, telling the students and faculty at Shanghai Normal University how she was tortured by Japanese soldiers during the war.

I was born in Jiucaigou Village, Helingeer County, Suiyuan Province [today's Inner Mongolia] on the Twelfth Day of the Twelfth Lunar Month in 1929. My original name was Liu Chunlian.[18] My father was named Liu Taihai and my mother Zhang Banni. I had an older brother, a younger brother, and two younger sisters. My father was addicted to opium and he spent all of our money on it, leaving my family destitute. My mother gave birth to my younger brother when I was about four years old. Unable to support so many children, my father decided to sell me. My mother wailed aloud and she repeated to me my birth date, my parents' names, and home village until I was able to remember them. I was taller than most girls of my age, so my father was able to sell me to the human trafficker as an eight-year-old. After that traffickers traded me again and again, and each time the trafficker increased the price. Eventually, I was sold in Yangquan Village in Yu County and became Li Wuxiao's child-bride.[19] Three other girls were sold in that village at the same time, but I was the only one who survived. Life was extremely hard, as was survival, in those days. My name was changed to Lingyu in Yangquan Village. I learned to do the work expected of a child-bride, and, growing up in hardship, I became a big, strong girl.

In 1938 the Japanese invaders entered Yu County, where the Japanese army ordered the local collaborators to form an Association for Maintaining Order and a puppet county government. In the spring of the following year, the Japanese troops built strongholds and blockhouses in the county seat, Donghuili, Shangshe, Xiyan, and other villages and towns. I hated the Japanese troops for the atrocious things they did to the Chinese people, so I followed the Chinese Communist Party [CCP] and actively participated in the resistance movement. I was among the first to join the Children's Corps and was elected the leader. Although I was still a child, I was tall in stature and had always worked with adults. Soon I became a CCP member through the recommendations of Li Yuanlin and Zhang Bingwu.[20] The people with whom I worked were deeply sympathetic to me because of what I had experienced at such a young age. Liu Guihua, Commander of the 19th Regiment of the Eighth Route Army, renamed me Kezai [The two characters in Chinese mean "to overcome misfortune"] to wish me smooth sailing in life. I worked very hard and served as a member of the CCP branch committee in Yangquan Village, which at that time was called "lesser district committee," and I also served as deputy village head and director of the Women's Association for Saving the Nation. My CCP membership was kept secret, and my activities were underground at the time so that the collaborators and the Japanese troops would not know.

Japanese troops set up strongholds in Shangshe, Jinguishe, and other places once they occupied Yu County. In the spring of 1943, I remember it was the season when plants just begin to grow in the yard, Japanese troops stationed at Jinguishe carried out a mop-up operation in Yangquan Village. My father-in-law was over seventy years old at the time and he was sick with typhoid. Although I was a child-daughter-in-law in the family, he had always treated me with kindness, so I didn't want to leave him behind to flee with the other villagers. The Japanese soldiers caught me.

The Japanese troops took all their captives to the riverbed. They announced that I was a member of the Communist Party. As a Japanese officer was about to kill me, an aged man in the village knelt down and begged him to spare me. He said that I was only a child and that I was a dutiful daughter to my parents-in-law, not a communist. The interpreter held the arm of the Japanese captain who had drawn his sword and translated the old man's words to him. That captain was a very cruel person and had buckteeth, so the villagers called him "Captain Donkey." Captain Donkey put his sword back after he heard the interpreter's words. I am forever grateful to that old man and to the interpreter. I didn't know if the interpreter was Japanese, but I believe there were kind people in the Japanese troops, just as there are today, when many Japanese people support our fight for justice.

The Japanese soldiers took me and the other four girls back to the Jingui stronghold. Jingui was a small village in the mountains. After the Japanese army occupied the area they built a blockhouse on top of the mountain, forced the villagers who lived in the cave dwellings in the surrounding area to move away, and confiscated their dwellings. The other four girls and I were locked in these caves. In the cave there was a mat, made of sorghum stalks, on the ground. A quilt, a pillow, and a blanket were put on the mat. I was not allowed to go out even when I needed to relieve my bowels. At the beginning of my captivity I still had the strength to empty the excrement pail but soon became too weak to do so.

Because a traitor revealed my anti-Japanese activities to the Japanese troops, they treated me more viciously than they did the other girls. During the daytime the Japanese soldiers hung me up on a locust tree outside the cave and beat me, forcing me to admit I was a communist and to tell them who else in the village were CCP members. I gritted my teeth tightly and refused to say anything. At night the Japanese soldiers locked me in the cave room and gang-raped me. The torture damaged my head, so I don't remember the details clearly now. I only remember that I was imprisoned there for days. I knew I would end up dying at the hands of the Japanese soldiers if I remained, so I planned to escape. One night when the guard wasn't paying attention I broke out through the window and ran back to Yangquan Village. When I was kept in the military stronghold the Japanese soldiers had local people deliver food to us. One of the deliverymen, named Zhang Menghai, saw how I was confined in the cave and what was done to me. According to him, I escaped from captivity by breaking the window lattice, which was in poor shape.

I still remember the quilt I used while in the cave. I knew the quilt had belonged to a villager named Hou Datu, who was my co-worker and a core member of the local resistance movement. Hou Datu is now over seventy years old and still lives in Xiangcaoliang Village on the other side of the mountain. Li Guiming knows this man.[21] Young people call him "Uncle Datu." I had seen this quilt when I visited Hou's house previously, so I knew it must be one of the things the Japanese troops had plundered during their mop-up operations. The cover of the quilt had a nice pattern, so I remembered it clearly. I tied up the quilt, the pillowcase, and the blanket and took them with me when I escaped. While escaping I ran into three village resistance movement leaders who were on their way to rescue me. They were surprised to see that I had already broken out from the confinement by myself. I asked the village leaders to return the bedding to Hou Datu. [Su Zhiliang and Chen Lifei spoke to Hou Datu on 11 August 2000 and verified what Wan Aihua said. Hou was seventy-four at the time of the interview, and he clearly remembered the Japanese army's torture of Wan Aihua. He was the only one still alive who had witnessed Wan Aihua's experience as the Japanese army's sex slave.]

When I got back to my home village, my husband-to-be, Li Wuxiao, wanted to cancel our marriage engagement because I had been raped by Japanese soldiers. A man called Li Jigui, who was also a resistance movement activist in the village and much older than I, was willing to help me out. However, Li Wuxiao asked him to pay for my release. With the help of the village head, Li Jigui paid Li Wuxiao dozens of silver dollars and took me home. Li Jigui married me and paid for the treatment of my injuries.

In late summer of 1943, I was captured by the Japanese soldiers again. I remember that it was when watermelons were ripe and many people were selling them. I was washing clothes by a pond when I heard someone shouting, "Japanese devils are here!" Before I turned around to run, a Japanese soldier grabbed my hair, and I was kidnapped by the Japanese troops yet again. This time a large number of Japanese troops stationed in Xiyan Town and in Jingui came from the south and the north simultaneously and surrounded Yangquan Village. I was taken to the Jingui stronghold and subjected to more brutal torture. The Japanese soldiers pulled one of my earrings off, tearing off part of my earlobe with it.

The Japanese soldiers raped me day and night. Sometimes two or three soldiers entered the room together and gang-raped me. They beat and kicked me when I resisted, leaving wounds all over my body. Later the soldiers came less often at night, perhaps disgusted at the purulent wounds on my body. The torture lasted for about half a month, until one night I found the blockhouse strangely quiet. "The devils must have gone on another mop-up action," I thought, "It appears there are not many soldiers here." I quietly jacked up the door and crawled out.

I was so weak that I had to rest many times when I was running away. I dared not return to Yangquan Village, so I ran to Xilianggou Village, where my *ganma* lived. [In China, people who are particularly fond of each other can form a fictive kinship and call each other by kinship terms plus the term "gan," such as *ganma* (fictive mother), *ganerzi* (fictive son), *ganjiejie* (fictive older sister). The relationship is only in name and the fictive child usually does not move in with the ganma's family and is not raised by her.] My *ganma's* family name was Wan. She had five sons; all of them were good men who had joined the Communist Party. Unfortunately, they have all died now. I hid at the Wans' house for about two months and, when my injuries healed, returned to Yangquan Village. My husband Li Jigui was sick in bed when I saw him; he was only skin and bones. I devoted all my time to taking care of him.

A few months later I was captured by Japanese troops for the third time. It was in the Twelfth Lunar Month [around January 1944]; Japanese troops encircled Yangquan Village at night just as the local people were eating Laba porridge. ["Laba" means "the Eighth Day of the Twelfth Lunar Month." The local people customarily eat a special porridge with nuts and dried fruits on this day.] They kicked my door open, came into my house, and took me away with them. This time the Japanese soldiers tormented me particularly cruelly to punish me for my previous escapes. I clearly remember the faces of the Japanese men who raped me. Among them, the "red-faced captain" and the "bucktoothed captain" were especially brutal. They let a group of Japanese soldiers hold my arms and legs while another soldier raped me. They took turns raping me in this manner and also tortured me for information until I passed out. The torment continued day after day up to the Preliminary New Year's Eve on the Twenty-Third Day of the Twelfth Lunar Month. That day I passed out again and didn't wake up for quite a long time, so the Japanese soldiers thought I was dead and threw me into a runnel by the village. I had no clothes on my body and the water in the runnel was frozen. Luckily, Zhang Menghai's father discovered me and saved my life. He said that my body was already freezing cold and that I had almost ceased breathing when he saw me. He watched over me for a day and a night, feeding me soup and massaging my body. When I finally came back to life, he secretly moved me to the home of an acquaintance of mine in Fengsheng-po Village.

I was unconscious for a very long time. When I woke up it was already New Year's Eve, so it must have been in February 1944. I was bedridden for three years, and my body was completely deformed. I could no longer stand straight because my hips and rib bones were broken. My arms were dislocated, my neck was knocked into my chest, and my lower backbone was compressed into my pelvis. My height had been more than 160 centimetres but was reduced to less than 150 after my torture. The earlobe of my right ear had been ripped off. The Japanese soldiers had beaten my head with a nail-studded board, which left a sunken spot on the top of my head that is still there today. Hair never again grew over the scarred areas. When the Japanese soldiers hung me up and beat me, they pulled out my armpit hair. Although I didn't die, for five years I had to be taken care of by others. Even today I suffer from severe uterine damage and body aches, and I rely on massage therapy to ease the pain. When the weather changes every bone in my body aches like hell.

My past was full of misery, full of horrible experiences. It was very hard for me to survive in the village. My husband died not long after I survived the Japanese torment for the third time. I adopted a two-year-old girl, who has been living with me. I moved from Yu County to Quyang and eventually came to Taiyuan and rented a small room here. We moved often and didn't have a stable place to live.

I still live in Taiyuan City. I moved from the countryside to the city and changed my name to Wan Aihua, using my *ganma*'s family name. I have made a living by doing needlework and by doing massage for people. I learned massage from a village doctor when I was young and have been helping local people with this skill. When I was in Yu County many people in my neighbourhood came to see me for massages. I am still doing massages for people now, and I don't charge poor people money.

My daughter has helped me tremendously ever since she was a little girl. She went out to beg for food by herself when I was too ill to work. She is a good daughter. I have worked hard to provide her with a good life, and I want to prove that she has a good mother who was a fighter during the Resistance War.

In 1992, a person contacted me saying that I had been a Japanese comfort woman, which made me very angry. I was not a "comfort woman," and I never comforted any Japanese troops! I came forward to tell people how the Japanese troops abducted me and forced me to be their sex slave. I want the world to know the cruel atrocities the Japanese soldiers perpetrated on Chinese people, and I want justice for all the women who suffered as I did. I don't consider myself a "comfort woman" for the Japanese army. I never comforted the Japanese troops and never wanted to. I attended the International Public Hearing Concerning Post-War Compensation of Japan in 1992 and testified on stage. When I recalled the torture I suffered and the unbearable things the Japanese military did to me I became so angry that I passed out.

From that point on I have sought to reinstate my CCP membership. I was an underground CCP member during the war, so not many people knew about my party membership and I didn't feel that I needed to prove it. Now I feel I must prove to people that I was a member of the resistance movement and Communist Party, and that I would never do anything to "comfort" the Japanese troops. It was not easy to verify my CCP membership because most of the people who knew my history had died. After much effort I finally found a few veteran local leaders, including Yu County head commissioner Zhang Guoying, Gao Changming, and Li Menghai, who witnessed my activities as a CCP member. All these people have died now. In 1994, after fifty years, my CCP membership was finally restored.

Since 1995, because my past work experience in the Resistance War was verified, I have received a monthly stipend of fifty yuan. Every month the government sends the money to my home. Fifty yuan is a small amount, and the money is not what I really care about. I wanted to prove I fought during the Resistance War. I have to admit, however, that even fifty yuan is a big help to me. I had major surgery in 1993 and am suffering from many medical problems now; I have a large number of medical expenses.

I want the Government of Japan to admit its war crimes. I am willing to go anywhere to tell about the atrocities the Japanese forces committed, and I went to Japan many times to testify in 1996, 1998, and 1999. In December 2000 I participated in the Women's International War Crimes Tribunal on Japan's Military Sexual Slavery in Tokyo as one of the plaintiffs. When I was giving my testimony and showed the audience the scars from my injuries, I passed out again. My health is getting worse and worse. I expressed my opinion strongly at the tribunal that the Shōwa emperor and the Japanese government must be found guilty. They must apologize to us and admit their wrongdoing. Only by doing so can we protect future generations from the kind of torture I suffered. I will continue fighting for that as long as I am alive.

On 30 October 1998, Wan Aihua and nine other Chinese victims of Japanese military sexual violence filed a lawsuit against the Government of Japan at the Tokyo District Court. She went to testify in person with survivors Zhao Cunni and Gao Yin'e in September 1999. Their claims were denied. Wan Aihua is currently seriously ill and bedridden.

(Interviewed by Su Zhiliang and Chen Lifei in 1999, 2000, 2001 2002, and 2007.)

7 Southern China Frontlines

Huang Youliang

Japanese troops landed on Hainan Island off the Guangdong coast on 10 February 1939.[1] In order to secure control of this important strategic position in the South China Sea, the occupation units built a large number of strongholds on the island. In Lingshui County alone fourteen strongholds, eight blockhouses, and two military airports were constructed.[2] The occupiers set up comfort stations in towns and cities as well as in military strongholds and village homes, for which they drafted women both abroad and locally. The troops also rounded up women with the help of the Association for Maintaining Order and the Self-Guard Corps. Huang Youliang's treatment by the Japanese military was commonplace: first she was raped, then kept as a sex slave by Japanese soldiers in her home village, and eventually taken to the Tengqiao Detachment Comfort Station. The Japanese troops later burned her village to the ground. The stronghold near the village no longer exists, but the Tengqiao military comfort station, where Huang Youlian was imprisoned, remains.

Figure 16 Huang Youliang, in 2000, speaking to interviewers about her experiences in a Japanese military "comfort station."

That year [1941] I was only fifteen.[3] Judging from the weather, I think it was around the Tenth Lunar Month. That morning, I carried two baskets on a shoulder pole to a rice paddy outside of the village [of Jiama]. All of a sudden I heard shouts. I raised my head and saw a group of Japanese soldiers standing not far away. I was very frightened, so I dropped the baskets and ran back towards the mountains. But the Japanese troops chased after me until I couldn't run any farther. I was caught. One of the soldiers said something loudly. I felt as if my head were swelling and I couldn't understand a word. One soldier with no beard on his shaved face suddenly grasped me in his arms. Another one moved his hands over my back and then began to rip off my shirt and skirt. The rest of the soldiers were laughing like crazy while watching. I was so angry that I wanted to kill them. I grabbed the hand that was roughly fondling my back and bit it with all my strength. The soldier gave a loud scream and pulled his hand away. He was furious and held up his bayonet. As he was about to stab me with it, another Japanese military man who looked like an officer stopped him with an ear-splitting yell. I was scared stiff. The officer smiled at me saying, "Don't be scared." He turned to the Japanese soldiers and said something I didn't understand, then waved his hand. The soldiers left. After the soldiers went away, the officer pulled me into his arms. I struggled to get away and he let me go. I thought I was free, so I put on my clothes and carried the baskets home. I didn't notice that the Japanese officer followed me all the way to my home. He stopped me at the door, carried me into my bedroom, and ripped off my shirt and skirt ... He left afterwards. I cried alone and tried to keep it to myself. By the afternoon, I could not bear it any longer, so I told my mother what had happened. My mother cried her heart out.

The following day, more Japanese soldiers came to look for me. I was frightened and hid. Unable to find me, the Japanese soldiers knocked my parents to the ground and beat them up. They made them crawl over the ground on their hands and feet doing what we called a "four-hoofed cow." When I heard what happened to my parents, I hurried home to see them, so the Japanese soldiers caught me and raped me again. From that time on I was forced to wash the Japanese soldiers' clothes during the day and at night the Japanese soldiers would come ... [Huang Youliang stopped talking. Her face had been expressionless while she was speaking; she looked down and fell into silence.]

That Japanese officer could speak a little Chinese; it sounded like Hainan dialect. People called him "Jiuzhuang." [Huang Youliang said the name in the local dialect. This is perhaps a nickname, but its meaning is unclear because Huang Youliang did not know how to write the name.] Because he was an officer, whenever he came soldiers followed him. Since "Jiuzhuang" knew where I lived, he came every day, and I was forced to wash his clothes in addition to submitting to rape. If I hid he would torture my parents. This situation continued until the spring of the following year when I was taken away to Tengqiao City of Ya County.

It was the Third or the Fourth Lunar Month when I was kidnapped by a group of Japanese soldiers. They put me in a military vehicle, drove to Tengqiao, and locked me in a house. I was locked in a room with a woman who had been abducted at the same time. Later I found out that there were other women locked in different rooms who had been abducted before us.

There were always soldiers guarding the gate and they didn't let us go anywhere. We laboured during the day, mopping the floor, washing clothes, and so on. At night the Japanese soldiers came to our rooms, usually three to five of them arrived together, but some days there were more than others. Sometimes one of them spent the whole night in the comfort station, but I didn't know if he was an officer. If I didn't do as they said, they beat me. I was very frightened and was forced to do whatever they asked ... sometimes they forced me to assume various positions ... [Huang Youliang could not continue. The interview was stopped to let her take a break and drink some tea. When the interview resumed, the interviewers changed the topic and asked her about her family.]

There were only three people in my family: my father, my mother, and I. My mother was blind. My father was a peasant and I helped him with the farm work. I missed my parents very much in that place [Tengqiao Comfort Station] and wanted to escape. My body felt as if it were falling apart due to the torments every night. Many times I looked for an opportunity to run away and secretly discussed it with the other girls there. But Japanese soldiers strictly guarded the house, and we didn't know any of the roads outside the house, so it was impossible to escape. Once one of my friends there, a girl of Han ethnicity,[4] escaped from the place, but she was captured by the Japanese soldiers and almost beaten to death. Then she was locked up, most likely killed. After that incident, I gave up my hope for escape and submitted myself to fate.

During that time I didn't see any woman given a medical examination in the station, nor did I see any man ever use a condom. I didn't know if any of the girls became pregnant, but I knew one woman, whose name was Chen Youhong, who was tortured to death. She didn't want to do what the Japanese soldiers told her to do, so she was beaten until blood gushed out of her vagina. She bled to death. I heard that another girl committed suicide by biting off her own tongue.

The Japanese soldiers never gave us anything or any money. They didn't even give us enough to eat, never mind paying us. I was kept in the Tengqiao Comfort Station for a long time, at least two years, until I became very sick and my family helped me escape. That was around the Fifth or the Sixth Lunar Month of the year. That day Huang Wenchang from my home village came to see me. He told me that my father had died. I cried loudly and bitterly, and went to beg the Japanese officer to let me go home to attend my father's funeral. The officer wouldn't let me at first, but Huang Wenchang and I begged and begged, kneeling on the floor to kowtow. Finally he agreed to let me go, with the condition that I would return to the comfort station as soon as my father's funeral was over.

That was in the evening. Huang Wenchang took me out of Tengqiao and, via a shortcut, towards home. We arrived at my home in the middle of the night. As I walked through the door, I was stunned to see my father in perfectly good health waiting for me. It turned out that my father and Huang Wenchang had made a plan to rescue me from that comfort station by deceiving the Japanese troops. They were afraid that I would have been unable to act as if it were real, so they didn't tell me the truth until I got home.

My father and Huang Wenchang worked overnight with hoes and shovels to make a fake grave for me on top of a desolate hill on the outskirts of the village. They told people that I had committed suicide because of excessive grief. My father and I fled from the village right after that. My mother had already died by that time. My father and I became fugitives and for a period lived as beggars. We stayed in one place for a while then returned to Jiama Village. People in our village told us that the Japanese officer "Jiuzhuang" had come with a group of soldiers to arrest me. The villagers told him that I had committed suicide. He saw the fake grave and believed them.

Since everyone in the village knew that I had been ravaged by the Japanese troops, no man in good health or of good family wanted to marry me. I had no choice but to marry a man who had leprosy. My husband knew about my past and used it as an excuse to beat and curse me for no reason other than that he was unhappy. I gave birth to five children: three daughters and two sons. Two of my older daughters are married and the youngest one is still living with us. My children have treated me well, particularly my daughters. However, since I had that horrible experience in the past, even my own children sometimes swear at me. But it was not my fault! What a cruel fate! I hate the Japanese soldiers!

During the Cultural Revolution, because of my awful past, people in the village, particularly those in the younger generations who weren't clear about history, said bad things about me behind my back; they said I was a bad woman who slept with Japanese troops. Because of this, my husband was not allowed to serve as a village official and my children were not allowed to join the Communist Youth League or the Communist Party.

I am willing to go abroad to testify to the atrocities the Japanese military committed, and I am also willing to go to Japan to testify to the faces of the Japanese. I demand an apology from the Japanese government. I am not afraid. [Visibly cheered by this idea, Huang Youliang's previously expressionless face broke into a big smile.]

After her interview in 2000, Huang Youliang led the interviewers to the site of Tengqiao military comfort station. The former comfort station is a run-down, two-story building made of bricks and wood; its roof and entrance door are gone. Local residents confirmed the accuracy of her recollection about the comfort station. The Japanese army's blockhouse and water tower nearby are still standing. Although Huang Youliang had not been allowed to leave the comfort station during her captivity, she had been able to see outside from the second floor of the building. She pointed and said, "Look, see that tree trunk over there? It was where the Japanese troops tied up and tortured their captives." On 16 July 2001, Huang Youliang and seven other Japanese military comfort station victims from Hainan Island filed a lawsuit against the Government of Japan in the Tokyo District Court. Huang Youliang is now living with her youngest daughter in Hainan.

(Interviewed by Chen Lifei and Su Zhiliang, interpreted by Hu Yueling in 2000)

Chen Yabian

Chen Yabian was abducted from Zuxiao Village and sent to the Japanese military comfort station in Ya County (today's Sanya) on Hainan Island. From February 1939, the Japanese military stationed a large number of troops in Ya County, using it as a major naval and air force base.[5] It has been confirmed that fourteen Japanese military comfort stations were in operation in the area between 1941 and 1945. During a research trip in 2000 Su Zhiliang and Chen Lifei were able to locate seven of the buildings or what is left of them.

Figure 17 Chen Yabian, in 2003, in front of her home.

I live in Zuxiao Village, Lingshui County, Hainan Island. I had one older brother and one older sister; I was the youngest child in the family and my parents loved me very much. People said I was a good-looking girl.

During the occupation, the Japanese army organized a puppet self-guard corps in the vicinity of Zhenban-ying Village. [According to the local historical record, the Self-Guard Corps comprised about fifty soldiers and was led by Chen Shilian.] They set up barracks on the hill near our village and ordered local collaborators to draft young women to work in the barracks. One day in 1942 four traitors came to my home and said that the head of the Self-Guard Corps had ordered me to harvest grains. Many girls from the Li ethnic villages in the area were taken into the barracks, including another girl from my village and me. I was forced to work there for months, doing all sorts of miscellaneous jobs, such as washing clothes, sewing gunnysacks, carrying water, and processing grains. At night girls were forced to "entertain" the soldiers. We never received any payment for the work we did at the camp.

After working in the corps camp for a few months, I was taken by force to a Japanese military comfort station in Ya County and locked in a dark room. I didn't know where in Ya County the station was. I only remember that it was a two-story wooden house and that I was held in a small room on the second floor. In the room there was a shabby bed, on which there was a very dirty quilt. There were also a table and two stools. The door was locked and the window was sealed completely with wooden boards, so the inside was pitch black even during the day. Japanese soldiers came at night, sometimes two or three, sometimes more. They made me bathe first and then raped me one after another. Some of the soldiers seemed to have been from Taiwan. The Japanese soldiers didn't wear condoms when they raped me, nor did the army provide me with medical examinations. I was so frightened and resisted them, but they encircled my neck with their hands, strangling me, and slapped my face ... [Chen Yabian stopped talking and cried. She demonstrated how the soldier strangled her.] I cried aloud and tried to push the door open, but the door was locked from outside. From that day on I was never allowed to step outside. They only opened the door to deliver a pail when I needed to move my bowels or to send in some food for me to eat. They sent food twice or three times a day, but I don't remember what the food was like; it was so dark in the room that I couldn't even see the food clearly.

I cannot remember clearly how long I was kept in the Japanese comfort station, perhaps for several months. I cried in horrible fear every day there. My parents were worried to death after I was taken away. They begged everyone they could possibly find to help obtain my release, but there was no hope. After having begged many people for help, but to no avail, my mother went to the head of the corps and kneeled before him. She cried, begged, and said she would die in front of him if he refused to help obtain my release. The head had no way to get rid of her so he, in turn, went to beg the Japanese troops and helped arrange my release.

I could not walk upon my release; my lower body was severely infected and was so swollen that I could not relieve my bowels without excruciating pain. My eyes were damaged by the torture in the comfort station, too. For all these years after the war my eyes have been red and have hurt; I cannot see clearly and my eyes water constantly. Yet I was drafted by the corps again after I was released from the comfort station and forced to work at the corps camp for another three years until Japan's surrender. [Su Guangming, chair of Lingshui County People's Political Consultative Committee, told the interviewers that Chen Yabian, fearing discrimination because she was a Japanese military comfort woman, lived alone in the mountains for a long time until local people prevailed on her to emerge after the liberation.]

My parents arranged for me to marry Zhuo Kaichun when I was a child. [Pang Shuhua, who was the interpreter for the interview, explained that this was called "child-engagement" *(wawaqin)*, a local custom whereby parents pre-arranged a marriage for their children in their childhood.] Zhuo Kaichun joined the Chinese forces when I was detained in the comfort station. He later left the Chinese force because one of his hands had been injured. We married after he returned home.

I had terrible difficulties trying to have a child after my marriage. [Chen Yabian cried again.] I had multiple miscarriages and stillbirths. Doctors said my uterus had been damaged by the torture. I always had severe pain during menstrual periods and intercourse. When I became pregnant again in my late thirties, my husband sent me to a hospital in central Hainan, and, under the doctors' diligent care, I finally gave birth to a healthy girl around 1964.

My husband died several years ago and my daughter is married and lives in another village now. I am in very poor health. I continue to have abdominal pain all these years later, and I have difficulty breathing. I also suffer from frequent nightmares resulting from the past horrors and constant fears. During the Cultural Revolution I was beaten and yelled at by local people. They tied up my hands and pushed me out, accusing me of "having slept with Japanese soldiers." How miserable I am for not having a son to look out for me ...

[Chen Yabian cried again. According to local tradition, male offspring take care of aged parents while daughters move away from their parents' home after marriage. Although Chen Yabian is covered under the Five Guarantees Program – a social welfare program that guarantees childless and infirm elderly people food, clothing, medical care, housing, and burial expenses – because of the high cost of her medical expenses the financial aid she has received from the government is insufficient to meet her needs.]

I could have had many children, but because of the torture by the Japanese troops I was unable to have a son. I want redress. I welcome all who come to interview me because I want to let people know my experiences. I demand an apology and compensation from the Japanese. I want to have a peaceful and good life in my late years.

On 30 March and 1 April 2000, Chen Yabian attended the First International Symposium on Chinese Comfort Women at Shanghai Normal University as an invited speaker. She had to rely on pain medication to ease her headaches, but despite the constant discomfort she gave a courageous speech on her war-time experience to an international audience. In poverty and poor health, Chen Yabian now relies on the "Five Guarantees Program" provided by the local government and the produce of a few fruit trees for daily life. She lives with constant body ache and abdominal pain, and continues to have horrifying nightmares.

(Interviewed by Su Zhiliang and Chen Lifei and interpreted by Pang Shuhua in 2000 and 2001)

Lin Yajin

Lin Yajin was kidnapped and imprisoned in the Dalang stronghold at Nanlindong (today's Nanlin Township), Baoting County, Hainan Island, in 1943, which was also the year that the United States began submarine warfare against Japanese shipping.[6] In order to reinforce its military bases on Hainan Island, the Japanese army brought more troops from northeastern China to the area that same year. Nanlin, which is only about twenty-five kilometres from (Ya County) Sanya and is surrounded by mountains, was chosen by the Japanese army as a base for military supplies and munitions. The Japanese troops drove the villagers out of their hiding places in the mountains. Villagers who didn't obey the military orders were killed. Those who followed the orders to register for a "Good Citizen ID" were sent to do hard labour on military highway construction sites, in iron mines, or on farms, where they grew tobacco, grains, and vegetables for the Japanese army.[7] Lin Yajin had been drafted to labour at a military highway construction site before she was kidnapped and taken to a military comfort station.

Figure 18 Lin Yajin, in 2007, attending the opening ceremony of the Chinese "Comfort Women" Archives in Shanghai.

I am a Li ethnic woman, born in Fanyuntao, Nanlindong, Baoting County, Hainan Island. My father's name was Lin Yalong, and my mother was Tan Yalong. I had five siblings. My older sister was named Yagan. I am the second child. I had two younger sisters and two younger brothers. My parents and most of my siblings have already died. Now only my youngest brother and I are still alive. I am living in Shihao Village in Nanlin District now. I don't have any children of my own. My siblings' children all live in Nanlin. They come to visit me when I need help.

I was about sixteen years old when the Japanese troops came to Nanlin. Three years later [1943], I was drafted by the Japanese military to build a highway that led to their arsenal. Many people in our area were drafted, including a lot of women. We received no pay and had to bring lunch to work from home. I was released two months later.

In the autumn of that year, I heard gunshots from the direction of Da'nao Village when I was harvesting rice with three girls named Tan Yaluan, Tan Yayou, and Li Yalun from neighbouring villages. [The names are transliterated according to Lin Yajin's pronunciation.] We realized that the Japanese troops had come. The rice paddy was very close to Da'nao, so we had no time to escape. We lay down next to the ridge between the fields, very scared. A long time passed. When we heard some sounds and raised our heads to look around, we found Japanese soldiers standing right behind us. The Japanese soldiers tied our hands behind our backs with ropes and took the four of us to their strongholds, first to the Japanese army's barracks at Nanlin and then to the Dalang stronghold in Ya County. I was nineteen years old at the time. ["Dalang" is the place-name "Shilou" in Li language].

We spent one night at the Nanlin stronghold in a room that was used to incarcerate labourers who attempted to escape. We saw torture instruments and feet cuffs. The Japanese soldiers placed the cuffs on our feet so that we could not move. The cuffs would break your bones if you sat down, so we could only stand. An interpreter who looked to be a native of Hainan came in and said to us: "Do not try to run away. You will be killed if you try to escape."

The following day, we were taken to the Dalang stronghold in Ya County by armed Japanese soldiers. The Japanese soldiers tied us up and forced us to walk very fast. They kicked us ruthlessly if we slowed down even a bit. We left Nanlin in the morning and arrived at Dalang when it turned dark. We were not allowed to eat or drink the whole day.

At Dalang we were locked up in a strange house. The house was divided into small rooms. Each girl was put into a room. The room had a wooden door but no window, so it was very dark inside. The door was double-locked and there were always Japanese soldiers standing outside guarding the house. The walls felt like metal sheets. The size of the room was about this big. [Lin Yajin indicated a length of about ten square metres.] There was no bed or bedding in the room. They only gave me one washbowl and a towel, and there was a container for urination at the corner of the room – nothing else. I slept on the earthen floor. Luckily the weather was not cold.

The Japanese soldiers only took me out of the house to empty the excrement container. They watched me closely and took me back when I was done. The room was filled with a filthy smell. After I was taken into the stronghold I was not given clothes. The only clothing I had on me was the top shirt and skirt I was wearing when I was abducted, which were almost torn into pieces by the Japanese soldiers later; both sleeves were ripped off.

Twice a day the Japanese soldiers sent us food. It was thin gruel served in a coconut shell. It smelled awful and looked like swill. Our first meal each day was near noon. The Japanese soldiers would come after we had eaten the meal and had emptied the excrement container. Normally three or four Japanese soldiers would come into my room together. One of them would guard the door. The others often fought to be the first to rape me. I was very frightened when they fought, so I stood against the wall to avoid being hurt. They were completely naked, one raping me while the others were watching.

[Lin Yajin cried. She squinted into the distance, and tears flowed from her eyes. Heartbreaking sobs filled the room. After about twenty minutes, Lin calmed down and continued.]

Some of the Japanese soldiers raped me more than once. At night a different group of soldiers would come. They never used condoms, but they gave us some pills to take. The pills were about the size of my pinkie nail, some white, some yellow, and some pink. I feared that the pills might be poisonous, so I spit them out when no one saw it. We were given a bowl of cold water to wash our lower bodies after each group left. I had already begun menstruating at that time. I resisted fiercely when I had my menstrual period, but the Japanese soldiers raped me even when I was bleeding. I developed some kind of disease and had horrible pains when urinating. The lower part of my body became swollen and festered.

The Japanese soldiers often beat me. If I showed the slightest resistance, they would grab my hair and hit my face and breasts. One day a Japanese soldier came to rape me, but I resisted. He punched my left breast so hard that my chest continues to hurt today. [Lin showed where she had been hit. The bones on the left side of her chest were noticeably uneven; the entire area looked bumpy while some parts were caved in. Lin cried again. Her whole body trembled like a leaf in the wind.]

One time a Japanese soldier pressed me to the floor with a cigarette between his lips. He crushed the cigarette onto my face. The burned area immediately swelled up. The wound left this scar next to my nose. [The scar, which is about the size of a large pea, is clearly visible on Lin's face.] No Japanese doctor ever gave us a medical exam or any treatment. If a girl fell sick, she would be thrown into cold water. As time passed I began to urinate blood and I had severe chest pains. The pain went from my chest to my left shoulder. Even today my chest often hurts, bringing back horrible memories of the past.

I was locked in the Dalang stronghold for a long time. Mother told me later that it was about five months. I cried every day. I also heard the crying of the girl in the next room and the sounds of the Japanese soldiers violating her since the rooms were separated only by metal sheets. Every night we cried in our rooms, talking about our parents, our families, and our fears that we might never see them again. I was already very sick. My injured chest bones hurt, my private parts festered, I urinated blood, and my whole body was swollen and ached like hell. I thought I was going to die soon.

My father heard that I was very sick, and he begged a relative who was a Baozhang to bail me out. [Baozhang was an official position in the old *Bao Jia.* administrative system, which was organized on the basis of households. Each *Bao* consisted of ten *Jia* and each *Jia* consisted of ten households. The Baozhang was the head of the *Bao.*] My father and the parents of the other girls sent chickens and rice, which were the best things they could find, to the Baozhang. The Baozhang, in turn, brought these things to beg the Japanese troops to let me and the other three girls out of the Japanese stronghold. By that time the four of us were all infected with the same disease and we were too ill to service the soldiers, so the Japanese troops let us out. I was too sick to walk and was carried back by members of my family. Yayou died soon after she got home. Yaluan and Yalun also died within a year. I was the only one who survived.

My father died not long after I was released from the Japanese stronghold. He had had a chronic disease and constantly had chills and a fever. After I was kidnapped by the Japanese troops, my father did hard labour for the Japanese army, hoping to earn my release. His health declined rapidly because of that. He did not live to see Japan's surrender.

I stayed in the Baozhang's village for about two months, receiving herbal treatments, but the infected area didn't heal and I continued bleeding. My mother then brought me back home. She gathered herbs to treat me herself.

I was so sick that I was unable to walk for a long time and had a bloody discharge with pus. My mother dug up herbs in the mountain, put them in liquor, and then used this herbal wine to treat my disease. She also invited someone to perform sorcery. Gradually I recovered, and by the spring of the following year, I was able to walk.

My mother helped me recover, but she fell sick. She died two years later. I wailed loudly in front of my mother's tomb. Life became much harder after my mother died. My older sister was already married at the time and lived in far-away Fanshabi Village at the foot of the mountain. Seeing the hardship my younger siblings and I suffered, she took me to her house. I lived with my older sister for about four years and met my late husband there.

My husband's name was Ji Wenxiu. He was from a well-off family that owned some rice land and betel nut trees, so he and his younger brother were able to attend school. His family paid for everything for our wedding.[8] Because of my past experience, I was afraid to be with him on our wedding night even though I knew this would be totally different because I was married to the man I loved. Still, I didn't want to tell him about my past. My husband had heard about what had happened to me, but he never asked me about it. He didn't want to hurt me. He was really nice to me. I became pregnant soon, but two months into my pregnancy I had a miscarriage.

Two years after I married Ji Wenxiu, he went to work in Ganzha. His younger brother was a military man at the time and he asked my husband to join him in doing work for the revolution. My husband helped collect grains for the Liberation Army and worked at the local tax bureau. He was later arrested when working as the head of the tax office. [Tears filled Lin's eyes when she was speaking about her husband. The interpreter explained that Ji Wenxiu was one of the many persons wronged during the chaotic 1950s, and it is still not clear why he was arrested.]

I received a note that my husband died of illness in the prison. I couldn't believe it and went to Baoting to look for him but was told that he had been moved to Sanya. I then went to Sanya, only to find that he had been sent to Shilou. I didn't know of a way to make the trip to Shilou, so I had no choice but to return home. I don't know exactly when my husband was arrested and died. I only remember that it was during the time when everyone was eating from the same big pot.[9]

Because of my husband's arrest I was discriminated against. When eating in the communal dining room, I was always given a smaller portion and worse food. I did farm work to support myself. Although I worked very hard, I was given the lowest number of work-points.[10] I was living with my in-laws at the time. My father-in-law had some land before the revolution so his family was classified as being of landlord status. His lands had been confiscated, but because of his family background, he was criticized and denounced at public meetings during the Cultural Revolution. When my in-laws died, no one in the village came to attend their funerals. My husband had seven siblings. Now all of them have died except his younger brother.

An investigative team came to check into my history during the Cultural Revolution. However, the three girls who were abducted by the Japanese along with me had all died. The investigative team couldn't find any witnesses. Moreover, those who knew I had serviced the Japanese troops didn't tell the team anything because most people in the village belonged to the same Ji family. Even today, people in my village don't like to talk to strangers. Therefore, I was not criticized publicly during the Cultural Revolution. I felt helplessly alone so I adopted a five-year-old boy named Adi from Fanyuntao after the Cultural Revolution ended. Adi has six children now, four boys and two girls. Adi's oldest daughter has two children already.

The Japanese soldiers did horrible things to me. The Japanese government must admit the atrocities it committed and compensate me before I die.

Since 2000, every month the Research Center for Chinese "Comfort Women" has sent two hundred yuan to Lin Yajin and other Japanese military comfort station survivors in China, using funds from private donors. With that money Lin's adopted son gradually rebuilt their house. Lin Yajin now lives with the family of her adopted son.

(Interviewed by Chen Lifei and Liu Xiaohong in 2007; interpreted by Chen Houzhi.)

Li Lianchun

Yunnan Province is situated between inland China, Burma, and India, and it occupied a key position on one of China's major supply lines during the Resistance War. In 1942 and 1943, the US Air Force built air bases in Yunnan, from which the Fourteenth Air Force provided assistance to Chinese military operations. The Japanese air units countered with major strikes, and the Japanese ground forces began the invasion of Burma in January 1942. The 56th Division entered Yunnan Province in the spring of the same year, and, by early 1943 it had taken control of the area west of the Nu-jiang River (known as Salween River in English) and established its headquarters at Longling.[11] *During the occupation the Japanese troops set up comfort stations from the Longling county seat all the way to the Songshan frontline.*[12] *Li Lianchun, whose home village of Bai'nitang lay to the west of Songshan and on the west bank of the Nu-jiang River, was abducted into one of these military comfort stations.*

Figure 19 Li Lianchun, in 2001, being interviewed in her daughter's house.

I was born in the Ninth Lunar Month [1924], but I don't know the exact date. My birth name was Yuxiu, and my nickname was Yaodi. Yaodi means "wanting a little brother." I was born in Bai'nitang Village, Lameng Township,

Longling County. When the Japanese attacked this place, I was eighteen years old. I had a younger sister named Guodi. My father smoked opium and didn't care about the family, so everything fell on my mother's shoulders. However, my mother became ill and died, so my father's younger brother took my sister and me to his house. Every day my sister and I went to the mountains to collect hay and sold it in the market, earning some money to help support the family.

On a market day in the summer around the Lunar Eighth Month [of 1942] we went to sell the hay as usual. All of a sudden a group of Japanese soldiers appeared. People at the market tried to hide anywhere they could. I hid in a shop nearby, but the Japanese soldiers found me and jerked me out. They tied my hands and feet with their puttees and stuffed cloth in my mouth to prevent me from crying out ... I was then raped by the Japanese soldiers right at the side of the road ... [Li Lianchun could not continue talking; she tried hard to control her emotions.] About twenty girls were raped that day. My younger sister barely escaped being raped. She was very small at the time and was not found. I had tried to hide behind the counter in the shop, but the Japanese soldiers found me ... [Field investigation indicates that the Japanese troops raped a large number of the local women that day and then moved to Changqing Village before returning to the Songshan stronghold. Soon after, the troops ordered the local collaborators to round up women for the Japanese military comfort stations.]

Around this time my father was drafted for hard labour. A man from the local Association for Maintaining Order said to him: "Send your two daughters to do laundry and to cook for the Imperial Army, then you don't have to do the hard labour. Your tax can be waived, too." My father didn't agree, so he was taken to perform hard labour. The Japanese troops beat him badly. He fell sick upon returning and died soon after. My uncle was unable to support my sister and me. After laying my father to rest, he married me off to a man of the Su family in Shashui Village deep in the mountains. The Su family was very poor and we barely had anything to eat or wear. As I nearly starved to death, I ran away from the mountain village. A team of Japanese soldiers caught me at Bai'nitang when I was almost home and took me to the comfort station at Songshan.

In the comfort station we were given two meals a day while the Japanese had three meals. They ate *baba* [a Yunnan delicacy made of rice powder] but we were given only crude rice. We wore our own clothes at first. Later the Japanese soldiers forced us to wear Japanese clothing. I hated that ugly clothing and didn't want to wear it. I also hated to do my hair as they asked, but we had no choice.

The Japanese soldiers didn't call me by my name. They called all of us *hua guniang* [flower girl], but most of the time they spoke Japanese. I didn't know any of the Japanese words and didn't want to learn them either. Some of the Japanese soldiers could speak a few Chinese words. When they wanted to call me, they would wave their hands and say, *"Wei, lai, lai"* ["Hey, come, come"]. At mealtimes I heard them say *"Mishi."* ["Mishi" is not a Chinese word. It might be an incorrectly pronounced Japanese word, *"meshi,"* which means "meal" or "rice."]

The Japanese army men made us take some sort of medicine, but I didn't know what it was. During the day when there were not many Japanese soldiers, we had to work, either sewing or making shoes. There were special guards watching us. Many Japanese soldiers came at night. The numbers were different, depending on the day of the week. They liked to pick good-looking girls, so pretty girls had to service more soldiers. The soldiers often beat us. I still have a scar on my left shoulder today. It was caused by a Japanese soldier when he bit me. I also saw the soldiers drag a woman out of her room and beat her. [When asked under what circumstances the Japanese soldier bit her, Li Lianchun seemed to have great difficulty speaking about it. She then showed us her left shoulder. The scar is very long and wide; it is hard to imagine it is a wound from a bite. In order to divert Li from the painful memory, Chen Lifei asked whether the Japanese soldiers paid fees when using the comfort station. Li Lianchun continued.]

Those Japanese soldiers never gave me any money. Money was useless at the time anyway. [Local history indicates that, during the Japanese occupation, Chinese currency was abolished. The Japanese authorities issued "military currency" *(junpiao)*, but many Chinese people refused to use it. Therefore, trade in the region at the time was virtually all by the barter system.] The Japanese soldiers didn't give us anything, and we had to work to support ourselves. During the day we sewed clothes and made shoes to earn food and other things for daily use.

I was kept in that comfort station for about a year. I escaped in 1943, if I remember the time correctly. I looked for opportunities to escape from the day I was taken into the comfort station. As time passed, the Japanese soldiers dropped their guard a little bit. During the day they let me go to the town to collect sewing work. Of course, I was never allowed to go out freely, and there was always a guard watching me. But I gradually made acquaintances among the local people. One of them was an old cowherd who was a distant relative. He agreed to help me escape.

One night, I changed into the old cowherd's clothes in a latrine before dawn and sneaked out of the comfort station in Dayakou. I left Dayakou, hiding myself from the eyes of the Japanese troops on the way. I didn't know where to go. I only knew that I must escape from the west side of the Nu-jiang River and go to the east side.[13] Fearing being caught again, I avoided the main roads and travelled through the mountains. I didn't have any money, so I begged for food and did labour along the way. Several months later I came to a little town. I had no means to go any further, so I stayed there and married a local man. However, life there became unbearable ...

[Li Lianchun fell silent. Later, local people told the interviewers what happened to Li Lianchun in that small town. In November 2001, Su Zhiliang and Chen Lifei travelled from Shanghai to Li Lianchun's home in Yunnan with the documentary film production team of the Shanghai Television Station. During this trip they went to Li Lianchun's birthplace Bai'nitang to gather more information about her experience before and after the military comfort station and also to verify the sites of her abduction and enslavement. At Bai'nitang they met Feng Puguo, whose cousin's wife is Li Lianchun's sister. According to Feng Puguo, the old cowherd who helped Li Lianchun escape was a native of Daqishu Village. He had come to know Li Lianchun through her aunt, who had married a man in the cowherd's village. After the cowherd helped Li Lianchun get out of the Songshan Comfort Station, she ran to Xiangshu Village in Lujiang-ba, where she crossed the river by raft. Li was later taken by a local warlord, whose surname was Cha, to be his concubine in a place near Pupiao Town. During the struggle to wipe out the local bandits and despots the warlord was killed and Li Lianchun was mistreated. She then ran into the mountains and lived under a cliff at Longdong for about half a year, until she was taken in by Gao Xixian, her late husband. Feng remembered that Li Lianchun had come back once to visit her relatives in 1999.

On the way to Li Lianchun's home, Su Zhiliang and Chen Lifei also made a trip to Changqing Village, which was the first of the places to which Li Lianchun had been abducted. During the war Changqing Village had been occupied by Japanese soldiers who were stationed in the ancestral temple of the Li clan. The village had over two hundred households, of which two-thirds had the family name "Li." The villagers referred to the temple as the "Lis' General Temple." The temple is on a hill and is a well-built, one-story wooden structure. The villagers hold their annual Lunar New Year ceremony in the temple. During the Japanese occupation, the Japanese army's 113th Regiment had three battalions stationed at Songshan and two companies at Changqing; their headquarters were located in the resident's house right next to the Lis' ancestral temple. It was not clear whether the temple had been used as a comfort station or whether this was the Changqing Comfort Station. According to Li Qinsong, an eighty-one-year-old man the interviewers met in the village, during the war the temple was occupied by Japanese troops and there were Chinese girls confined inside. He said that, during the chaos of the Japanese occupation, most of the women in the village hid themselves deep in the mountains. The Japanese soldiers looted pigs and chickens, but they didn't stay there for very long. Judging from what he said, the Japanese troops seemed to have launched a "mop-up operation" in the Bai'nitang area, during which they raped Li Lianchun and other Chinese girls. On their way back, the Japanese soldiers stayed at Changqing temporarily and then returned to their Songshan fortress.]

[As Li Lianchun stopped talking, her daughter Gao Yulan, who accompanied Li to the interview, told what happened to Li after she fled into the mountains.]

My mother ran away from that village and fled deep into the mountains in Bingsai, where my father found her and took her to his house. My father was about ten years older than my mother. He was a village doctor and his first wife had died. He was in the mountains gathering medicinal herbs when he saw her hiding under a huge rock. [Li Lianchun's daughter later took the interviewers to that huge rock. It sticks out from a slope, less than two metres above the ground. Vines growing on the slope hang over the front of the rock, forming a space that had become Li Lianchun's shelter.] She was almost dead, eating wild fruits and barely surviving. Too much crying had damaged her eyes, so she was nearly blind. She looked like a beggar, wrapped in ragged clothes with her hair tangled. My father felt very sorry for her. He took her home, gave her food, and then treated her illnesses.

My mother was not the only person to whom my father provided refuge. Before my mother, he had taken in another person from a neighbouring village. That person suffered from dropsy and his entire belly was swollen. He had crawled to my father for help. My father let him stay in his house.

My grandfather and my uncle were both veterinarians. They opposed taking my mother in, but my father insisted. My mother's health gradually improved. She was a very neat and able person, good at both farming and housework. She worked very hard, keeping the house very clean. As time passed, my father fell in love with her. But my grandfather and uncle were against their relationship. My father then moved out of the house; he had no other choice since he wanted to marry her. My father knew about my mother's past, but he didn't mind. He often said, "Your mother has suffered a lot, a lot." [Gao Yulan choked with tears.]

My grandfather lived in Tuanshan-ba in Xia-longdong. My father moved up the mountain to Shang-longdong. To go from my grandfather's house to my father's house he had to climb for about thirty minutes. My father built a little thatched house on the mountain where they got married. My father treated my mother's illness, first her eye disease and then her venereal disease. My mother said that she had several miscarriages before she gave birth to me.

My father Gao Xixian was truly great. He saved many people's lives. When he married my mother in the mountain hut, he took the person who had dropsy with them. He even thought of adopting him as his son because my mother might not be able to bear children. That person later had his own family and moved out. When my father died, he came to his funeral like a filial son. We still remain very close, like relatives. My father never charged fees when villagers sought medical help from him, so people would bring him things to show their appreciation. He was well liked by all.

My father built the best house in the village for my mother. He once went to visit my mother's hometown. He walked several days to the village, only to find that my mother's elderly relatives had all died. My mother sobbed bitterly. Later she asked me to teach her how to read so that she could travel to her hometown by herself. She learned quite a few characters. She could read some characters, such as those in her name.

My father died in 1971 during the Cultural Revolution. People in the village kept their distance from us after my father died and gossiped about my mother's past. When my mother went to work, people would stay away from her, so she was always alone. She worked in the field day and night. Life was very, very difficult then. I will never forget what my mother said: "No matter how hard our life is, you must attend school. Only learning can save you from being trodden upon."

One day it was raining heavily. My mother came to the school to pick me up. Coming directly from the field, she was barefoot and drenched to the skin. Something punctured her sole and pierced through her foot. Seeing that, I cried, "Mum, I don't want to attend school anymore." People in the village also urged my mum to let me help her work instead of going to school. But my mother would not agree. She wanted my siblings and me to continue school no matter how difficult it was. Therefore, all the children in my family received an education. My mother supported us single-handedly.

Every day I walked fifteen kilometres through the mountains to the school. I left home before dawn and came back in the evening. It was thirty kilometres roundtrip, but the hardship did not stop me. I studied really hard; I wanted to be a good student as my mother expected. I received very good grades and was the only female student who got into the county high school. Later I graduated from the normal school and became a teacher. I was so happy that I could help my mother then. My mum is a great mother. She raised us four children and took good care of my grandfather after my father died. My grandfather was a hot-tempered man. Although my uncle treated him very well, he could not get along with him, so my grandfather came to live with us. He often got angry with us, too. Once he flew into a temper and broke the door. When my grandfather became angry, he would move his bedding to the mountain and sleep under a cliff. My mother would fix meals for him and we would take them to him in the mountains. My mother said we could not return home without my grandfather, so my sister and I would kneel in front of my grandpa and beg him to go home with us. My mother took very good care of my grandfather in his old age.

My mother wants justice. I hope she is able to fulfill her wish in her remaining years. [Gao Yulan turned to Li Lianchun and urged her to speak: "Mum, tell them what you said at home last time. Don't be afraid." Li Lianchun grasped Chen Lifei's hand and began to speak again.]

My son died a month ago. He had esophageal cancer. He was only thirty-six … I am so sad … Too many sad things in my life … Now I am getting too old and these sad things are fading away from me … There are a lot of things I want to say, but it's so hard to talk about … I've suffered my entire life, and I have been poor my whole life, but I have one thing that is priceless to me. That is my body, my dignity. My body is the most valuable thing to me. The damage to it cannot be compensated for with money, no matter how much money they pay. I am not seeking money, and I am not trying to get revenge. I just want to see justice done.

Li Lianchun died due to illness in January 2004. She was unable to realize her wish to see justice done during her lifetime. In July 2005, Li Lianchun's grandson Aji passed the Guizhou University entrance examination. Chen Lifei and Su Zhiliang sponsored him for high school as well as college, paying his school expenses. Her granddaughter Adan's education was paid for by one of the documentary film production team members from the Shanghai Television Station.

(Interviewed by Su Zhiliang and Chen Lifei in 2001)

The twelve survivors' accounts reveal the appalling nature of the military comfort women system. It was with remarkable courage and strength that these women survived, both during the war and in the postwar era, and continued their struggle to seek justice. The following pages situate the Chinese comfort women's postwar struggles within the larger context of the international redress movement.

PART 3

The Postwar Struggles

8 Wounds That Do Not Heal

The Second World War ended in 1945. However, for the women who suffered in the comfort stations, the end of the war failed to bring justice, even though the information about imperial Japan's military comfort women was available. At the time of Japan's surrender, the Allied forces took many comfort women into custody as POWs; photographs of Korean, Chinese, and Indonesian comfort women captured by the Allied forces are preserved in the Public Record Office in London, the US National Archives, and the Australian War Memorial.[1] In addition, the prosecutors representing China, the Netherlands, and France prepared documents relating to the Japanese commission of military sexual slavery and presented them to the International Military Tribunal for the Far East (IMTFE).[2] Nevertheless, the tribunal did not specifically identify the military comfort women system as one of the common war crimes committed by the Japanese forces,[3] although the judges recognized some individual cases. One such case, presented by a Chinese prosecutor, is mentioned in the tribunal judgment: "During the period of Japanese occupation of Kweilin, they [the Japanese forces] committed all kinds of atrocities such as rape and plunder. They recruited women's labour on the pretext of establishing factories. They forced the women thus recruited into prostitution with Japanese troops."[4] However, after having recognized that forced prostitution constituted a war atrocity, the tribunal stopped short of unequivocally ruling that the leaders of the Japanese military and government were responsible for the perpetration of the military comfort women system.[5]

Why did the IMTFE fail to pursue this further? Researchers have offered various explanations. One suggests that this failure is a result of racial prejudice since most of the victims of this enforced sexual slavery were not white women.[6] The IMTFE has been criticized as "fundamentally a white man's tribunal."[7] John Dower notes that, although the countries invaded and occupied by Japan were all Asian and an enormous number of Asian people died and were victimized as a result, only one of the nine justices of the initially envisioned tribunal was Asian. That one justice was the representative of China. Justices from India and the Philippines were added after agitation from their respective countries. Other Asian people who suffered as a result of the Japanese invasion and colonization, including those in Korea, Indonesia, Vietnam, Malaya, and Burma, had no representatives of their own.[8] Dower sees the issue of "white men's justice" as also a factor in "the localized trials of 'B/C' Class war criminals, which, with the exception of China and the Philippines were conducted by the European and American powers and focused primarily on crimes involving Caucasian prisoners."[9] In these B Class and C Class war crimes tribunals, among the defendants about three-quarters were accused of crimes against prisoners;[10] there were only two exceptional cases in which Japanese military personnel were prosecuted for enforced prostitution. One of these prosecuted cases involved Dutch women who were forced to work in Japanese military brothels in Indonesia,[11] and the other involved women from Guam, but that case was conducted in conjunction with a Japanese affront to the American national flag.[12]

Another explanation for the IMTFE's failure to follow up is the fact that patriarchal views of gender are deeply rooted in military forces of all nations, and they foster a general insensitivity to women's rights.[13] The behaviour of some Allied and American occupation troops toward the comfort women they encountered is considered indicative of this attitude. A large number of Japanese and Taiwanese nurses, as well as comfort women, were reportedly raped by Allied soldiers at the end of the war.[14] Furthermore, after the war, the Japanese government created comfort women facilities for the occupation forces.[15] Tokyo Keizai University professor Takemae Eiji writes that, on 18 August 1945, three days after Japan accepted the Potsdam Proclamation Defining Terms for Japanese Surrender, Japan's Security Bureau of the Ministry of Home Affairs "instructed law enforcement agencies across the nation to set up 'special comfort establishments,' later renamed Recreation and Amusement Associations," "to protect the daughters of the well-born and middle classes by having lower-class women satisfy the sexual appetites of battle-weary GIs."[16] Indeed, evidence for the operation of such comfort facilities can be found in newspaper advertisements at the time. On 3 September 1945, for example, *Yomiuri Shimbun* carried the Association of Special Comfort Facilities' *(Tokusho ian shisetsu kyōkai)* Urgent Ad *(Kyūkoku)* to recruit "special women employees."[17] If the leaders of the Allied forces gave tacit consent to the idea that women were obligated to offer sexual services to men who fought in the war, or considered it acceptable for soldiers of the occupying forces to rape the women of the occupied nation, then it is not surprising that the victimization of comfort women was ignored.

Recent studies of the IMTFE offer other explanations of why the comfort women issue was largely ignored. Yuma Totani examines the prosecutorial strategies of the IMTFE and points out that, because the prosecutors representing the victimized nations failed to introduce sufficient court exhibits, the tribunal judges concluded that the prosecution did not meet the burden of proof for establishing the responsibility of Japanese state leaders for perpetrating the comfort women system.[18] Totani demonstrates that, in making their case about Japanese war crimes, the Allied prosecutors relied on the strategy of substantiating the recurrence of atrocities by demonstrating common patterns throughout the war. This is because, due largely to "the Japanese government's coordinated effort in the last days of the war to destroy military records,"[19] they had great difficulty providing conclusive evidence of the personal culpability of individual defendants. This prosecutorial strategy ultimately produced mixed results as each prosecution team had its own priorities and ways of presenting evidence. The Chinese team, for example, treated the Nanjing Massacre as the representative case and took great care to document it in full; however, for war crimes in other parts of China, it only introduced a small selection to show the widespread nature of Japanese atrocities. Consequently, although the Chinese team attempted to introduce various exhibits concerning the Japanese commission of rape, organized sexual enslavement, and other forms of sexual violence, it fell short of presenting enough corroborative evidence to establish the responsibility of the wartime Japanese leaders for the sexual crimes committed by the Japanese troops.[20]

In studying the Nuremberg and Tokyo trials, Nicola Henry finds that, in both trials, "rape did not fit the dominant discourse of post-conflict justice, nor did it conform to the political will of the victors."[21] She suggests that, in the eyes of the prosecutors, the systemic sexual enslavement of the comfort women may not have been "political enough" to warrant serious attention at these proceedings. And, "[b]ecause victory in warfare is an overly masculinized concept, victor's justice is also marked by the absence of gender justice." Therefore, at both trials, when rape was mentioned it was often to highlight the heroism of one side as opposed to the barbarity of the other, and victims – as individuals – were overlooked. Henry sees this as a form of "legal amnesia" rooted both in political factors and in the patriarchal (and hence gendered) nature of legal discourse.[22]

The International Military Tribunal for the Far East was adjourned in November 1948. As the tribunal proceedings were coming to a close, Chinese Communist forces were winning battles in the civil war and the military control of the Nationalist government was deteriorating. Western politicians, worrying about the communist takeover of China, concentrated on their Cold War strategy, which required the help of their former enemies, including Japan. Due to the postwar military and political situations, Jiang Jieshi's (also known as Chiang Kai-shek) government had difficulty carrying out thorough investigations of war crimes not only on matters related to sexual violence but also in general. Reportedly, the Nationalist government of China constituted thirteen military tribunals in China from 1946 to 1949 to try Japanese war criminals as well as their Chinese collaborators; a total of 504 of the 883 accused and tried were convicted, and "rape" and "forcing women to become prostitutes" were among the crimes.[23] Yet the number brought to trial for sexual crimes was very small compared to the vast scope of victimization, and the tribunals did not attempt to establish the responsibility of the Japanese state and military leaders for perpetrating the military comfort women system. In 1956, the newly established People's Republic of China held two special military tribunals in Shenyang, Liaoning Province, and in Taiyuan, Shanxi Province, to bring Japanese war crime suspects to trial. Emphasizing reformation through education, the tribunals were generally lenient.[24] The Taiyuan Tribunal, for example, sentenced only nine Japanese war criminals, and none of them was given the death penalty; the tribunal did not prosecute the other 120 suspects, even though their crimes had been confirmed.[25] The declassified trial documents show that three of the nine convicted war criminals had committed rape and that, among those who were not prosecuted, forty-three had confessed that they had committed rape, gang-rape, and/or had abducted Chinese women and forced them into military comfort stations during the war; some admitted that they had committed sexual violence dozens of times, some as many as seventy.[26]

Consequently, issues surrounding comfort women remain unacknowledged, justice has not been served, and the resulting lack of compensation has left the survivors suffering severe hardship (see Figure 20). Recent investigations reveal that living conditions for surviving Chinese comfort women are substandard and unacceptable. In Yu County, Shanxi Province, for example, all identified survivors are poor and struggling. The Yu County Seat was occupied by the 14th Infantry Battalion of the 4th Independent Mixed Brigade, North China Area 1st Army, in early 1938, and in subsequent years the region was repeatedly devastated by the Japanese army's Operation Destroy All *(jinmetsu)*. Uchida Tomoyuki's investigation reports that 275 villages in the county had been burned to the ground by 1943;[27] the total population of the county was reduced from 215,000 in 1936 to 146,000 in 1946;[28] hundreds of local women became sex slaves to the Japanese army; and their families were exploited, being rendered financially destitute after being forced to pay huge ransoms. In one example of the latter, Nan Erpu's father sold the family's land to raise the money demanded for her ransom after she had been raped and taken to a military stronghold in Hedong Village in the spring of

Figure 20 "Comfort station" survivor Zhu Qiaomei's home after the Second World War; her family became destitute as a result of the Japanese invasion.

1942. However, the Japanese troops refused to release her even after the money was paid. Nan was forced to service a Japanese captain for a year and a half. She attempted escape but was recaptured and brought to a block-house on nearby Yangma Mountain, where she was gang-raped by a group of soldiers every night for two months. Finally, she was able to run away when the Japanese troops left the stronghold to engage in a mop-up operation. Outraged, the Japanese soldiers tortured her little brother and burned their house. Nan Erpu was unable to return home until the Japanese army retreated from the area in 1945. Having had to sell all their property, her family fell into abject poverty.[29]

There are many cases similar to Nan Erpu's in Yu County. Wang Gaihe was captured in the spring of 1942 when the Japanese army raided the Chinese Communist Party members' meeting at Nanbeizi. Wang's husband, a member of the CCP and anti-Japanese forces, was arrested and shot to death before Wang's eyes. The Japanese soldiers tried to force her to reveal information about other CCP members, torturing her until she lost consciousness. She was then taken to the Hedong Village stronghold and raped every day. One of Wang Gaihe's legs was broken, her abdomen became swollen, her teeth were knocked out, and she became incontinent. She was almost dead when her father sold their land and other properties to ransom her. Wang was bedridden for two years after her release, and for another three years she required support to walk. In her old age, Wang led a lonely life, depending on a small pension of about sixty yuan from the Chinese government,[30] along with the produce from a 0.13-hectare plot of land. For more than half a century, incontinence and pain from her old injuries caused her daily agony, and at night she was haunted by nightmares filled with Japanese soldiers. "I don't have much time left," Wang said, "I want to see justice done for my torture while I am still alive."[31] Wang Gaihe died on 14 December 2007 without having attained that longed-for justice.

The twelve survivors whose experiences are related in Part 2 all lived in poverty once they escaped or were finally released from military comfort stations. Zhu Qiaomei's family, for example, became destitute after her husband was killed by Japanese troops and their restaurant was destroyed. For decades they lived in an old, tattered shed. When Su Zhiliang and Chen Lifei visited her in 2000, Zhu Qiaomei's health was declining and she suffered from renal disease and constant headaches. Zhu Qiaomei and her family depended mainly on her son's retirement pension of 460 yuan (less than US$70 at the time) per month to meet daily living expenses. Other than that, she received financial aid of thirty-six yuan a year from the local government of Chongming County (see Figure 21). Chen Yabian lives in a decrepit mud-brick house in Hainan, and daily she eats dark-coloured weeds like those that the interviewers noticed boiling in a big pot in her kitchen in 2000. With no other source of income, Chen Yabian relies on selling coconuts to make ends meet.

In addition to living in poverty, the survivors strive constantly to live with the physical and mental wounds that are the direct result of the torment they endured in the comfort stations. Uterine damage and sterility are common among the victims, and a variety of psychological symptoms, including post-traumatic stress disorder, depression, chronic headache, insomnia, nightmares, nervous breakdown, and fear of having sex haunt them to this day. More than half a century has passed since Lin Yajin was tortured in the military comfort station, but she still suffers as a result of her traumatic experiences. She rarely smiles and does not like to talk to people. When she was invited to be one of the representatives of the survivors and to attend the opening ceremony of the Chinese "Comfort Women" Archives at Shanghai Normal University, Shanghai, in June 2007, she locked herself in her room and did not talk to anyone. Even at mealtimes, she hardly ever said a word to her companions. There was always a sad, absent look on her face. Among the twelve survivors whose narratives are presented in this book, seven have permanent scars or injuries as a result of physical torture in the comfort stations; six suffer from injuries of the uterus or urinary tract as a result of sexual

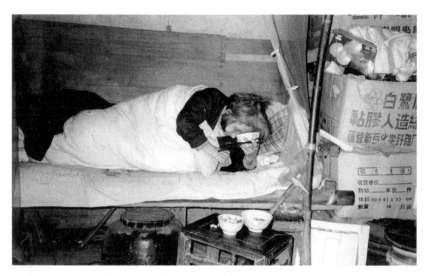

Figure 21 "Comfort station" survivor Zhu Qiaomei was sick at home in 2001.

abuse; seven suffer from constant headaches and nightmares as a result of beatings and/or psychological trauma; three had pregnancies that ended in miscarriages; and five were unable to give birth as a result of the torture experienced in the comfort stations.

Being unable to bear children is especially significant in a society in which one becomes dependent on one's children for care in one's old age. Childlessness often relegates a survivor to devastation and decreases her societal value since, traditionally, a woman's worth is determined by her ability to produce offspring. Gao Yin'e, a native of Nanshe Township, Yu County, was married when she was kidnapped in the spring of 1941 by the Japanese troops stationed in the stronghold in Hedong Village. Her husband sold their land to raise money for her ransom. By the time she was released, sexual abuse had already caused her serious damage; Gao Yin'e suffered severe abdominal pain and irregular bleeding, but her family had no more money to obtain treatment. Gao became sterile and, consequently, was divorced because she could not bear children. She remarried but was divorced again for the same reason. During her third marriage Gao adopted a daughter. However, her family never overcame economic hardship;[32] on 14 January 2008, Gao Yin'e died in poverty.

An oppressive socio-political environment added another level of misery to many survivors' lives. It is true that, in the postwar era, some survivors did receive warm support from local people. For example, Grandma M, a Korean woman who adopted a Chinese name, was tricked into a Japanese military comfort station in Wuhan, Hubei Province, in May 1945. She escaped three months later during the chaos of Japan's surrender in August 1945. Feeling disgraced because she had been a comfort woman, she did not return to Korea and settled in Huxi Village, Hubei Province. Over the years she received affectionate support from the local people and was covered under the village's Five Guarantees Program. The local Civil Administration Department has provided her with a monthly allowance of sixty yuan for living expenses. The villagers call her "grandma," and she proudly considers herself to be Chinese.[33] However, in many cases the former comfort women faced social and political discrimination. The patriarchal ideology that permeated Chinese society rated a woman's chastity higher than her life. Thus, a woman whose virginity was spoiled or whose chastity was violated became socially unacceptable. During the war, this patriarchal ideology was combined with political prejudice, with the result that many comfort station survivors were regarded not only as immoral but also as betrayers of the nation. The survivor's family was also affected; reportedly, three of Nan Erpu's family members in Yu County were killed by unknown assailants because she was a military comfort woman.[34]

In this social and cultural environment, many comfort station survivors felt so ashamed that, after the war ended, they lived alone and in silence. Often, they did not even speak to their families. Unable to overcome the horrible memories and emotional distress, some survivors receded into insanity or committed suicide. Those whose wartime experiences were revealed were often humiliated and persecuted. After the war, as has been mentioned, Yuan Zhulin was accused of having "slept with" Japanese soldiers and was sent to the far north to perform hard labour. Nan Erpu was charged as a "counter-revolutionary" because she had serviced Japanese soldiers. She was imprisoned for two years and persecuted as an "old-line counter-revolutionary" during the Cultural Revolution. Unable to bear the physical and mental agony resulting from her wartime torture and postwar mistreatment, Nan committed suicide in 1967.[35] Patriarchal ideology, and the sexism that is inseparable from it, is still so widely influential in Chinese society that, when victim Li Lianchun was invited to attend the Women's International War Crimes Tribunal on Japan's Military Sexual Slavery in Tokyo in 2000, the local official refused to issue her the necessary travel documents because he believed it was inappropriate for her to speak of her "shameful past" abroad.[36] This patriarchal sexism almost certainly plays a role in explaining why China, as the largest victimized nation, failed to pursue timely justice for the hundreds of thousands of Chinese comfort women. Although the "Committee for Investigating the Enemy's War Crimes" *(Diren zuixing diaocha weiyuanhui),* established by the Chinese Nationalist government at the end of the war, listed "Rape," "abduction of women," and "Enforced Prostitution" as war crimes,[37] there was no thorough investigation into what had occurred in the comfort stations.[38]

International and domestic social, political, and cultural postwar conditions ensured that survivors suffered in silence. However, these conditions began to change, and, inspired by the international redress movement in the late 1980s and early 1990s, the endeavour to seek justice for the victims of the Japanese military comfort women system has finally gained momentum in China.

9 The Redress Movement

The sexual slavery practised by the Japanese military was largely unrecognized during the first decades after the Second World War. While descriptions of comfort women occasionally appeared in memoirs and literary texts in Japan, most of the victims and former Japanese military men remained silent about the issue. In the 1970s, two pioneering books on the subject were published, one by Senda Kakō, a Japanese journalist and non-fiction writer, and the other by Kim Il Myon, a Korean resident in Japan.[1] In addition, three personal stories of former Japanese and Korean comfort women were published in Japan.[2] Memoirs of former Japanese officers, who describe their wartime involvement in establishing the comfort stations, have also been published.[3] Yet the issue failed to attract wide public attention until, in the 1980s, a coalition of Korean and Japanese women's groups elevated it to the status of a political movement within the global context of feminist and grassroots politics.[4] The South Korean Church Women's Alliance initiated action to condemn sexual violence against women, defining it as a basic human rights issue, and Professor Yun Chong-ok, who had engaged in years of research on the comfort women issue, started to work with some concerned Japanese scholars.[5]

The Japanese government initially denied any involvement with comfort women and dismissed the request for an investigation when Motooka Shōji, a Socialist Party member of the Japanese National Diet, raised the issue at a budget committee meeting on 6 June 1990. The government was forced to change that position after a series of key events over the following year and a half. In August 1991, a Korean woman, Kim Hak-sun, came forward to testify publicly about her experience as a military sex slave. On 6 December 1991, Kim and two other Korean comfort women survivors filed a lawsuit against the Japanese government at the Tokyo District Court, asking for an apology and compensation. This was the first of a series of lawsuits filed by surviving Korean comfort women against the Japanese government. About a month later, on 11 January 1992, a major Japanese newspaper, *Asahi Shimbun,* reported Chūō University professor Yoshimi Yoshiaki's finding of documentary evidence of the Japanese military's direct involvement in establishing the

comfort women system. Five days after the publication of Yoshimi's findings, Prime Minister Miyazawa Kiichi expressed his regret and extended an
apology during his visit to South Korea, promising further investigation of
the issue.

On 6 July 1992, the Japanese government published the result of its investigation, which involved an examination of 127 documents, including those
first unearthed by Professor Yoshimi and other investigators.[6] However,
critics are sceptical about the results; as George Hicks notes, there were no
relevant documents released from the Police Agency or to the Ministry of
Labour, even though these two government agencies were frequently impli-
cated in the forced recruitment of women.[7] In addition, the Ministry of Justice
was not investigated, although it was known to house the records of the war
crimes trials. The investigation also failed to include data from individuals
(such as telephone reports collected in Japan) and from foreign documents
(such as US Army reports).[8] Not surprisingly, the limited scope of the investigation provoked widespread criticism from women's groups and concerned
researchers.[9]

On 4 August 1993, the Japanese government published its second report,
presenting the results of further investigations. Based on this report, Chief
Cabinet Secretary Kōno Yōhei stated that the Japanese imperial forces had
been involved, directly or indirectly, in the establishment and administration
of comfort stations and that there had been cases in which women had been
gathered against their will. He also indicated that these women had been
forced to live under miserable conditions.[10] The Kōno statement was wel-
comed as a step toward the recognition of the Japanese military's involvement in the victimization of comfort women, but its careful wording was
criticized for enabling the government to avoid its legal and political responsibilities. Yoshimi Yoshiaki found three aspects of the Kōno statement
particularly unacceptable. First, the statement implied that the main perpetrators of comfort station atrocities had been private traders and that government involvement was largely tangential. Second, while acknowledging that
a large number of comfort women had been taken from the Korean peninsula,
the Kōno statement paid little attention to comfort women of other ethnic
and national backgrounds (except for those from Japan). In fact, Yoshimi
observed that the Japanese government had conducted no hearings that took
into account the voices of surviving victims in Mainland China, Taiwan, and
Southeast Asia-Pacific areas. Third, although it expressed "a feeling of apology and reflection," the report failed to recognize the matter as a war crime
and as constituting a violation of international law; nor did it specify any
government plans for further investigation and compensation.[11]

In Japan, in the years following the publication of the Kōno statement, public opinion concerning government responsibility became more divided. While many Japanese researchers, journalists, legal experts, and ordinary citizens urged their government to assume responsibility for its war crimes, the conservatives opposed the redress movement. In 1995, a group of Liberal Democratic Party legislators sponsored a research association that issued publications that disputed the historical veracity of accounts of the Japanese military's wartime atrocities, including the Nanjing Massacre. At the same time, the anti-redress activists insisted that comfort women were mostly prostitutes and that the Japanese military had not forced them into the comfort stations. They also claimed that, at the time, the way in which the women were treated did not violate international law. For these reasons, they concluded that Japan bore no responsibility and that it had no reason either to apologize or to offer compensation.[12]

With regard to compensating former comfort women, the Japanese government maintained that Japan had settled all claims of compensation through the San Francisco Peace Treaty and various bilateral agreements with other nations. However, under increasing international and domestic pressure to compensate former comfort women, in July 1995 the coalition cabinet of Socialist Murayama Tomi'ichi announced the establishment of the Citizens' Asia Peace Fund for Women *(Josei no tame no Ajia heiwa kokumin kikin)*, often referred to as the "Asian Women's Fund," or AWF, to raise funds through private donations for surviving comfort women. This initiative, as Philip A. Seaton points out, was overshadowed by a series of statements made by government officials around that time. Seaton cites that in May 1994, newly appointed justice minister Nagano Shigeto called the Nanjing Massacre a "fabrication" and said that Japan had had no "aggressive intent." On 12 August 1994, the director general of the Environment Agency, Sakurai Shin, stated that Japan had not fought with the intention of waging an aggressive war and that, thanks to Japan, Asia could now "throw off the shackles of colonial rule." On 8 November 1995, the director general of the Management and Co-ordination Agency, Etō Takami, told his press club "off the record" that he believed that Japan had also done good things during its colonial rule in Korea.[13] These statements evoked protests from neighbouring countries as well as doubts about the sincerity of the Japanese government's apologies.

According to the AWF's records, during its twelve years of operation, from 1995 to 2007, it had raised about 565 million yen from citizen donors to fund compensation, in addition to the approximately 750 million yen given by the government to fund medical welfare and support. Reportedly, 285 former comfort women in the Philippines, South Korea, and Taiwan received payments from the AWF, and each of seventy-nine women in the Netherlands was provided medical welfare support worth three million *yen*.[14] However, the AWF failed to enter into official discussions with either the Government of China or the Government of North Korea, even though vast numbers of women from these countries had been victimized by the military comfort women system. Since its formation, the AWF has been criticized both by Japanese nationalists (for paying "compensation in practice") and by progressive intellectuals (for not paying "official compensation"); many believe that the murky nature of the AWF creates "more confusion than resolution."[15] Takemae Eiji commented, "By limiting its campaign to corporate and private donations, the government purposely sidestepped the question of state responsibility for the sex-slave programme."[16] He notes that "Japan's efforts pale beside the efforts of Germany to compensate Jews and Eastern Europeans for Nazi depredations": under a 1956 federal relief law, Germany contributed a total of 6 trillion *yen* ($50 billion) to Jewish and non-German war victims.[17] From the viewpoint of the advocates who are demanding state redress, the AWF was simply a device designed to enable Japan to evade its legal responsibility.[18]

In 1997, in order to support the surviving comfort women who declined the AWF payment, the Taipei Women's Rescue Foundation organized a fundraiser. Li Ao, a renowned writer and critic, donated a large portion of his antique collection to this fundraiser. Ma Yingjiu (mayor of Taipei at the time), Wang Ching-feng (who has played a leading role in the redress movement in Taiwan), and many other public intellectuals and celebrities also made generous donations for the event. The association raised over 40 million new Taiwan dollars, from which the foundation provided each of the surviving Taiwanese comfort women who had declined the AWF payment with 500,000 new Taiwan dollars in financial aid. This amount was matched by the Government of Taiwan, providing a substantial amount of money to improve the living conditions of these women.[19]

In 2000, the AWF informally contacted Su Zhiliang, director of the Research Centre for Chinese "Comfort Women," about the possibility of providing AWF payments to Chinese victims. After consulting with the survivors, Su declined the AWF offer. Yuan Zhulin, one of the Chinese survivors who sought an official apology and compensation from the Japanese government, said to the centre's Chen Lifei: "My young daughter died because I was forced into the Japanese comfort station, and I lost the ability to ever have children again because of the torture. I will never accept this kind of settlement even if I die of starvation. If I accept the money from the AWF, that will be a grave disgrace to my country." In this regard, Yuan Zhulin's opinions were shared by Jan Ruff O'Herne, a Dutch woman who had been taken into a Japanese military comfort station from central Java, and other survivors, all of whom viewed the AWF as "an insult to comfort women."[20]

As the Japanese government continued to maintain its stance against state compensation for individual civilian victims, leaders of the redress movement as well as the surviving comfort women and legal experts sought international support; they urged the United Nations to investigate the issue. On 4 January 1996, Special Rapporteur Radhika Coomaraswamy submitted her investigative report to the UN Commission on Human Rights, confirming that the comfort women system constituted both military sexual slavery and a crime against humanity. In its response to Radhika Coomaraswamy's report, the Japanese government based its denial of legal liability on a number of substantive grounds, the most significant of which include:

(a) that recent developments or advances in international criminal law may not be applied retroactively; (b) that the crime of slavery does not accurately describe the system established through the "comfort stations" and that the prohibition against slavery was not, in any event, established as a customary norm under applicable international law at the time of the Second World War; (c) that acts of rape in armed conflict were not prohibited by either the regulations annexed to the Hague Convention No. IV of 1907 or by applicable customary norms of international law in force at the time of the Second World War; and (d) that the laws of war would only apply, in any event, to conduct committed by the Japanese military against nationals of a belligerent State and would not, therefore, cover the actions of the Japanese military with respect to Japanese or Korean nationals, since Korea was annexed to Japan during the Second World War.[21]

On 22 June 1998, Special Rapporteur Gay J. McDougall submitted to the UN Sub-Commission on Prevention of Discrimination and Protection of Minorities her final report, which contained the results of further investigations and presented a rebuttal to the Japanese government's arguments. The appendix of the report detailed the findings regarding Japan's guilt and liability, including, in particular, the following points:

(a) Japan's military comfort women system falls under the international definition of slavery at the time. "By 1932, at least 20 international agreements suppressing the slave trade, slavery or slavery-related practices had been concluded" and "the 1926 Slavery Convention, which was developed by the League of Nations and provided a definition of slavery as 'the status or condition of a person over whom any or all of the powers attaching to the right of ownership are exercised,' was clearly declaratory of customary international law by at least the time of the Second World War"; (b) Rape (including forced or coerced prostitution) was a war crime at the time. "Several early authoritative sources on the rules of war, most prominently the 1863 Lieber Code [and the Hague Convention Regulations of 1907, and article 27 of the Fourth Geneva Convention], explicitly prohibited rape or the mistreatment of women during war"; (c) "The widespread or systematic enslavement of persons has also been recognized as a crime against humanity for at least half a century." In crimes against humanity, the nationality of the victim is irrelevant; therefore, the Japanese government is liable for these offenses whether the crimes were committed against its enemies' citizens or its own.[22]

The report points out that, even relying exclusively on the facts established in the Japanese government's own review of the involvement of Japanese military officials in establishing, supervising, and maintaining the rape centres during the Second World War, it is clear that the Japanese government should be held legally liable for these crimes:

> Under customary international law, the Government of Japan must provide redress for the atrocities perpetrated against the "comfort women." Redress should take the form of individual compensation to the former "comfort women" by the Government of Japan. Alternatively, compensation could also be sought by States on behalf of their citizens who were former "comfort women." These States must then establish mechanisms to distribute those funds to the aggrieved victims. In addition, as indicated above, government and military personnel must also be prosecuted for their culpability in establishing and maintaining the rape centres.[23]

Although the UN report sets out the legal framework for individual criminal liability, state responsibility, and liability for compensation, the Japanese government has not followed the UN's recommendation to punish those responsible for the comfort women system and to compensate its victims.[24]

Beginning in the early 1990s, the Japanese government's denial of its responsibilities to its victims prompted Chinese legal scholars and activists to re-examine the postwar international legal practices and the treaties between China and Japan concerning war compensation. On 25 March 1991, Tong Zeng, a leading redress movement activist trained in international law at

Peking University, submitted a memorandum – "Demanding War Compensations from Japan Is of Great Urgency to China" (Zhongguo yaoqiu Riben shouhai peichang keburonghuan) – to the Administrative Office of the National People's Congress. In this document he traces how, in international legal practice, the concept of war compensation was changing, and he calls for legislators to distinguish the war indemnity paid by the defeated state to the victorious state from compensation paid to individual victims. He points out that, although, in the Sino-Japanese Joint Communiqué of 1972, which was concerned with restoring a normal diplomatic relationship between the two nations, the Chinese government relinquished its claim for war indemnity from Japan, China never waived the individual victim's right to claim such compensation. If Japan denies the historical truth of its wartime atrocities and permits the revival of militarism, then this would be a violation of the principles established by the Joint Communiqué and the 1978 Sino-Japanese Peace and Friendship Treaty. And, in that case, China would have the right to reclaim war compensation from the Japanese state.[25]

The individual victims to whom Tong Zeng refers include more than just comfort women. The memorandum enumerates many Japanese atrocities committed in China, including the Nanjing Massacre, military sexual slavery, the killing and torture of POWs, forced labour, biological and chemical warfare, indiscriminate aerial bombing, and the selling of opium and illegal drugs. It urges the Japanese government to take responsibility and to compensate the Chinese victims who suffered as a result of Japanese war crimes, and it suggests that the Chinese government take steps to support its citizens' pursuit of redress. Tong's memorandum represented the opinions of many Chinese legal experts and scholars who specialized in Sino-Japanese relationships at the time, and it had a huge impact in China.

After the Cultural Revolution, in the late 1980s, Chinese intellectuals whose voices had long been suppressed began to assert individual human rights and citizens' rights. Riding this current, Li Guping and others questioned the government's 1972 decision to abandon its right to claim war reparations from Japan.[26] The re-examination of the war compensation issue was also a reaction to the Japanese neo-nationalist denial of Imperial Japan's war atrocities. On 18 August 1987, Li Guping, then a young employee of Dongfeng Automobile Company, sent "A Citizen's Open Letter to the National People's Congress Regarding the Compensation Issues of Japan's Aggressive War in China" (Yige putong gongmin jiu Riben qin-Hua zhanzheng peichang wenti gei Quanguo renmin daibiao dahui de yifeng gongkaixin), in which he stresses that, as, after the signing of the Sino-Japanese Joint Communiqué, Japanese government officials and right-wing activists continued to whitewash the history of Japan's aggressive war, taking measures to redress the damages of the Japanese invasion could effectively counter such denials and place the Sino-Japanese relationship on a more solid foundation.[27]

The open letters of Li Guping, Tong Zeng, and others in the late 1980s and early 1990s sparked a vigorous response from Chinese citizens. Thousands of war victims wrote to Tong Zeng when the media reported his article, and many of them went to talk to him in person.[28] After the publication of Tong's memorandum, the members of the National People's Congress (NPC) drafted ten proposals to address the issue when the congress was in session in 1991. In the following year, two NPC members – Wang Lusheng, a China National Democratic Construction Association member from Guizhou Province, and Wang Gong, a lawyer from Anhui Province – again raised the issue for discussion by the NPC.[29] At the same time, Shen Panwen, a chemistry professor at Nankai Univerisity, made a proposal at the Chinese People's Political Consultative Conference (CPPCC) to allow individual war victims and NGOs to file claims for compensation from the Government of Japan.[30] There was no report about whether or not these proposals resulted in any resolution, but the inclusion of the issue in the NPC and CPPCC agendas indicated the impact of the issue on China's political centre at the time.

What, then, was said about Japan's responsibility for war compensation in the Sino-Japanese Joint Communiqué? Article 5 of the Joint Communiqué, signed in 1972 by the governments of both China and Japan, states: "The Government of the People's Republic of China declares that in the interest of the friendship between the Chinese and the Japanese peoples, it renounces its demand for war reparation from Japan."[31] The wording of the article does not waive the rights of individual victims to file compensation claims. The Chinese government never officially interpreted this article as allowing lawsuits against Japan; however, since the rise of the redress movement in Asian countries, government officials have openly criticized Japan's denial of its responsibilities for war crimes. In a 1992 statement, the Chinese ambassador to Japan, Zhang Zhenya, called the comfort women system "a shameful atrocity committed by the Japanese militarists" and stated: "It is reported that Chinese women were among the victims. We are paying close attention to the matter and hope further investigation will be done to reveal the truth."[32] On 7 March 1995, Minister of Foreign Affairs Qian Qisen stated that the Joint Communiqué waived only the Chinese government's right to claim reparations against the Japanese government, not those of private Chinese citizens. For this reason, he said, the Chinese government would not prohibit individual citizens from filing claims for redress.[33] The Chinese government, however, provided no substantive support to these individual victims.

Action seeking redress for comfort station survivors began as a grassroots movement in China in the late 1980s. In 1982, Zhang Shuangbing, a school-teacher in Yu County, Shanxi Province, came to know a surviving Chinese comfort woman. As he was returning from a school trip in the fall, Zhang was struck by the sight of a solitary old woman, who, with great difficulty, was harvesting millet. Zhang helped her with the farm work and later learned that this woman, Hou Dong'e, had been held in a Japanese stronghold and raped during the Japanese occupation of Yu County. About a decade later, in a newspaper, Zhang Shuangbing read Tong Zeng's article concerning the right of Chinese war victims to claim compensation, and he immediately brought this news to Hou Dong'e. At first Hou did not want to speak of her experience as a sex slave; however, Zhang Shuangbing's wife joined the conversation and was able to persuade her. Hou Dong'e finally broke her silence and cried for a long time. The miseries she revealed far exceeded anything Zhuang Shuangbing could have imagined.[34]

Hou Dong'e was one of many Chinese women in the area who had been forced to become a sex slave for the Imperial Japanese Army. From that point on, Zhang Shuangbing, Li Guiming (a native of Zhenxi Village, Yu County), and other local volunteers worked to confirm the identities of local surviving comfort women and to support them. On 7 July 1992, the fifty-fifth anniversary of the Lugouqiao Incident, which marked the beginning of Japan's full-fledged invasion of China, Hou Dong'e and three other survivors sent a written document to the Japanese Embassy in Beijing. The document stated the facts of their devastating experience as sex slaves for the Japanese army during the war and demanded an official apology and monetary compensation from the Japanese government. This was the first time that former Chinese comfort women voiced their demand for redress. In December 1992, the International Public Hearing Concerning the Post-War Compensation of Japan was held in Tokyo.[35] With the support of Chinese researchers, local volunteers, and Lin Boyao (a member of an activist group representing ex-patriate Chinese in Japan), Wan Aihua and other Chinese survivors spoke at this hearing. The meeting between Chinese survivors and activists in Japan hastened the formation of transnational support groups for the Shanxi comfort women's redress movement.[36]

In southern China, research on Chinese comfort women survivors also began in the early 1990s. On Hainan Island, where Japan established its strategic bases during the Asia-Pacific War, a well-trained history scholar, Fu Heji, who was the deputy of the Hainan Province Historical Records Bureau, coordinated a provincewide investigation. The investigation engaged both historians and officials such as Su Guangming from the local People's Political Consultative Committee and volunteers such as Chen Houzhi from the Baoting Farm. Their research located sixty-two former comfort station sites on the island and found the largest group of survivors in China.[37] Zhang Yingyong, of the Baoting County Local History Bureau in Hainan Province, began his research on comfort women in the area in 1992, when he was working on local history regarding the Japanese invasion. He visited a number of villages and towns on foot and by bicycle, and he helped to identify twenty-three surviving comfort women, including Chen Jinyu, who later participated in the Hainan comfort women's lawsuit against the Japanese government.[38]

About the same time, Chinese intellectuals and volunteers from all walks of life joined the movement. Sponsored by a Hong Kong businessman, Jiang Hao and a group of volunteers began a nationwide investigation of former Chinese comfort women. This resulted in the 1993 publication of the first book on Chinese comfort women, *Zhaoshi: Zhongguo weianfu* (Exposé: Chinese comfort women). In 1993, based on her independent investigation, journalist Li Xiuping published a monograph entitled *Shiwan weianfu* (One hundred thousand comfort women). Subsequently, a large number of studies and findings relating to Chinese comfort women have been published, including: Su Shi's research on how the Japanese military drafted Chinese women to comfort stations; Gao Xingzu's investigation of the sexual violence perpetrated by the Imperial Japanese Army in Nanjing and the establishment of the comfort women system; Guan Ning's discussion of the relationship between the comfort women issue and its impact on Japan's relationship with the international community; and He Ji's collection of archival documents.[39] Field investigations of the sites of former comfort stations were conducted both in big cities and in rural areas of the provinces. Su Zhiliang and Chen Lifei, whose research contributed crucially to this book, were among the first to conduct investigations into the comfort stations in China.

Despite the massive scale of the comfort women system, documenting these crimes has been very difficult. This is because the Japanese military destroyed its records at the end of the Second World War, and many records were also lost during the chaos of China's civil war immediately thereafter. Moreover, most of the Chinese comfort women died in the comfort stations or as the result of the torture, and those who survived have been silenced. It often took many visits before researchers were able to succeed in helping a survivor to find her voice. In addition, Chinese authorities did not encourage this research, leaving investigators on their own, without government support. Lack of funding has been a common plight among Chinese researchers and activists, most of whom have been volunteering their time and providing their own funding. Su Zhiliang and Chen Lifei paid for many of their research trips with their own savings, especially during the initial years. Attorney Kang Jian, who, together with Japanese lawyers, has represented surviving comfort women from Mainland China in three of four lawsuits, made sixteen trips to Shanxi Province and six trips to Hainan in order to investigate their cases. And she has devoted countless hours to their lawsuits free of charge. In spite of all the obstacles, field investigations led by university researchers, legal experts, and local historians have produced first-hand evidence of the scope of the Japanese military's comfort women system in China.

10 Litigation on the Part of Chinese Survivors

In the Chinese survivors' redress movement Japanese public intellectuals, legal experts, and citizen groups played a vital supporting role. In May 1994, invited by the Institute of Law, Chinese Academy of Social Sciences, the Japan Democratic Lawyers' Association sent a judicial research delegation to China. During their trip the Japanese lawyers saw for themselves the Chinese people's anger regarding the Japanese government's denial of Japan's war crimes.[1] Attorney Onodera Toshitaka, secretary-general of the association, visited China again in July 1994 to meet victims of Japanese war crimes. He was shocked by Chinese victims' testimonies describing the brutal atrocities committed by the Japanese military while carrying out operations that involved "burning all, killing all, and looting all."[2] From that point on, Onodera and progressive Japanese lawyers committed themselves to supporting the lawsuits of Chinese war victims.

After a year of preparation, the Japanese Legal Team for Chinese War Victims' Compensation Claims (Chūgokujin sensō higai baishō seikyū jiken bengodan) was formed in August 1995. The legal team was headed by Oyama Hiroshi, Onodera Toshitaka served as the secretary-general, and Watanabe Shōgo was in charge of administrative matters. Surviving Chinese comfort women's lawsuits were included among the cases they planned to represent, and Attorney Ōmori Noriko headed this special team. Attorneys from different parts of Japan joined the cause, and Japanese citizens rallied various support groups behind them. In addition to devoting a tremendous amount of time to working on the cases of the Chinese victims, these Japanese attorneys also contributed immensely to funding the investigations, and they even paid plaintiffs' travel expenses so that they could appear in court in Japan. The Chinese media reported that, in order to finance the Chinese plaintiffs' legal pursuits, Onodera Toshitaka took out huge loans.[3] Oyama Hiroshi also spent many of his personal funds to help pay for the Chinese victims' lawsuits.[4] According to Kang Jian, who has worked closely with the Japanese legal team since 1995, during the first ten years of the litigation process, Japanese attorneys and citizens' support groups financed almost all the investigations as well as the travel and legal expenses of Chinese war victims. The litigation brought forward by the Chinese comfort women would have been impossible without their generous support. After August 2005, the All China Lawyers Association and the China Legal Aid Foundation set up a special fund for the Chinese victims of Japanese war crimes in order to support the Chinese litigators.[5]

The efforts of Japanese lawyers, researchers, and citizen groups are particularly remarkable because they are working under extremely difficult circumstances: those in Japan who pursue the issue of Japan's responsibility for war crimes continue to face abusive messages and threats of violence. Attorney Ōmori Noriko, whose meeting with Kang Jian at the United Nations' Fourth World Conference on Women in Beijing in September 1995 led to a transnational collaboration representing Chinese comfort women, views her effort to support these people as a meaningful service to her own country as well. "If we truly care about Japan's future," she said, "we must ensure that Japan can obtain full trust from the world in terms of moral principles, and particularly that Japan can form a truly friendly relationship with Asian countries. Now concerning the 'comfort women' issue, so many countries are still seeking a sincere apology and, above all, they want to see the Japanese government take responsible action to help heal the victims' wounded hearts in the remaining days of their lives. It is not acceptable to say that the issue belongs to the past."[6] Onodera said to a Chinese newspaper reporter at an interview that these Japanese lawyers, scholars, and citizens shared a firm belief: "Japan and Japanese people cannot win the trust of Chinese people and other people of Asian nations unless we assume our responsibilities for the war victims."[7] Words and actions such as theirs have won the hearts of the Chinese people. In 2003, Oyama Hiroshi became the first non-Chinese national chosen to receive the China Central Television annual award, People Who Moved All China.

Since 1995, several transnational groups have been formed to support the litigation brought forward by former Chinese comfort women. Among these is the Association to Support the Lawsuits of Chinese Comfort Women, which is led by Ōmori Noriko and consists of peace activists and Japanese citizens. This group has worked with the Japanese organization known as the Association to Support the Claims of Chinese War Victims as well as with the Chinese lawyer Kang Jian on the Shanxi victims' lawsuits. Another group, led by Japanese historian Ishida Yoneko and called the Association for Uncovering the Facts of Sexual Violence Committed by the Japanese Military in China and Supporting the Legal Cases for Redress *(Chūgoku ni okeru*

Figure 22 "Comfort station" survivor Mao Yinmei (middle) in front of her house with Su Zhiliang (second from right) and researchers from Germany and Japan.

Nihongun no seibōryoku no jittai o akiraka ni shi, baishō seikyū o shiensuru kai),[8] made multiple trips to Shanxi Province beginning in 1996 to work with local Chinese victims and volunteers. Members of the association are volunteers and come from different areas of Japan. The results of their investigation contributed to the supporting evidence for the Shanxi women's lawsuits. In southern China a joint investigation into the comfort women system on Hainan Island was conducted by a transnational group and local supporters: Onodera Toshitaka and members of the Japanese Legal Team for Chinese War Victims' Compensation Claims, along with Kang Jian, participated in the investigation. Another transnational group, this one led by Su Zhiliang, Chen Lifei, and the Japanese writer Nishino Rumiko, also engaged in multi-year investigations into the issues of comfort women, forced labour, and other atrocities committed by the Japanese military in the Hainan area. In Taiwan, Tsuchiya Kōken, president of the Japan Federation of Bar Associations, and Arimitsu Ken, chief coordinator of the Japanese Post-War Compensation Network, helped form a transnational legal team representing the Taiwanese victims. Japanese attorney Shimizu Yukiko and Taiwanese attorney Wang Ching-feng headed the team.[9] Assisted by local volunteers, these transnational groups played an important role in the Chinese comfort women's redress movement.

With the support of the non-governmental transnational groups, surviving Chinese comfort women filed five lawsuits with Japanese courts between 1995 and 2001; four of these suits were filed by women from Mainland China and one was filed by women from Taiwan. As of 3 March 2010, all the cases have been denied. The decisions of the Japanese courts, as seen in the brief summaries below, were based on nullification defence arguments – namely, "statutory time limitation," "state immunity," and "abandonment of the right to claim."

The First Lawsuit Brought Forward by Former Chinese Comfort Women

On 7 August 1995, Li Xiumei, Liu Mianhuan, Zhou Xixiang, and Chen Lintao of Yu County, Shanxi Province, filed a lawsuit with the Tokyo District Court, demanding an official apology from the Japanese government and 20 million *yen* (about $US211,000) per victim for having been taken by the Japanese army and used as sex slaves between 1942 and 1944.[10] A Japanese legal team led by Ōmori Noriko and Chinese attorney Kang Jian represented the plaintiffs. Li Xiumei and Liu Mianhuan attended the court hearing on 19 July 1996 and alleged that, at ages fifteen and sixteen, respectively, they were kidnapped from their home village by Japanese soldiers, confined in a Japanese fortress, and continually raped. Torture inflicted by Japanese soldiers permanently damaged Li's right eye and injured Liu's left shoulder. Six years later, on 30 May 2001, the Tokyo District Court dismissed the case on the grounds that an individual had no right to sue a state for compensation. The plaintiffs appealed to the Tokyo High Court on 12 June 2001. On 15 December 2004, the Tokyo High Court rejected the plaintiffs' appeal, stating that the Japanese government had no responsibility for damages and that the statute of limitations had expired, even though the court recognized that the four plaintiffs had been taken to Japanese military bases by force and repeatedly raped and that they continued to suffer from post-traumatic stress disorder after the war.[11] The plaintiffs immediately appealed to Japan's Supreme Court. On 27 April 2007, the Supreme Court delivered a half-page judgment rejecting the plaintiffs' claims.[12]

The Second Lawsuit

On 22 February 1996, Guo Xicui and Hou Qiaolian from Yu County sued the Government of Japan in the Tokyo District Court, asking for an official apology and 20 million *yen* (about US $190,000)[13] per individual as compensation for sufferings endured as sex slaves for the Japanese military.[14] A Japanese legal team led by Ōmori Noriko and Kang Jian represented the plaintiffs. Reportedly, Guo was fifteen and Hou was thirteen years old when each was kidnapped, confined, and raped by Japanese soldiers on a daily basis for more than a month in 1942.[15] Again the Tokyo District Court waited for six years to hand down its verdict. One of the plaintiffs, Hou Qiaolian, died on 11 May 1999 while the case was pending. The court rejected the victims' compensation claims on 29 March 2002. The decision cited a rule stipulating that the current government could not be held responsible for any acts by the state under the former Constitution of the Empire of Japan.[16] The surviving plaintiff appealed to the Tokyo High Court. Three years later, on 18 March 2005, the Tokyo High Court upheld the earlier district court's ruling. While acknowledging the fact that the Japanese troops forcibly kidnapped, confined, beat, and raped the two women, and that, as a result, they suffered from post-traumatic stress disorder, the court held that China had waived its right to seek compensation from Japan under the 1952 peace treaty between Japan and the Nationalist regime in Taiwan and that the twenty-year statute of limitations had elapsed.[17] On the day the Tokyo High Court ruled, the following groups presented a joint statement protesting the judgment: the All China Lawyers Association, the All-China Women's Federation, the China Foundation for Human Rights Development, and the Association on the History of the Resistance War.

The surviving plaintiff, Guo Xicui, lodged an appeal with the Supreme Court of Japan on 30 March 2005. On 27 April 2007, the Supreme Court issued a final judgment on the appeal, upholding the Tokyo High Court ruling against the compensation claim. Despite its recognition of the damage done to the plaintiffs, the Supreme Court took the position that, under the 1972 Sino-Japanese Joint Communiqué, Chinese people lost their rights to judicially claim war compensation from Japan.[18] It interpreted the communiqué as "a framework like the San Francisco Peace Treaty," which was signed between Japan and the Allied powers in 1951 and that waived all Allied reparation claims, including the right of individuals to seek compensation.[19] At a press conference after the court decision, Chinese foreign ministry spokesman Liu Jianchao strongly opposed the Japanese Supreme Court's interpretation of the Joint Communiqué and asked the Japanese government to deal seriously with China's concerns and to handle the war reparation issue properly.[20]

The Third Lawsuit

On 30 October 1998, ten more Chinese victims of the military comfort women system, including Wan Aihua, Zhao Runmei, Gao Yin'e, Wang Gaihe, Zhao Cunni, Yang Shizhen, Yin Yulin, and the daughter of deceased victim Nan

Erpu, filed a lawsuit against the Government of Japan at the Tokyo District Court, demanding a public apology from the Japanese government and 20 million *yen* for each individual victim. A Japanese legal team headed by Nakashita Yūko represented the plaintiffs. The court did not rule until nearly five years later, when, on 24 April 2003, it denied the plaintiffs' claim for compensation.[21] At the end of the judgment, Presiding Judge Takizawa Takaomi recognized all the allegations made by the plaintiffs, stating that "The actions of the Japanese soldiers were abnormal, contemptible and barbaric, even if they were carried out in wartime," but he had "no choice but to deny judicial relief through the application of (existing) laws."[22] The plaintiffs appealed to the Tokyo High Court on 8 May 2003, and on 31 March 2005 the High Court upheld the verdict of the district court. By that time four of the plaintiffs had died.[23] The plaintiffs appealed to Japan's Supreme Court, but their appeal was denied in December 2005.[24]

The Fourth Lawsuit

On 16 July 2001, Huang Youliang and Chen Yabian, both from Lingshui County, and Lin Yajin, Deng Yumin, Chen Jinyu, Tan Yadong, Tan Yulian, and Huang Yufeng, all from Baoting County, Hainan Province, sued the Government of Japan in the Tokyo District Court. A Japanese legal team led by Onodera Toshitaka and Chinese attorney Kang Jian represented the plaintiffs. Reportedly, all eight ethnic minority women had been between fourteen and eighteen years old when Japanese forces occupied their hometowns and forced them into sexual slavery. Initially, the plaintiffs demanded only that the Government of Japan publish an official apology and compensate each individual with 3 million *yen* (about US$24,096).[25] As the Japanese government did not respond to their demands, after three years had passed, the plaintiffs increased the claim for compensation to 20 million *yen* for each victim.[26] The court did not issue a judgment until five years later, during which time two of the plaintiffs died. In support of the former comfort women's lawsuit, 20,166 residents of Hainan Province signed a petition in March 2006.[27] The Tokyo District Court finally made a decision on 30 August 2006, denying the victims' claims and maintaining that an individual Chinese person had no right to sue the Japanese state. The surviving plaintiffs lodged an appeal with the Tokyo High Court, but, on 26 March 2009, it upheld the initial verdict of the district court. Indignant over the ruling, the plaintiffs pledged to appeal to the Japanese Supreme Court.[28] On 3 March 2010, the Supreme Court of Japan rejected the appeal of the eight Chinese comfort women, upholding the verdicts of the first and second trials. On 8 March 2010, commenting on the Japanese Supreme Court's argument that the plaintiffs lost

Figure 23 Gravestone erected by the Research Center for Chinese "Comfort Women" commemorating the life of Yang Wubang, a Hainan Island "comfort station" survivor who died on 31 August 2006, the day after the Tokyo District Court denied the Hainan victims' claim for compensation.

the right to claim individual compensation when China signed the Sino-Japanese Joint Communiqué, Qin Gang (China's foreign ministry spokesperson), made the following remarks: "The Sino-Japanese Joint Statement is a serious political document between the two governments. Any unilateral interpretation of the document by the Japanese court is illegal and invalid."[29]

In addition to the four cases described above, all of which were lodged by survivors in Mainland China, nine survivors from Taiwan filed a lawsuit against the Government of Japan in the Tokyo District Court on 14 July 1999, demanding 10 million *yen* (about US$80,300) per individual as compensation and an official apology.[30] Taiwanese lawyers, Wang Ching-feng and Chuang Kuo-ming, and Japanese lawyer, Shimizu Yukiko led the legal team for the women. Reportedly, these women were lured into Japanese comfort stations between 1938 and 1945 by deceptive job offers and have suffered physically and mentally ever since. Huang A-tau, one of the plaintiffs, stated that she applied for a nurse's job only to find herself forced into a brothel in China and then transferred to similar facilities in Indonesia and Burma, where she remained until the end of the war. She stated that she returned to Taiwan but was too ashamed to tell her parents what had happened and has lived alone ever since.[31] The Ministry of Foreign Affairs in Taiwan joined the lawyers in demanding compensation and an apology from the Japanese government. The ministry stated that, since 1992, the Taiwan government has commissioned private groups to investigate the situation of former comfort women. Their research shows that at least 766 Taiwanese women were forcefully conscripted as comfort women.[32] The Taiwanese research group conducted oral interviews with fifty-eight women who pleaded their cases and confirmed that at least forty-eight of them had clearly been forced to work as comfort women. The government in Taiwan granted humanitarian aid of US$15,384 to each of the forty-two comfort women who were still alive and living in Taiwan.[33] On 15 October 2002, the court handed down its initial verdict, rejecting the plaintiffs' claims. By that time two of the plaintiffs had already died.[34] The plaintiffs appealed to the Tokyo High Court, which denied their appeal on 9 February 2004. On 25 February 2005, the Japanese Supreme Court issued a final ruling dismissing the victims' claims.[35] On 26 February 2005, the support groups from Taiwan decided to bring the case to the United Nations and to continue their efforts for redress.

A total of ten lawsuits, including the five cases mentioned above, have been filed with Japanese courts by the victims of Japan's military comfort women system. The plaintiffs are from South Korea, China, Taiwan, the Philippines, and the Netherlands. In addition, one plaintiff is a Korean resident living in Japan. The Japanese courts denied all the former comfort women's claims except one: on 27 April 1998, the Shimonoseki branch of Yamaguchi District Court ordered the Japanese government to pay each of the three Korean comfort women 300,000 *yen* (about USD$2,272). In this case, the district court found that the Japanese government had a duty to enact legislation to compensate the comfort women and that, by neglecting them for so many years, Japan had exacerbated their pain and committed new harm. Moreover, the court notes: "Upon examination of facts presented in this case, the comfort women system was extremely sexist and racist, disgraced women, trampled on racial pride, and can be seen as a violation of fundamental human rights relating to the core values expressed in Section 13 of the Japanese National Constitution."[36] This verdict, however, was overturned by the Hiroshima High Court on 26 March 2001. The Japanese courts' main arguments are: (1) that "any civil or criminal case concerning the Second World War rape centres would now be time-barred by applicable statute of limitations provisions"; (2) that individuals have no right to claim compensation from the state of Japan; and (3) that "any individual claims these victims may have had for compensation were fully satisfied by peace treaties and international agreements between Japan and other nations following the end of the Second World War."[37]

The Japanese government's nullification defence arguments have been repeatedly refuted by legal experts both in Japan and in the international legal community. As Special Rapporteur Radhika Coomaraswamy restates: "Statutes of limitations shall not apply in respect to periods during which no effective remedies exist for human rights violations. Claims relating to reparations for gross violations of human rights shall not be subject to a statute of limitations."[38] Furthermore, the Japanese government's argument that individual comfort women do not have the right to lay a claim against Japan cannot be upheld because, "by the late 1920s international law recognized that when a State injured the nationals of another State, it inflicted injury upon that foreign State and was therefore liable for damages to make whole the injured individuals," and that individuals are "subjects of rights conferred and duties imposed by international law."[39] As is shown in the cases summarized above, as the redress movement gathered force, even some Japanese courts rejected the arguments of the Japanese government.[40] Yet the official stance of the Japanese government is that Japan had settled its war compensation issues with China and other countries through the peace treaties that were signed after the war. For this reason it does not recognize that it has any legal obligations toward former comfort women.

Do the peace treaties it signed after the Second World War justify Japan's claim that it has adequately addressed its war compensation issues with neighbouring countries? When the Allied Powers worked out the San Francisco Peace Treaty in the fall of 1951, China and Korea were not invited, not only because the Allied Powers could not agree which government was the legitimate representative of these politically divided countries but also because of the political agendas of the treaty's designers.[41] Consequently, when the signatories of the treaty allocated Japanese compensation to the Allied POWs and the occupied countries, China and Korea, which had suffered longer than any other country under the Japanese, were not included. Japan later signed separate treaties with the Nationalist regime in Taiwan in 1952, the Republic of Korea in 1965,[42] and the People's Republic of China in 1972. The Sino-Japanese Peace Treaty that the Japanese government signed with Taiwan in 1952 does not include an article specifying war compensation, but it does state that all issues resulting from the war between the two countries should be resolved according to the San Francisco Peace Treaty. In turn, in Article 14, the San Francisco Peace Treaty specifically details Japan's compensation to the former Allied Powers, although it also includes a section waiving all claims not set forth in the treaty. Relying on this waiver section, the Japanese government argues that the Sino-Japanese Joint Communiqué (between Japan and the People's Republic of China) was signed on the understanding that the Sino-Japanese Peace Treaty of 1952 had already resolved the issue of war compensation and that the right of Chinese victims to claim such compensation had long been abandoned with the signing of that treaty.[43] However, concerning this argument, the McDougall report states:

> Although China is not a signatory to the 1951 peace treaty, the treaty does discuss China's rights vis-à-vis Japan following the war. Interestingly, the treaty states in article 21 that China is entitled to benefits under article 14 (a) (2), which sets forth the specific reparations owed by Japan, but does not state specifically that China is subject to the waiver provision in article 14 (b). Because the waiver does not apply to China, there is no basis for the Japanese Government to argue that the treaty bars Chinese nationals from seeking reparations from Japan.[44]

In refuting the Japanese government's arguments, Chinese researchers and legal experts made the following points: first of all, the San Francisco Peace Treaty has no binding effect on the People's Republic of China because it was not a signatory to the treaty. Moreover, the Sino-Japanese Peace Treaty was nullified when China and Japan signed the Joint Communiqué in 1972 because Article 2 of that communiqué states that the Government of Japan recognizes the Government of the People's Republic of China as the only legitimate government of China. It was under this condition that the diplomatic relationship between the two countries was normalized. Using the Sino-Japanese Peace Treaty as its defence, therefore, contradicts Japan's position as defined in the Sino-Japanese Joint Communiqué.[45]

Moreover, McDougall's final report states that, even though the San Francisco Peace Treaty contains a waiver section, "the Japanese government's attempt to escape liability through the operation of these treaties fails on two counts: (a) Japan's direct involvement in the establishment of the rape camps was concealed when the treaties were written, a crucial fact that must now prohibit on equity grounds any attempt by Japan to rely on these treaties to avoid liability; and (b) the plain language of the treaties indicate that they were not intended to foreclose claims for compensation by individuals for harm committed by the Japanese military in violation of human rights or humanitarian law."[46] In fact, in certain instances, the Government of Japan argues that the San Francisco Peace Treaty does not altogether negate the individual's right to claim compensation. For example, Kang Jian notes that, during the lawsuits involving Japanese nationals detained in Siberia and Japanese atomic bomb victims, the Japanese government stated that, with regard to seeking compensation from another nation, its position had always been that what was abandoned by the San Francisco Peace Treaty was not the individual right to claim but, rather, the government's right to claim on behalf of the individual.[47] Interestingly, however, when it comes to claims put forward by victims of war crimes committed by the Japanese military, the Japanese government offers a totally different interpretation of the treaty.[48]

While, since the rise of the redress movement, the Japanese government has been referring to the San Francisco Peace Treaty as evidence that compensation issues have already been settled, John Price's research reveals that, in 1951, the Japanese government recognized that the treaty could not extinguish the right of victims to claim compensation. According to diplomatic records that were declassified in 2000, the Dutch government refused to accept the proposal that the treaty would extinguish the rights of its citizens to seek redress, and it threatened to boycott the proceedings. In his letter to the Dutch government, Japan's prime minister Yoshida Shigeru stated that the peace treaty did "not involve the expropriation by each Allied government of the private claims of its nationals."[49] Price calls for concerned governments to work toward reconciliation by fully investigating the war claims of survivors and creating a supplementary pact that will allow justice to finally triumph.[50]

Although the Japanese courts denied the victims' claims for compensation, the litigation brought forward by the comfort women forced them to recognize Japan's wartime atrocities against women and to admit that the victims are still suffering. Through these lawsuits, the former comfort women's voices directly confronted and contradicted Japan's official narrative of the war, providing a powerful educational platform within the Japanese nation-state, where the dominant ideology had constructed an image of Japan as the liberator of Asia (which had hitherto been oppressed by Western colonialism) and as the real victim of the Second World War. Indeed, the comfort women's redress movement has had a significant impact on the "public memory" of the war both in Japan and in the rest of the world.[51]

Together with the war victims of other countries, the former Chinese comfort women also presented their cases to jurisdictions outside Japan and at international tribunals. On 18 September 2000, fifteen former comfort women from Korea, China, the Philippines, and Taiwan filed a class action lawsuit with the US District of Columbia Circuit Court in Washington, demanding a formal apology and compensation from the Japanese government. This was the first time the issue was addressed in the US courts.[52] Chinese survivors Zhu Qiaomei, Lu Xiuzhen, Guo Yaying, and Yuan Zhulin were among the plaintiffs, and Chen Lifei of the Research Center for Chinese "Comfort Women" acted as their representative. The comfort women's lawsuit received strong support from members of the US Congress and numerous lawyers, but the court sided with the Government of Japan, arguing that Japan was not subject to the jurisdiction of the US court.[53] On 4 October 2001, the court dismissed the comfort women's class action lawsuit.

In December 2000 another major event brought the issue of Japan's military sexual slavery to international attention. Organized by Asian women and human rights organizations, and supported by international NGOs, the Women's International War Crimes Tribunal on Japan's Military Sexual Slavery was held in Tokyo from 8 to 12 December. More than sixty survivors from the Asia-Pacific region gathered at the tribunal. Four legal experts of international renown served as judges: Gabrielle Kirk McDonald (United States), former president of the International War Crimes Tribunal on the Former Yugoslavia; Carmen Maria Argibay (Argentina), president of the International Women's Association of Judges; Christine Chinkin (United Kingdom), expert on gender and international law; and Willy Mutunga (Kenya), president of the Commission on Human Rights. Patricia Viseur Sellers, legal adviser for gender-related crimes in the Office of the Prosecutor for the International Tribunal for the former Yugoslavia and the Rwanda Tribunal, and Ustinia Dolgopol, professor of law, Flinders University, Australia, acted as the chief prosecutors. Specialists in the fields of history, post-traumatic stress disorder, and sexual violence served as expert witnesses.[54]

Eight regional teams of prosecutors presented cases on behalf of the surviving comfort women. Headed by Su Zhiliang, the delegation from Mainland China consisted of thirty-five members, including six surviving comfort women (Wan Aihua, Yuan Zhulin, Yang Mingzhen, He Chuangshu, Guo Xicui, and Li Xiumei)[55] and eight prosecutors (Zhou Hongjun, Gong Bohua, Su Zhiliang, Guan Jianqiang, Zhu Chengshan, Kang Jian, Chen Zuliang, and Chen Lifei).[56] During the first three days, testimonies were given by survivors, scholars, and two former Japanese soldiers who had committed sexual violence against women during the war. Because the Japanese government did not respond to the invitation, three Japanese lawyers acted as *amicus curiae* to explain its position. On 12 December 2000, the tribunal issued its preliminary judgment based on the evidence and testimonies presented before it, finding both the State of Japan and Emperor Hirohito guilty of war crimes and crimes against humanity. As the judgment was announced, lasting applause from the audience filled the meeting hall.

The Final Judgment of the tribunal was issued on 4 December 2001 in The Hague. The two-hundred-page judgment details the factual findings of the tribunal, citing laws applicable to the case, and finds the defendants accused in the Common Indictment guilty. Although the tribunal does not have the authority to execute the judgment, it expressed the unified voices of the survivors and their supporters, and it established the comfort women issue as a contemporary international human rights issue.[57] Scholars and legal experts also stress that the tribunal highlighted the demand to punish those responsible for the crimes of the Japanese military, including sexual slavery, something that had not been addressed by Japanese courts. As the McDougall Report reiterates, the cycle of impunity with regard to crimes of sexual violence committed during armed conflicts ensures that similar crimes recur today; the prosecution and punishment of those responsible for such crimes are essential both for the healing of the victims and for the prevention of similar incidents in the present and the future.[58] The tribunal's judgment, based on the principles of humanitarian law, contributed significantly to the development and application of humanitarian law in international legal practice. It has been referred to as the voice of the "international community" – a voice that, from the position of "universal justice,"[59] speaks against the Japanese government.

11   International Support

The Women's International Tribunal effectively increased the visibility of the issues related to comfort women as an item on the international political agenda. Since 2001, resolutions or recommendations urging the Government of Japan to accept full responsibility for its enslavement of comfort women have passed a number of parliaments of different countries and regions, including: the British Parliament, the South Korean National Assembly, the Philippine House of Representatives, the US Congress, the Dutch Parliament, the Canadian House of Commons, the European Parliament, and the Legislature of Taiwan. Yet Japanese government officials have continued their denial. When, in a clear and unequivocal manner, Michael Honda of the US House of Representatives proposed House Resolution 121 in January 2007 to urge Japan to accept historical responsibility for the comfort women issue, Prime Minister Abe Shinzō asserted that private agents, not the military itself, had coerced the women.[1] His foreign minister, Asō Tarō, also attacked the US resolution, saying that it was "not based on the facts."[2]

The Japanese government's denial served to enflame the worldwide movement for justice for comfort women. In the past decades activist organizations supporting the comfort women's redress movement have been formed in many countries and regions, including Korea, Japan, China, the Philippines, Indonesia, Taiwan, the Marshall Islands (and other Pacific Islands), Guam, Australia, New Zealand, the Netherlands, Germany, the United Kingdom, Canada, and the United States.[3] International networks have also been established, including the Washington Coalition for Comfort Women Issues,[4] the Global Alliance for Preserving the History of WWII in Asia,[5] and the International Solidarity Council Demanding Settlement of Japan's Past.[6] In commemoration of the 101st anniversary of the 1907 Hague Convention, the International Solidarity Council held its fifth conference in The Hague, Netherlands, from 2 to 4 October 2008. The members of the delegations included victims of Japanese wartime atrocities, activists, researchers, and lawyers from the Netherlands, South Korea, North Korea, Japan, Taiwan, the United States, Germany, Canada, England, and Ireland. In urging the

Figure 24 Chen Lifei (second from left), of the Research Centre for Chinese "Comfort Women," attending the funeral of "comfort station" survivor Lu Xiuzhen, who died on 24 November 2005.

Government of Japan to follow the example set by Germany in officially compensating both the countries and individuals victimized during the war, the resolution adopted by the conference also expressed deep concerns about the attitude of the Japanese cabinet members who would not recognize the past.[7]

In the absence of appropriate action by the Japanese government in response to the voices of the international community, supporters among Japanese legal experts and National Diet members sought legislative solutions to the issue. The proposal to seek a legislative solution was first raised in 1995 by the delegation of the Japan Federation of Bar Associations headed by Tsuchiya Kōken at the United Nations' Fourth World Conference on Women in Beijing. Tsuchiya Kōken later served as the president of the Association Seeking Resolution of the Comfort Women Issue through Legislation (Ianfu mondai no rippō kaiketsu o motomeru kai). Following this proposal, Motooka Shōji and a group of Democratic Party, Communist Party, and Social Democratic Party members of the National Diet jointly proposed to enact A Proposed Law for the Timely Resolution of the Issues Concerning the Victims of Wartime Forced Sexual Slavery *(Senji seiteki kyōsei higaisha mondai no kaiketsu no sokushin ni kansuru hōritsu [An])* in March 2001. The bill is based on two earlier proposals put forward by the Japanese Democratic Party and Communist Party members, respectively, the previous year. Since 2001, the proposal has several times been resubmitted to the Upper House. The 2008 version of the bill contains thirteen articles and an appendix. It recognizes Japan's responsibility as a state to restore the dignity of the women who were victimized by organized and continual military sexual violence, and it requires the government to take immediate and effective action to apologize and to compensate the victims. It urges the Japanese government to consult with the governments of the relevant nations and to conduct thorough investigations of the issue. Furthermore, it requires the government to set up a special legislative body and committee to oversee the process of policy making and enforcement, to make regular progress reports to the National Diet, to respect the human rights of the victims, and to make an effort to obtain the understanding and support of the people of Japan.[8] However, due to the opposition of conservative members, the proposal has been shelved and has not received any serious consideration in the Upper House.[9]

Two thousand and eleven marks the twentieth year since surviving Korean comfort women filed the first lawsuit against the Japanese government, and nearly half of the survivors who came forward to testify have since died (see Figure 24).[10] As the survivors die one by one, the Japanese government has been criticized for waiting for "what it calls a 'biological solution to the Comfort Women problem.'"[11] As of May 2012, only nine of the self-identified former Taiwanese comfort women are still alive, with their average age being eighty-seven. The Taipei Women's Rescue Foundation has continued to provide services and care for the aged women, including regular home visits, referrals to medical subsidy and homecare services, and group therapy workshops. The foundation is also working on the second documentary project to record the survivors' lives and is preparing for the opening of a comfort women's museum in Taiwan in 2014.[12] Racing against time, researchers and activists in Mainland China have been working on improving the lives of the survivors and documenting their wartime experiences. Since its establishment in 1999, the Research Center for Chinese "Comfort Women" has coordinated the efforts of NGOs nationwide as they research the lives of, and provide financial aid to, former Chinese comfort women. In order to increase international awareness of the Imperial Japanese Military's victimization of Chinese women, the centre hosted a series of international symposiums, the first of which was held in 2000. Beginning in 2000, the centre has been distributing monthly financial aid and medical assistance to individual survivors. Funding has been provided by private donors. From 2001 to 2007, a large

Figure 25 "Comfort station" survivor Tan Yuhua (sitting second from left) with history teachers from North America after giving a talk in July 2008 about her experience during the Japanese occupation.

portion of monthly aid was made possible through the Global Alliance for Preserving the History of WWII in Asia, a non-profit worldwide federation formed in 1994 and comprising over forty grassroots organizations. A total of fifty-seven Chinese comfort station survivors have received aid since 2000; as of 2013, only twenty-six are still alive. The aged survivors are all in poor health and are living in poverty. Unlike the survivors in Korea and Taiwan, who received financial aid from their own governments,[13] the former comfort women in Mainland China have received no special aid from the government, although a few of them receive a small amount of money from local welfare programs or pensions. Currently, since large donations are difficult to secure, the centre has relied on a small number of donations and on the savings of Su Zhiliang and Chen Lifei to continue to provide a small amount of monthly financial aid to each comfort station survivor in Mainland China.

Despite all the difficulties, support for the survivors from NGO groups kept increasing in China. In 2006, the All China Lawyers Association and the China Legal Aid Foundation launched the Committee for the Investigation of the Victimization of Former Chinese "Comfort Women" (Zhongguo yuan "weianfu" shouhai shishi diaocha weiyuanhui). To date, the committee has published three reports of its investigations.[14] Its new-found documentary evidence includes the confessions of fifty-seven captured Japanese military officers, police officers, and government officials concerning their direct involvement in setting up comfort stations and kidnapping, detaining, and raping Chinese women in such facilities in Anhui, Hubei, Jiangsu, Shanxi, Inner Mongolia, Manchuria, Shandong, Beijing, Tianjin, Hebei, Henan, Liaoning, Jilin, and Heilongjiang.[15] The committee's investigations also reveal that, after Japan's surrender in 1945, one Japanese unit left behind in Shanxi and renamed the "6th Security Brigade" (Baoan diliu dadui), affiliated with Yan Xishan's Nationalist force, continued perpetrating the comfort women system. This brigade notified Japanese soldiers still remaining in the area that they had established a comfort station in Taiyuan, Shanxi.[16] During the Japanese invasion an extremely large number of Japanese troops were stationed in China, but thus far very few of the former Japanese servicemen have come forward to speak about the imperial army's comfort women system. The records of the confessions of Japanese war criminals often focus on killing, while sexual violence and slavery are mentioned only in passing. As the investigation progresses in China, researchers hope to unearth more confessions pertaining to military sexual slavery.

At the same time, grassroots-initiated memorials became important sites for the commemoration of comfort women. After the 1998 establishment of the Museum of Sexual Slavery by Japanese Military in South Korea, the Women's Active Museum on War and Peace (WAM) opened in Tokyo in the summer of 2005, the sixtieth anniversary of the end of the Second World War. The museum was initiated by the late Matsui Yayori, the former chairperson of Violence Against Women in War – Network Japan (VAWW-NET Japan), and supported by Japanese citizens. Since its opening the museum has regularly held exhibitions and symposiums on the comfort women system and wartime sexual violence committed by the Japanese military. One of the latest exhibitions it co-sponsored with Japanese and Chinese NGOs – Panel Exhibition: Japanese Military Sexual Violence *(Nihongun seibōryoku paneruten)* – has been touring China. The executive committee of the panel exhibition, led by Ikeda Eriko (head of WAM), comprises Japanese citizen groups, scholars, and legal specialists. Since November 2009, five panel exhibitions have been held in Wuxiang, Beijing, Xi'an, Guangzhou, and Nanjing in China. The personal panels portraying the Chinese victims had a powerful impact on audiences and were reported by major Chinese media networks.

On 5 July 2007, which marks the seventieth anniversary of the beginning of China's Resistance War against Japan, the Chinese "Comfort Women" Archives opened at Shanghai Normal University. The archives, founded by history professor Su Zhiliang, preserve former Chinese comfort women's testimonials, research findings, video recordings, and historical relics from former comfort station sites. In the past decades, Su and Chinese researchers have been calling for the preservation of historical evidence of Japanese military comfort stations by establishing museums at their former sites, but this proposal has encountered difficulties. On 2 September 2010, after years of joint efforts by local people, researchers, and administration, China's first such museum, the Japanese Military Comfort Women System Atrocities Museum, opened at Dongjia-gou, Longling County, Yunnan Province. The museum was established at the Dong Family Compound *(Dongjia dayuan)*, which was seized by the Japanese army and turned into a comfort station during the Japanese occupation of Longling, from 1942 to 1944. The houses were left unoccupied after the Japanese troops withdrew. In 2005, the Dong family donated the compound to the local government and, at the request of local researcher Chen Zuliang and the Baoshan Committee of the China Zhi Gong Party,[17] it was designated a historic site. Longling Cultural Relics Bureau restored the dilapidated buildings with government funding and established the museum to commemorate the victims.[18]

Longling was an important fortress on the vital wartime supply line in China. According to the West Yunnan NGO Research Association for the Unresolved Issues of the Anti-Japanese War (Dianxi kang-Ri zhanzheng yiliu wenti minjian yanjiuhui), the Imperial Japanese Army's 56th Division occupied Longling County on 4 May 1942 and, within two weeks, set up a military comfort station at Zhen'an-jie Street. Reportedly, the first comfort station had four Burmese comfort women, and fighting among the soldiers took place frequently for the opportunity to use it. So, before the end of May, troops transported about a hundred comfort women from Taiwan and set up two more comfort stations at the Duan Clan Ancestor Temple and the Jesuit church in Longling County. Soon after that, the occupation army organized a puppet association for maintaining order and instructed it to submit six hundred local women to "comfort the Emperor's army." However, the association was unable to comply with this order because most local women had fled into the mountains to escape the invading troops. Japanese soldiers then went on mop-up missions in the surrounding mountains. They first raped the captured women and then detained them, setting up more comfort stations in sites such as the Dong Family Compound of Dongjia-gou, Longshanka, Baita, Pingjia, and Lameng. Besides local women, local people also saw Japanese and Korean women confined in these comfort stations.[19] The comfort station at the Dong Family Compound was in operation for two years, until the Chinese Expeditionary Army defeated the Japanese army at Longling on 3 November 1944 after five months of bloody fighting. What happened to the comfort women in this station when the Japanese forces withdrew remains unknown, although there have been reports that, in nearby Lameng Township and Tengchong County, Japanese troops forced Korean comfort women to take mercuric chloride, while they shot and killed Chinese comfort women.[20]

During the restoration of the buildings at the Dong Family Compound museum workers unearthed a large number of relics of the former comfort station, including Japanese medicine bottles, women's sandals, a toothbrush made in Japan, combs, lipsticks, pens, and a leather wallet embossed with Japanese words indicating that it was an award given by the "Military Government of the Great Manchuria Imperial State" (Dai Manshū teikoku gunseibu). Who had used and left these things in the comfort station? What happened to them during the war? The answers to these questions are forever buried in the dust of history, but the relics and the museum stand as a vivid reminder of the individual lives of the women who were raped, enslaved, tortured, and murdered.

Twenty years after the comfort station survivors broke their silence, museums and memorials commemorating the history of comfort women continue to proliferate. On 5 May 2012, the War and Women's Human Rights Museum opened in Seoul, and memorials, artwork, and websites memorializing the comfort women spread from Korea, Japan, and China to other countries in the world. In its introduction WAM writes: "The Women's Active Museum of War and Peace is a place where the reality of war crimes is recorded and kept for posterity. We come here to remember historical facts about 'comfort women,' and to listen to their stories. And we raise our voices and say, 'Never Again, anywhere in the world.'"[21] Despite the Japanese government's denial, the comfort women's stories have become part of the emerging transnational memory of the Second World War.

Epilogue

The two-story greyish buildings at Lane 125, Dong-Baoxing Road, Shanghai, don't attract any attention from passersby today, but to local residents they are important historic locations: eighty years ago these buildings housed Japan's first military comfort station, "Daiichi Saloon" (*Dayi shalong* in Chinese). Entering the compound one sees decrepit walls and stairways, where traces of a fire, which occurred in the 1990s and burned a flight of wooden stairs, are still visible. Rubble and trash lie scattered in the yard. The former dance hall, consisting of over fifty square metres on the right side of the ground floor, has been turned into small rooms. The passage connecting the three buildings is now a space with a shared kitchen and three small bathrooms. Only a few Japanese-style movable doors and wooden carvings of Japanese landscapes left in some of the rooms tell people of the buildings' wartime past.

Daiichi Saloon is one of the 164 sites of Japan's military comfort stations found in Shanghai in recent years. At most of those sites the buildings had been demolished during the urban development after the war, and the existing ones have atrophied due to lack of maintenance. The buildings of Daiichi Saloon were made into residential houses soon after Japan's defeat in 1945; currently about seventy families live here.[1] In order to preserve this historic site, Su Zhiliang and other Chinese researchers have appealed to the government to convert it into a museum, like those at the sites of Hiroshima and Auschwitz-Birkenau. Local authorities have agreed to the idea but claim to be stifled by lack of funds. Scholars from Europe and Japan who have visited the place have also suggested that a memorial museum be set up here to record the crimes of the Japanese army, but thus far nothing has been done. Funding such a project is certainly not easy since repairing the buildings would be expensive, as would relocating the current residents. However, researchers believe that it is not beyond the government's ability, given the nation's rapid economic growth in the past two decades. The real obstacle seems to be political concerns. According to *Global Times*, a press officer for the cultural department of Hongkou District said that, due to the sensitive nature of the matter, the museum would not be built in the near future.[2]

The situation concerning the museum at the Daiichi Saloon site is a microcosm of the socio-political memoryscape surrounding the comfort women issue in China: while, at the grassroots level, researchers and activists are struggling to commemorate the traumatic experiences of hundreds of thousands of military comfort women, authorities are held hostage to state politics and so avoid dealing with the issue. However, avoidance cannot heal the wounds of the past: on the contrary, it creates a void in social memory and leaves a space in which amnesia and narrow, nationalistic understandings of history take root and grow. True healing and reconciliation begin with the formation of a transnational memory of the traumas of the past.

One of the political concerns implied by the "sensitive nature of the issue" seems to be that the museum, by memorializing the traumas of the past, may harm the current diplomatic relationship between China and Japan. However, as demonstrated by the narratives of the Chinese survivors presented in this book, the stories of the comfort women are not simply about hatred and revenge. These women, whose very bodies were taken as war supplies, were tortured and exploited by the Japanese imperial forces. Then, when the war ended, they were discarded as shamed and useless by members of their own patriarchal society. Indeed, in China many of them were ignored, treated as collaborators with the enemy, or otherwise persecuted. Yet what the survivors remember and recount is not only suffering and anger but also humanity – no matter how little they themselves have received. We see in the stories that Wan Aihua, though gang-raped multiple times and nearly beaten to death by Japanese troops, never forgot the army interpreter who saved her from an officer's sword and the local people who helped her. "I didn't know if the interpreter was Japanese," Wan Aihua emphasized, "but I believe there were kind people in the Japanese troops, just as there are today, when many Japanese people support our fight for justice." We also hear Yuan Zhulin speak of her grateful feelings toward a Japanese officer. Yuan lost everything during the Japanese occupation: her first marriage was destroyed as the battle zone kept the couple apart; her father starved to death and her mother was driven away from her hometown; her only daughter died while she, Yuan, was detained in the military comfort station; and her body was violated and damaged, resulting in her inability to have a child. Despite all the sufferings the Japanese army inflicted on her, Yuan Zhulin recalls Nishiyama, a lower-ranking officer who not only treated her kindly but also helped other local Chinese people during the war. Yuan Zhulin was treated as "a whore working for the Japanese" in the postwar era and sent to do hard labour for seventeen years. At the time she was interviewed, political conditions in China had changed, but there was little room for the idea of affection between a Chinese comfort woman and a Japanese officer. It was with great courage and from a deep faith in humanity that Yuan Zhulin revealed her fondness for Nishiyama, saying that to this day she believes he was a kind person. The comfort women's stories teach us that the fundamentals of humanity transcend the boundaries of the nation-state. They force us to think deeply about what led to the atrocious behaviour of the Japanese troops and how to prevent such behaviour from reoccurring.

The wounds the war left on the bodies and hearts of the comfort women were so deep that, more than half a century later, in the 1990s, when Ishida Yoneko and a group of Japanese researchers first interviewed a comfort station survivor in Shanxi Province, she began to shake and to panic as soon as she heard the voice of a Japanese man. Only with the psychological support of local people and female researchers was she able to speak of her wartime experience as a comfort woman.[3] This difficulty in recalling the traumas of the past is experienced by all the survivors, and they experience it whenever they are re-interviewed. In order to minimize their distress in retelling their extremely painful wartime experiences, the researchers who collaborated in producing this book worked closely with local researchers in order to provide the survivors with the necessary psychological and physical support during each interview. By the time this book was written, the twelve women had been interviewed a number of times by different researchers, activists, and media reporters; and some of their testimonies had also been collected by legal experts for litigation against the Japanese government. While the interviews and legal investigations helped the women break their silence and provided them with a supportive space in which to recall their traumatic memories, the process also created a narrative structure, beginning with self-identification and ending with a call for justice. This structure may give the impression that the narrators' understanding of their experiences was influenced by interviewers and/or activists. This impression, whether accurate or not, should not be viewed negatively. Having little education and living in imposed silence for most of their lives, these women needed to be empowered through a larger socio-political discourse in order to overcome their fear, and they also needed a venue in which they could articulate and reframe their narratives. The international redress movement for comfort women provided this discourse and this venue. Yet each individual survivor's life story, as is evident in this book, is personal and unique.

By its very nature, memory is subjective and temporal, and it can present itself as partial and inconsistent. It is for this reason that the testimonies and memories of former comfort women have often been contested. It is true that, due to old age, wartime trauma, poor education, and the time lapse between the experience and the recounting of the experience, comfort station survivors may not be clear on dates and details surrounding past events. Wan Aihua, for example, due to head injuries suffered when she was beaten by Japanese soldiers, could not remember certain details of her abduction and torture. After her interview Su Zhiliang and Chen Lifei spoke to many local people, including Hou Datu, who witnessed Wan Aihua's abduction, to confirm the information obtained through the interview. All the narratives presented in this book were subjected to such verification. Since the abduction and enslavement of these women were witnessed by local people, their stories are verifiable. As the testimonies of former comfort women have frequently been denied due to the tenuous nature of memory, the Chinese survivors' narratives constitute a strong voice, and it asks: In the reconstruction of history, whose words count?

The Chinese comfort women's stories are painful to read, revealing, as they do, the darkest crimes on the spectrum of sexual violence carried out under the aegis of the military comfort women system. As the women's accounts show, the wanton murder of Chinese women and the brutal mutilation of their bodies was part of the sexual violence that occurred in the comfort stations throughout Japan's aggressive war in China. These atrocious acts cannot simply be explained by sexual starvation on the part of the troops or lack of discipline. They were politicized acts made possible within the context of war and the violent nature of imperialist conquest. This politicized and militarized mentality dehumanized Japanese military men, enabling them to perceive brutality toward enemy nationals as a necessary part of the war effort and as an expression of their loyalty to the emperor.

The symbolic nature of the bodily damage Japanese troops inflicted on comfort women may be seen in the imperial soldiers' testimonies. The recollections of Kondō Hajime, a former Japanese military man of the 13th Infantry Battalion of the 4th Independent Mixed Brigade, are a telling example. Kondō was sent to the battlefields in China in 1940, and his unit was stationed at Liao County, Shanxi Province, not far from Yu County, where survivors Yin Yulin and Wan Aihua were detained as military comfort women. Kondō recalled that the new recruits in his troops were trained to kill enemies with a bayonet by tying Chinese people to trees and using them as targets. When he was made to thrust his bayonet into a Chinese man, he did not feel that he was killing a living person. Kondō said this numbness toward killing came from the education soldiers received from childhood, which taught them that "Chankoro [a derogatory term for Chinese] are worse than pigs." In addition, the Imperial Japanese Army trained its troops to treat Chinese nationals as non-humans to whom they could do anything they wished.[4] Kondō witnessed and reported two revealing incidents of violence. One concerned the commander of his unit, Captain Maekawa, who had a village woman stripped naked and walk with the soldiers during a mopping-up action. The woman, who had been gang-raped by the troops on being captured, was holding a baby in her arms. As the unit was marching on a mountain ridge, a soldier grabbed the baby from the woman and threw the infant off the cliff. Following her baby, the woman threw herself over the cliff as well.[5] The other incident concerns Commander Yamamoto of the advance unit, who liked to cut local civilians with his sword. He ordered the soldiers to kill Chinese people by smashing their heads with large rocks. He said: "When killing Chinese people, using a gun would be inexcusable to our emperor. Use a rock instead!"[6] These two military commanders' acts demonstrate how raping and killing were seen as symbolic of imperial conquest and service to Imperial Japan: the body destroyed, tortured, raped, and humiliated was perceived as that of the nation of China. With the women's bodies transformed into the symbolic site of the enemy nation, their suffering was perceived by the Japanese troops as signifying the victory of the occupiers and the humiliation of the occupied. This political symbolism seriously increased Chinese women's suffering during the war.[7]

Tragically, the imperialist symbolism associated with the suffering bodies of Chinese women fuelled a prejudice, parading as nationalism, toward their suffering: their violated bodies were seen by many of their compatriots as signifying China's shame and the failure of its citizens to defend it. This reaction helps to explain why the suffering of Chinese comfort women was excluded from China's heroic postwar narrative for a long time. In fact, the few Chinese women who survived the torture of the comfort stations were not only silenced but also often treated, by the authorities and the public alike, as collaborators who served the nation's enemy.

This nationalistic prejudice combined with patriarchal ideology to demean the sufferings of the comfort women. According to this ideology, women had to be virgins before marriage and chaste thereafter. A woman who died resisting sexual violence was deemed a martyr, while one who survived was deemed shameful. The patriarchal requirement of feminine chastity was further politicized during the war, with the result that a comfort woman who serviced the enemy's troops, even though forced to do so, was regarded not only as immoral but also as disgracing the nation and her family. During the

Mao era, the nationalistic and patriarchal prejudices against former comfort women were transformed into political persecution when a series of political movements aimed at eradicating all dissidents labelled numerous innocent people "public enemies." Thus, the women who survived the brutality of the comfort stations were persecuted after the war. As is seen in the survivors' stories, Chen Yabian and Li Lianchun hid themselves in the mountains to escape harassment; Yuan Zhulin was exiled to do hard labour; and many of the women suffered from explicit or implicit ostracism. The continued suffering of the surviving Chinese comfort women reveals how social and political institutions joined together to prolong their victimization. Their stories teach us that the comfort women issue is not simply a historical matter: they pose a fundamental challenge to those contemporary institutions that have perpetuated their suffering.

The Chinese comfort women's narratives of their prewar lives expose how women were abused and maltreated by a male-dominated culture that regarded girls as unwanted goods and women as mere tools for producing offspring to ensure the continuation of the family line. As seen in Zhou Fenying's and Tan Yuhua's narratives about their mothers, in such a cultural environment a woman's personal identity was often ignored and her name forgotten; she was referred to either as the daughter of her parents or the wife of her husband. We also see that, in order to survive economic hardship, daughters of poor families were frequently abandoned or sold to be the "child-daughters-in-law" of richer families and that wives were divorced or discriminated against when they lost the ability to produce children. This patriarchal culture contributed to the life-long suffering of these women and made them easy prey for the violence of Japanese troops.

Commonly, rape has been considered a private, individualized experience of bodily violation.[8] To the contrary, the experience of the Chinese comfort women is highly politicized, first by Japan's imperialist war and then by China's patriarchal ideology and nationalistic politics. This politicization both increased their victimization during the war and prolonged it afterwards, causing a lifetime of suffering. Yet, as is seen in the stories in this book, these women demonstrate remarkable agency, which they sustained through wartime brutality and postwar persecution. Their life stories show that they were not mere sex slaves and victims but also historical actors and heroes. The escape stories of Lei Guiying, Lu Xiuzhen, Wan Aihua, Huang Youliang, and Li Lianchun, each filled with danger and accomplished through the courageous help of local people, portray the strength to resist violence and to overcome hardship. Such agency and strength is also demonstrated in the narratives of their postwar lives, a time when many of them were subjected to discrimination, ostracism, and poverty due to prejudice and political exigency. As Li Lianchun's daughter tells us, during the Cultural Revolution the people in a small mountain village all shunned Li Lianchun and her family. Not succumbing to this hardship, Li Lianchun worked in the fields day and night and single-handedly supported all three of her children through their schooling. In a place where many children were not able to complete their elementary education, this was a remarkable achievement. Wan Aihua, whose body was severely deformed by Japanese soldiers, suffered physical pain the rest of her life. Yet, in spite of her own suffering, over the years she offered free massage therapy to those who could not afford medical treatment. The resilience and humanity demonstrated by these women, who continued loving others even though they themselves were abused, is their most important legacy.

When this book was completed, Lei Guiying, Li Lianchun, Lu Xiuzhen, Yin Yulin, Yuan Zhulin, Zhou Fenying, and Zhu Qiaomei had all died. Tan Yuhua's health has been deteriorating rapidly since 2011, and Wan Aihua has been hospitalized. The other women are also suffering from poor health and the trauma induced by their torture in the comfort stations. Before Li Lianchun died, she said the following words in an interview in 2001:

> I've suffered my entire life, and I have been poor my whole life, but I have one thing that is priceless to me. That is my body, my dignity. My body is the most valuable thing to me. The damage done to it cannot be compensated for with money, no matter how much money they pay. I am not seeking money, and I am not trying to get revenge. I just want to see justice done.

Poignant words. Indeed, the voices and memories of the former comfort women constitute a legacy that has profound and far-reaching social, political, and cultural implications. When the rape of women is still used as an instrument of armed conflict and the sexual exploitation of women continues to be globally prevalent, the legacy of the comfort women plays an important role in the attempt to attain a more just and humane world. As more and more of the comfort women's individual memories become part of our collective memory, this legacy will continue to educate us as well as future generations, thus sustaining the transnational endeavour to prevent the occurrence of yet more crimes against humanity.

Notes

Foreword

1 Daisuke Shimizu, "'Comfort Women' Still Controversial in Japan, S. Korea," *Asahi Shimbun*, 14 July 2012. Available at ajw.asahi.com/ (viewed 30 July 2012).

2 Available at http://petitions.whitehouse.gov/ (viewed 6 June 2012).

3 Josh Rogin, "Japanese Comfort-Women Deniers Force White House Response," *Foreign Policy*, available at http://thecable.foreignpolicy.com/ (viewed 6 June 2012).

4 This point has been made by Timothy Brook, "Preface: Lisbon, Xuzhou, Auschwitz: Suffering as History," in *Beyond Suffering: Recounting War in Modern China*, ed., James Flath and Norman Smith (Vancouver: UBC Press, 2011), xviii.

Introduction

1 The "Chinese Comfort Women" in the title refers mainly to the narratives of former comfort women drafted from Mainland China. Information on comfort women drafted from Taiwan, then Japan's colony, has been published in English. See, for example, Nihon Bengoshi Rengōkai, *Investigative Report in Relation to Cases of Japan's Imperial Military "Comfort Women" of Taiwanese Descent* (Tokyo: Japan Federation of Bar Associations, 1997); Taipei Women's Rescue Foundation, "Comfort Women," available at http://www.twrf.org.tw/; and Yoshiaki Yoshimi, *Comfort Women: Sexual Slavery in the Japanese Military during World War II*, trans. Suzanne O'Brien (New York: Columbia University Press, 2000), 115-17.

2 For postwar/postcolonial publications on comfort women, see C. Sarah Soh, *The Comfort Women: Sexual Violence and Postcolonial Memory in Korea and Japan* (Chicago: University of Chicago Press, 2008), 145-73.

3 For survey and analysis of the controversy over the comfort women issue, see George Hicks, *The Comfort Women: Japan's Brutal Regime of Enforced Prostitution in the Second World War* (New York: W.W. Norton, 1994), 194-266; and Soh, *Comfort Women*, 29-77.

4 Ustinia Dolgopol and Snehal Paranjape, *Comfort Women: An Unfinished Ordeal* (Geneva, CH: International Commission of Jurists, 1994).

5 Linda Chavez, "Contemporary Forms of Slavery," working paper on systematic rape, sexual slavery, and slavery-like practices during wartime, including internal armed conflict, submitted in accordance with sub-commission decision 1994/109, UN Doc. E/CN.4/Sub.2/1995/38.1995; Radhika Coomaraswamy, *Report on the Mission to the Democratic People's Republic of Korea, the Republic of Korea and Japan on the Issue of Military Sexual Slavery in Wartime*, UN Doc. E/CN.4/1996/53/Add.1, 4 January 1996; and Gay J. McDougall, *Contemporary Forms of Slavery: Systematic Rape, Sexual Slavery and Slavery-Like Practices during Armed Conflict*, final report submitted to United Nations Commission on Human Rights, Sub-Commission on Prevention of Discrimination and Protection of Minorities, 50th Session, UN Doc. E/CN.4/Sub.2/1998/13, 22 June 1998. The three reports can be found under United Nations documents at http://www.unhchr.ch.

6 Dai Sil Kim-Gibson, *Silence Broken: Korean Comfort Women* (Parkersburg: Mid-Prairie Books, 2000); Sangmie Choi Schellstede, ed. *Comfort Women Speak: Testimony by Sex Slaves of the Japanese Military* (New York: Holmes and Meier, 2000); and Nelia Sancho, ed. *War Crimes on Asian Women: Military Sexual Slavery by Japan during World War II; The Case of the Filipino Comfort Women* (Manila: Asian Women Human Rights Council, 1998).

7 See, for example, Yoshimi, *Comfort Women* (English translation [2000] of the 1995 Japanese book); Hicks, *Comfort Women*; David A. Schmidt, *Ianfu: The Comfort Women of the Japanese Imperial Army of the Pacific War – Broken Silence* (Lewiston: Edwin Mellon Press, 2000); Margaret Stetz and Bonnie B.C. Oh, eds. *Legacies of the Comfort Women of World War II* (Armonk, NY: M.E. Sharpe, 2001); Yuki Tanaka, *Japan's Comfort Women: Sexual Slavery and Prostitution during World War II and the US Occupation* (New York: Routledge, 2002); and Soh, *Comfort Women*.

8 I have borrowed the term "memory change" from Carol Gluck's "Operations of Memory: 'Comfort Women' and the World," in *Ruptured Histories: War, Memory, and the Post-Cold War in Asia*, ed. Sheila Miyoshi Jager and Rana Mitter, 47-77 (Cambridge, MA: Harvard University Press, 2007). My discussion here is inspired by her work.

9 Hirofumi Hayashi, "Disputes in Japan over the Japanese Military 'Comfort Women' System and Its Perception in History," *Annals of American Academy of Political and Social Science* 617 (2008): 123-32.

10 For more detailed information on English publications on the subject, see Soh, *Comfort Women*, 46-56.

11 *Japan Times* online, 11 March 2007, available at http://www.japantimes.co.jp. For a summary of the disputes in Japan over the comfort women system, see Hayashi, "Disputes in Japan."

12 For major publications of this perspective, see Fujioka Nobukatsu, *Jigyakushikan no byōri* [An analysis of the masochistic views of history] (Tokyo: Bungeishunjū, 1997); and Hata Ikuhiko, *Ianfu to senjō no sei* [Comfort women and sex in the battlefield] (Tokyo: Shinchōsha, 1999).

13 Nicola Henry, *War and Rape: Law, Memory and Justice* (London: Routledge, 2011), 51.

14 Soh, *Comfort Women*, 235-36. The characterizations she quotes are from Yoshimi, *Comfort Women*, 66; and Tanaka, *Japan's Comfort Women*, 173.

15 Soh, *Comfort Women*, 235.

16 Ibid., xii-xiii.

17 A few cases of Dutch, Philippine, Indonesian, and Chinese comfort women are mentioned very briefly, but the author's arguments are based primarily on the experiences of Korean and Japanese comfort women.

18 Su Zhiliang, *Weianfu yanjiu* [A study of the comfort women] (Shanghai: Shanghai shudian chubanshe, 1999), 275-79.

19 Many researchers have revealed that the Japanese military destroyed its own documents at the end of the Second World War, including those concerning the operation of comfort stations. Among these researchers, Yoshimi Yoshiaki conducted extensive investigations in *Jūgun ianfu* (Tokyo: Iwanami shoten,1995). In his 1995 article, "Korean Women Drafted for Military Sexual Slavery by Japan," Chin Sung Chung also cites recently uncovered documents to demonstrate that the Japanese military not only secretly operated the comfort women system but also instructed soldiers to destroy records at the end of the war. See Keith Howard, ed., *True Stories of the Korean Comfort Women* (New York: Cassell, 1995), 11. For evidence of the murder of Chinese comfort women by the Japanese military at the end of the war, see Part 1 of this book.

20 Diana Lary and Stephen MacKinnon, eds. *Scars of War: The Impact of Warfare on Modern China* (Vancouver: UBC Press, 2001), 3-4.

21 An abbreviated term for the Great Proletarian Cultural Revolution, a political movement initiated by the leader of the CCP, Mao Zedong, from 1966 to 1976. The political power struggles between rival factions during the movement brought the whole nation into social and economic chaos. Tens of thousands of people were persecuted, abused, or died, and Chinese people have since referred to the movement as "ten years of catastrophe" *(shinian haojie)*.

22 For a brief summary of the varied estimations of the numbers of comfort women, see Yoshimi, *Jūgun ianfu*, 78-81; Hata, *Ianfu to senjō no sei*, 397-407; and Soh, *Comfort Women*, 23-24. Yoshimi reports an estimated range of between 50,000 to 200,000.

23 Su Zhiliang, *Weianfu yanjiu*, 275-79.

24 Cited in Yuma Totani, *The Tokyo War Crimes Trial: The Pursuit of Justice in the Wake of World War II* (Cambridge: Harvard University Asia Center, 2008), 126-27.

25 See, for example, Kasahara Tokushi, "Chūgoku sensen ni okeru Nihongun no seihanzai: Kahokushō, Sanseishō no jirei" [The Japanese army's sexual crimes at the frontlines in China: The cases of Hebei and Shanxi Provinces], *Sensō sekinin kenkyū* [Studies of war responsibilities] 13 (1996): 2-11; and Su Zhiliang, Rong Weimu, and Chen Lifei, eds., *Taotian zuinie: Erzhan shiqi de Rijun weianfu zhidu* [Monstrous atrocities: The Japanese military comfort women system during the Second World War] (Shanghai: Xuelin chubanshe, 2000).

26 These statistics are based on Su Zhiliang's record and do not include cases recorded by other Chinese researchers and institutions.

27 Tomishima Kenji, "Inu" [Dog], in *Sankō: Kanzenban* [The three alls: A complete collection], comp., Chūgoku kikansha renrakukai, 102-8 (Tokyo: Banseisha, 1984).

28 Soh, *Comfort Women*, 117.

29 Yoshimi, *Jūgun ianfu*, 74.

30 Tanaka, *Japan's Comfort Women*, 18-19.

31 Soh, *Comfort Women*, 117-32.

32 Ibid., 117-18.

33 Ibid., 118 and 134.

34 Ibid., 235-36.

35 One of the cases, for example, is reported by Guan Wenhua, "Rijun dui Beipiao funü de lingru" [Japanese troops' sexual violence against women in Beipiao], in *Qin-Hua Rijun baoxing zonglu* [Collection of investigative records of the atrocities committed by the Japanese forces during Japan's invasion of China], ed. Li Bingxin, Xu Junyuan, and Shi Yuxin, 69 (Shijiazhuang: Hebei renmin chubanshe, 1995).

36 Su Zhiliang's investigative record. See also Wang Yufeng, "Scholars Propose Memorializing 'Comfort Stations': The Ravages of Time," *Global Times*, 22 September 2011.

37 Fu Heji, "Qin-Qiong Rijun 'weianfu' shilu" [The reality of the Japanese military "comfort women" in Hainan], in Su et al., *Taotian zuinie*, 188. The article was originally published in *Kang-Ri Zhanzheng yanjiu*, 1996 (4): 34-50.

38 For more detailed information on the conditions in which Chinese comfort women were confined, see Part 1 of this book.

39 Soh, *Comfort Women*, xvi.

40 A political advisory body in China, which consists of delegates from a range of political parties and organizations as well as independent members.

41 Zhang Jiliang, "Weishan Hong: Wei Zhongguo zhanzheng shouhaizhe daili susong 40 nian" [Oyama Hiroshi: Forty years of representing Chinese war victims' litigations] *Renmin ribao haiwaiban*, 7 July 2005.

Chapter 1: Japan's Aggressive War and the Military "Comfort Women" System

1 Mark R. Peattie, "The Dragon's Seed: Origins of the War," in *The Battle for China: Essays on the Military History of the Sino-Japanese War of 1937-1945*, ed. Mark Peattie, Edward J. Drea, and Hans van de Ven (Stanford: Stanford University Press, 2011), 48-78.

2 Yoshihisa Tak Matsusaka, *The Making of Japanese Manchuria (1904-1932)* (Cambridge: Harvard University Asia Center, 2001), 1-16.

3 Peattie, "Dragon's Seed," 66.

4 Matsusaka, *Making of Japanese Manchuria*, 381-87.

5 Peattie, "Dragon's Seed," 66-67. See also, Ienaga Saburō, *The Pacific War: World War II and the Japanese, 1932-1945* (New York: Pantheon Books, 1978), 65.

6 Peattie, "Dragon's Seed," 67.

7 Ibid., 67.

8 Zhang Xianwen, *Zhongguo kang-Ri zhanzhengshi* [A history of China's resistance war against Japan] (Nanjing: Nanjing daxue chubanshe, 2001), 92-105.

9 Guan Wenhua, "Rijun dui Beipiao funü de lingru" [Japanese troops' sexual violence against women in Beipiao], in *Qin Hua Rijun baoxing zonglu* [Collection of investigative records of the atrocities committed by the Japanese forces during Japan's invasion of China], ed. Li Bingxin, Xu Junyuan, and Shi Yuxin (Shijiazhuang: Hebei renmin chubanshe, 1995) 69.

10 Ibid.

11 Ibid.

12 For a survey of the Chinese wartime publications on Japanese military sexual violence against Chinese women during the war, see Egami Sachiko, "Rijun funü baoxing he zhanshi Zhongguo funü zazhi" [Japanese military's violence against women and wartime Chinese women's magazines] in *Taotian zuinie: Erzhan shiqi de Rijun weianfu zhidu* [Monstrous atrocities: The Japanese military comfort women system during the Second World War], ed. Su Zhiliang, Rong Weimu, and Chen Lifei (Shanghai: Xuelin chubanshe, 2000), 56-70.

13 Timothy Brook, *Collaboration: Japanese Agents and Local Elites in Wartime China* (Cambridge, MA: Harvard University Press, 2005), 23-24.

14 Besides the evidence recorded in the Chinese source cited above, Korean survivor Ch'oe Il-rye's testimony also dates the establishment of Japanese military comfort stations in the Manchuria area to 1932. See Sarah Soh, *The Comfort Women: Sexual Violence and Postcolonial Memory in Korea and Japan* (Chicago: University of Chicago Press, 2008), 125.

15 Based on the reliable documents discovered and the field investigations conducted since the 1990s, several researchers have concurred that the earliest comfort stations were set up by the Japanese imperial military in Shanghai. See, for example, George Hicks, *The Comfort Women: Japan's Brutal Regime of Enforced Prostitution in the Second World War* (New York: W.W. Norton, 1994), 45-49; Chin Sung Chung, "Korean Women Drafted for Military Sexual Slavery by Japan," in *True Stories of the Korean Comfort Women: Testimonies Compiled by the Korean Council for Women Drafted for Military Sexual Slavery by Japan and the Research Association on the Women Drafted for Military Sexual Slavery by Japan,* ed. Keith Howard, trans. Young Joo Lee (London: Cassell, 1995), 13-15; Yoshimi Yoshiaki, *Jūgun ianfu* [Military comfort women] (Tokyo: Iwanami shoten, 1995), 14-19; Su Zhiliang, *Weianfu yanjiu* [A study of the comfort women] (Shanghai: Shanghai shudian chubanshe, 1999), 23-40; Yuki Tanaka, *Japan's Comfort Women: Sexual Slavery and Prostitution during World War II and the US Occupation* (New York: Routledge, 2002), 8-12. The Korean survivors' testimony and evidence in China also indicate that comfort facilities were set up in the Manchurian area around the same time. See Soh, *Comfort Women*, 125.

16 Morisaki Kazue, *Karayuki san* [Overseas prostitutes] (Tokyo: Asahi shimbunsha, 1976), 92.

17 Su, *Weianfu yanjiu*, 24.

18 Ibid., 24.

19 "Shōwa jūsannenjū ni okeru zairyū hōjin no tokushu fujo no jōkyō oyobi sono torishimari narabi ni sokai tōkyoku no shishō torishimari jōkyō," in *Jūgun ianfu shiryōshū* [A collection of documents on military comfort women], ed. Yoshimi Yoshiaki, 184-85 (Tokyo: Ōtsuki shoten, 1992).

20 For more detailed discussion of this point, see, Chin-Sung Chung, "Wartime State Violence against Women of Weak Nations; Military Sexual Slavery Enforced by Japan during World War II," *Korean and Korean American Studies Bulletin* 5 15, 2-3 (1994): 16-17; Yoshimi, *Jūgun ianfu*, 18-19; and Tanaka, *Japan's Comfort Women*, 10-12.

21 Su, *Weianfu yanju*, 31-34.

22 Ibid., 30.

23 Okabe Naozaburō, *Okabe Naozaburō taishō no nikki* [General Okabe Naozaburō diary] (Tokyo: Fuyō shobō, 1982), 23. Cf. See also the translation of this passage in Yoshimi, *Comfort Women*, 45.

24 Inaba Masao, ed., *Okamura Yasuji taishō shiryō: Senjō kaisō hen, jō* [Sources of General Okamura Yasuji: Recollections of the battlefield, vol. 1] (Tokyo: Hara shobō, 1970), 302. Many scholars have discussed why Okamura chose to draft comfort women from Nagasaki and suggested that this had to do with the history of the area. Nagasaki was known as the hometown of a large number of *karayuki-san*, women of poor families who had been sold to overseas brothels or had worked as indentured prostitutes in many Asian countries since the Meiji period. See, for example, Yoshimi, *Jūgun ianfu*, 45; Su, *Weianfu yanjiu*, 23-40; Tanaka, *Japan's Comfort Women*, 10.

25 Yoshimi Yoshiaki, "Jūgun ianfu to Nihon kokka" [Military comfort women and the Japanese nation-state], in *Jūgun ianfu shiryōshū* [A collection of documents on military comfort women] (Tokyo: Otsuki shoten, 1992), 28-50.

26 Translation of this title follows Suzanne O'Brien's translation of Yoshimi, *Comfort Women*, 58. The discussion here also owes much to O'Brien's translation.

27 Yoshimi, *Jūgun ianfu shiryōshū*, 105-6.

28 Ibid.

29 Yang Tianshi, "Chiang Kai-shek and the Battles of Shanghai and Nanjing," in Peattie et al., *Battle for China*, 143.

30 Zhang, *Zhongguo kang-Ri zhanzheng shi*, 229-58.

31 Yang, "Chiang Kai-shek," 146.

32 Ibid., 147.

33 Edward J. Drea and Hans van de Ven, "An Overview of Major Campaigns during the Sino-Japanese War, 1937-1945," in Peattie et al., *Battle for China*, 31.

34 Ibid.

35 Ibid.

36 Many books and research articles have detailed the atrocities committed by the Japanese forces in and around Nanjing at this time. See, for example, John Rabe, *The Good Man of Nanking: The Diaries of John Rabe* (New York: Knopf Publishing Group, 1998); Hora Tomio, *Nankin daigyakusatsu: Ketteihan* [Nanjing massacre: An authoritative edition (Tokyo: Gendaishi shuppankai, 1982); Nankin jiken chōsa kenkyū kai, ed., *Nankin jiken shiryōshū* [Documents on the Nanjing incident] (Tokyo: Aoki Shoten, 1992); Iris Chang, *The Rape of Nanking: The Forgotten Holocaust of World War II* (New York: Penguin Group, 1998); Honda Katsuichi, *The Nanjing Massacre: A Japanese Journalist Confronts Japan's National Shame* (London: M.E. Sharpe, 1999); Yang Daqing, "Atrocities in Nanjing: Searching for Explanations," in *Scars of War: The Impact of Warfare on Modern China*, ed. Diana Lary and Stephen MacKinnon (Vancouver: UBC Press, 2001), 76-96; and Suping Lu, *They Were in Nanjing: The Nanjing Massacre Witnessed by American and British Nationals* (Hong Kong: Hong Kong University Press, 2004). On the other hand, conservatives and nationalists in Japan have denied the occurrence of the Nanjing Massacre. For a detailed study of the debate, see Takashi Yoshida, *The Making of the "Rape of Nanking": History and Memory in Japan, China, and the United States* (Oxford: Oxford University Press, 2006).

37 Chinese sources generally estimate that more than 300,000 Chinese citizens and unarmed soldiers were killed during the massacre. A newly unearthed document in the US archives reveals that William Edward Dodd, the US ambassador in Germany, reported in his telegram to the president of the United States on 14 Dcember 1937 that Shigenori Tōgō, a Japanese ambassador in Germany, said the Japanese army had killed 500,000 Chinese people. See Yuan Xinwen, "Nanjing datusha zai tian tiezheng" [New evidence of the Nanjing massacre], *Renmin ribao,* 6 December 2007.

38 HyperWar Foundation, "HyperWar: International Military Tribunal for the Far East," IMTFE Judgement (English Translation), Chapter 8, "Conventional War Crimes (Atrocities)," 1015. Available at http://ibiblio.org/ (viewed 26 April 2008).

39 Ibid., 1012. The Chinese Nationalist government's investigation indicated a much larger number, determining that approximately eighty-thousand Chinese women were raped during the Nanjing massacre. See Zhu Chengshan, "Nanjing datusha shi Rijun dui renlei wenming shehui de jiti fanzui," [Japanese army's collective crimes against humanity during the Nanjing massacre], in *Taotian zuinie: Erzhan shiqi de Rijun weianfu zhidu* [Monstrous atrocities: The Japanese military comfort women system during the Second World War], ed. Su Zhiliang, Rong Weimu, and Chen Lifei (Shanghai: Xuelin chubanshe, 2000), 128.

40 Rabe, *Good Man of Nanking,* 81. Format as it is published.

41 Yoshimi, *Jūgun ianfu shiryōshū,* 210.

42 According to the Japanese military codes, those who committed rape would be punished, receiving a sentence ranging from seven years imprisonment to death. See Yuma Totani, *The Tokyo War Crimes Trial: The Pursuit of Justice in the Wake of World War II* (Cambridge: Harvard University Asia Center, 2008), 120.

43 Aiko Utsumi, "How the Violence against Women Were Dealt with in War Crime Trials," in *Common Grounds: Violence against Women in War and Armed Conflict Situations* (Quezon: Asian Center for Women's Human Rights, 1998), 191.

44 Totani, *Tokyo War Crimes Trial,* 120. See also, Eguchi Keiichi, *Jūgonen sensō shōshi* [A history of the fifteen-year war] (Tokyo: Aoki shoten, 1986), 117; Kasahara Tokushi, *Nankin jiken* [The Nanjing incident] (Tokyo: Iwanami shoten, 1997), 191-200.

45 Yoshimi, *Jūgun ianfu,* 23.

46 Nankin jiken chôsa kenkyûkai, ed., *Nankin jiken shiryō shū,* [Documents on the Nanjing incident] (Tokyo: Aoki shoten, 1992), 411; cited and translated by Tanaka in *Japan's Comfort Women,* 13.

47 Jiang Gonggu, *Xian jing sanyue ji* [The fall of the capital: A journal of the three months], private publication, August 1938. Reprint: (Nanjing: Nanjing chubanshe, 2006), 14-24.

48 Susan Brownmiller, *Against Our Will: Men, Women and Rape* (New York: Simon and Schuster, 1975), 58.

49 Li Shimin, "Qiao Hongnian choushe weiansuo" [Qiao Hongnian prepared and set up comfort stations], *Dadi zhoubao* [Land weekly] 31 (1946): 2.

50 Chen Juan, "Nanjing Rijun 'weianfu' zhidu de shishi" [The implementation of the Japanese military "comfort women" system in Nanjing], in Su et al., *Taotian zuinie,* 157-58.

51 Jing Shenghong, "Qin-Hua Rijun zai Nanjing shishi 'weianfu' zhidu shimo" [The Japanese invaders' implementation of the "comfort women" system in Nanjing] in Su et al., *Taotian zuinie,* 166-67.

52 Chen Juan, "Nanjing Rijun," in Su et al, *Taotian zuinie,* 158.

53 Yoshimi, *Jūgun ianfu,* 25.

54 Yoshimi, *Jūgun ianfu shiryōshū,* 195-96.

55 Many researchers have made this observation. See, for example, Senda Kakō, *Jūgun ianfu* [Military comfort women] (Tokyo: Kōdansha, 1984), 72-76; Chin Sung Chung, "Korean

Women Drafted for Military Sexual Slavery by Japan," in *True Stories of the Korean Comfort Women*, ed. Keith Howard (London: Cassell, 1995), 16-17.

56 After the outbreak of the Pacific War, women from other Asian-Pacific regions, including the Philippines, Singapore, Thailand, Indonesia, East Timor, Malaya, Burma, and Vietnam, were also forced to be comfort women for the Japanese military.

57 Asō Tetsuo, *Shanhai yori Shanhai e: Heitan byōyin no sanfujinkai* [From Shanghai to Shanghai: A gynecologist at the commissariat hospital] (Fukuoka: Sekifūsha, 1993), 215.

58 Yoshimi, *Jūgun ianfu shiryōshū*, 183-84, and 258-68.

59 Hokushi keimubu, "Hōjin shokugyōbetsu jinkō tōkeihyō" [Statistics of population by occupations in northern China], 1 July 1939, in Gaimushō gaikō shiryōkan [Foreign Ministry Diplomacy Archive]; cited in Yoshimi, *Jūgun ianfu*, 30-31.

60 Yoshimi, *Jūgun ianfu shiryōshū*, 214-15.

61 Kinbara Setsuzō, "Rikugunshō gyōmu nisshi tekiroku" [Excerpts from the work logs of the Department of the Army], entry for 15 April 1939, kept in Bōeichō Bōei kenkyūjo toshokan. Cited in Yoshimi, *Jūgun ianfu*, 32.

62 Shanghaishi City Archive, document no. R36, *Quanzong 1 hao mulu*. For detailed information, see Chen Zhengqin and Zhuang Zhiling, "Dang'an zhong faxian de youguan Shanghai Rijun 'weianfu' wenti" [Newly discovered archival evidence of the Japanese military 'comfort women' in Shanghai], in Su et al., *Taotian zuinie*, 110-22.

63 Su Zhiliang, Chen Lifei, and Yao Fei, *Shanghai Rijun weiansuo shilu* [Investigative records of Japanese military comfort stations in Shanghai] (Shanghai: Shanghai sanlian shudian, 1995), 2-3.

64 The Third Report of Committee on the Investigation of the Victimization of Former Chinese Comfort Women, published on All China Lawyers Association website, www.ACLA.org (viewed on 30 June 2010).

65 "Shanghai de diyu – Dikou xinglesuo" [A hell in Shanghai – the enemy's entertainment facility] in *Dagongbao*, 27 February 1938, cited in Li Xiuping, *Shiwan weianfu* [One hundred thousand comfort women] (Beijing: Renmin Zhongguo chubanshe, 1993), 34.

66 Gao Xingzu, "Rijun Nanjing qiangjian shijian yu weiansuo de chuxian" [The rapes committed by Japanese forces in Nanjing and the establishment of the comfort stations], in Su et al., *Taotian zuinie*, 123-26.

67 Su, *Weianfu yanjiu*, 124-30.

Chapter 2: The Mass Abduction of Chinese Women

1 This summary of these battles is based on Edward J. Drea and Hans van de Ven, "An Overview of Major Military Campaigns during the Sino-Japanese War, 1937-1945." In *The Battle for China: Essays on the Military History of the Sino-Japanese War of 1937-1945*, ed. Mark Peattie, Edward J. Drea, and Hans van de Ven (Stanford: Stanford University Press, 2011), 33-35.

2 The war resulted in enormous casualties in China, for which there is no accurate number, although figures of between 20 million and 30 million are widely used. See Stephen R. MacKinnon, Diana Lary, and Ezra Vogel, eds. *China at War: Regions of China, 1937-1945* (Stanford: Stanford University Press, 2007), 1-2. China's official statistics for the total Chinese civilian and military casualties during the Japanese invasion from 1937 to 1945 are about 35 million: 20 million dead and 15 million wounded. See Guo Rugui, Huang Yuzhang, and Tian Zhaolin, *Zhongguo kang-Ri zhanzheng zhengmian zhanchang zuozhan ji* [Major battles during China's Resistance War] (Nanjing: Jiangxu renmin chubanshe, 2001), 31.

3 Complete statistics on Chinese forced labour during the Japanese invasion are not available. According to the Japanese Foreign Ministry Report, beginning in April 1943, as the draft had resulted in severe labour shortages, 38,935 Chinese men between the ages of

eleven and seventy-eight were brought to Japan to advance Japan's war effort by performing harsh physical labour in mines and on construction sites and docks from Kyūshū to Hokkaidō. Within barely two years, 17.5 percent of them had died. Some individual worksites posted death rates in excess of 50 percent. The official fatality figure of 6,830 excludes the thousands of victims who died in China during detention or while trying to escape prior to reaching the coast. See William Underwood, "Chinese Forced Labor, the Japanese Government and the Prospects for Redress," *Asia-Pacific Journal: Japan Focus,* available at http://www.japanfocus.org/ (viewed 2 July 2010).

4 Sakurada Takeshi and Shikanai Nobutaka, *Ima akasu sengo hishi,* vol. 1 [A secret postwar history now revealed] (Tokyo: Sankei shuppan, 1983), 40-41, cited in Yoshimi Yoshiaki, *Jūgun ianfu* [Military comfort women] (Tokyo: Iwanami shoten, 1995), 37.

5 It was believed that the term came from the pronunciation of "p" in "prostitute." Another explanation is that it was an imitation of the sound of a Chinese slang word for female genitals.

6 Senda Kakō, *Jūgun ianfu* [Military comfort women] (Tokyo: Kōdansha, 1984), 72-76. The military physician Asō Tetsuo, who conducted medical examinations of the comfort women at Yangjiazhai comfort station, wrote: "The special military comfort station is not a place for hedonistic pleasure; it is a hygienic public toilet." See Asō Tetsuo, *Shanhai yori Shanhai e: Heitan byōin no sanfujinkai* [From Shanghai to Shanghai: A gynecologist at the commissariat hospital] (Fukuoka: Sekifūsha, 1993), 222.

7 Senda, *Jūgun ianfu,* 73-74. The former Japanese soldiers' testimonies cited in Nishino Rumiko's *Jūgun ianfu: Moto heishi tachi no shōgen* [Military comfort women: Testimonies of former soldiers] (Tokyo: Akashi Shoten, 1992), 34 and 42-60, attest to the same fact.

8 Yoshimi, *Jūgun ianfu,* 22.

9 Chen Lifei, *Rijun weianfu zhidu pipan* [A critical analysis of the Japanese military comfort women system] (Beijing: Zhonghua shuju, 2006), 202.

10 *Dagong bao,* 27 February 1938.

11 Jiang Hao, *Zhaoshi: Zhongguo weianfu – kuaguo kuashidai diaocha baipishu* [Exposé: Chinese comfort women – An investigation across the boundaries of nations and times] (Xining: Qinghai renmin chubanshe, 1998), 172-88.

12 This estimated figure is used in Chinese, Japanese, and Western sources. See, for example, Zhang Xianwen, chief compiler, *Zhongguo kang-Ri zhanzheng shi* [A history of China's resistance war against Japan] (Nanjing: Nanjing daxue chubanshe, 2001), 25 and 1263-64; and "Second Sino-Japanese War," *New World Encyclopedia,* available at http://www.newworldencyclopedia.org/ (viewed 11 July 2010). Hata Ikuhiko also indicates that Japan had 1,980,000 military personnel in China and the pacific region in December 1941 and that this number had reached 3,240,000 by the end of the war (the majority of these were in China). See Hata Ikuhiko, *Ianfu to senjō no sei* [Comfort women and sex in the battlefield] (Tokyo: Shinchōsha, 1999), 401. In assessing the total number of women victimized by the Japanese military comfort stations, Korean and Japanese scholars have estimated the total number of Japanese soldiers at roughly 3,000,000.

13 Yoshimi, *Jūgun ianfu,* 78-81.

14 Senda, *Jūgun ianfu,* 119-20. Yuki Tanaka arrives at a slightly different figure of 800,000 as the number of soldiers involved during the Guangdong Army Special Manoeuvre. See Yuku Tanaka, *Japan's Comfort Women: Sexual Slavery and Prostitution during World War II and the US Occupation* (New York: Routledge, 2002), 18.

15 Yoshimi Yoshiaki, comp., *Jūgun ianfu shiryōshū* [A collection of documents on military comfort women] (Tokyo: Ōtsuki Shoten, 1992), 83.

16 Kim Il-myon, *Tennō no guntai to Chōsenjin ianfu* [The emperor's forces and the Korean comfort women] (Tokyō: Sanichi shobō, 1976), 50.

17 Hata, *Ianfu to senjō no sei,* 405.

18 Yoshimi, *Jūgun ianfu shiryōshū*, 83.

19 Su Zhiliang, *Weianfu yanjiu* [A study of the comfort women] (Shanghai: Shanghai shudian chubanshe, 1999), 277-79.

20 Li Xiuping, *Shiwan weianfu* [One hundred thousand comfort women] (Beijing: Renmin Zhongguo chubanshe, 1993), 6-7.

21 Su, *Weianfu yanjiu*, 278.

22 Wen Yan, "Anhui Rijun 'weiansuo,'" in Li Bingxin, Xu Junyuan, and Shi Yuxin, eds. *Qin-Hua Rijun baoxing zonglu* [Collection of investigative records of the atrocities committed by the Japanese forces during Japan's invasion of China] (Shijiazhuang: Hebei renmin chubanshe, 1995), 742-43.

23 Fu Heji, "Qin-Qiong Rijun 'weianfu' shilu," in *Taotian zuinie: Erzhan shiqi de Rijun weianfu zhidu* [Monstrous atrocities: The Japanese military comfort women system during the Second World War], ed. Su Zhiliang, Rong Weimu, and Chen Lifei (Shanghai: Xuelin chubanshe, 2000), 194-95.

24 For Philippine comfort women's experiences, see, for example, Maria Rosa Henson's memoir, *Comfort oman: A Filipina's story of prostitution and slavery under the Japanese military* (Lanham, MD: Rowman and Littlefield, 1999).

25 Mrs. Andrew Levinge's testimony, submitted to the International Tribunal for the Far East, Ex. 1590, 5089B. Published in Yoshimi Yoshiaki (editor-in-chief), Utsumi Aiko, Udagawa Kōta, Takahashi Shigehito, and Tsuchino Mizuho, eds. *Tōkyō saiban: Seibōryoku kankei shiryō* [Tokyo trial: Documents regarding sexual violence]. (Tokyo: Gendai shiryō shuppan, 2011), 183-86.

26 Wu Liansheng (narrator), Lin Liangcai, Liang Chuntian, and Fu Heji (recorders), "Chuguan beige hongyan xuelei: Rijun Nada weiansuo qindu ji" [Tragic stories of the suffering women: The Japanese military Nada comfort station I witnessed], in *Tietixiade xingfeng xueyu: Rijun qin-Qiong baoxing shilu, Xu* [Sequel to Bloody crimes of the occupation rule: Records of the atrocities committed by the Japanese military in Hainan], ed. Fu Heji, 272-79 (Hainan: Hainan chubanshe, 1995). Hereafter Fu, *TXXX*.

27 Li Qin, "Xin faxian de Rijun qiangzheng Tianjin funü chongdang 'weianfu' shiliao xi" [An analysis of the newly discovered historical documents relating to the Japanese military forcing Tianjin women to be "comfort women"], in Su et al., *Taotian zuinie*, 639.

28 Ibid.

29 "Jin Ji Lu Yu bianqu banian kang-Ri zhanzheng zhong renmin zaoshou sunshi diaocha tongji biao" [Statistics based on the investigations of civilian damages during the eight-year resistance war against Japanese forces at the Jin Ji Lu Yu border region] (January 1946), preserved in Hebei Province Archives, Quanzong-hao 576, Mulu-hao 1, Anjuan-hao 31, Jian-hao 3, cited in He Tianyi, "Lun Rijun zai Zhongguo Huabei de xingbaoli" [The Japanese military's sexual violence in northern China], in Su et al., *Taotian zuinie*, 255.

30 "Diren zai Huabei de baoxing," in Central Archives of China (Zhongyang Danganguan), Document 190, published in Zhongyang Danganguan, Zhongguo Dier Lishi Danganguan, Hebeisheng Shehui Kexueyang, comp., and Tian Susu, ed., *Riben qinlüe Huabei zuixing dangan 9, Xingbaoli* [Documented war crimes during Japan's invasion of north China, volume 9, Sexual violence] (Shijiazhuang: Hebei renmin shubanshe, 2005), 154-58. Hereafter Zhongyang et al., *RQHZD*.

31 Quanzong-hao 91, Mulu-hao 1, Juan-hao 6, Jian-hao 1, cited in He, "Lun Rijun zai Zhongguo Huabei de xingbaoli," in Su et al., *Taotian zuinie*, 260-62.

32 Ibid.

33 He Tianyi, "Lun Rijun zai Zhongguo Huabei de xingbaoli," in Su et al., *Taotian zuinie*, 262. See also, Xie Zhonghou, Tian Susu, and He Tianyi, eds., *Riben qinlüe Huabei zuixing shigao* [A history of atrocities: Japan's invasion of northern China] (Beijing: Shehui kexue wenxian chubanshe, 2005), 424. Hereafter Xie et al. *RQHZS*.

34 Yoshimi, *Jūgun ianfu*, 113-15.

35 Yamada Sadamu, *Kempei nikki* [A military policeman's diary] (Tokyo: Surugadai shobō, 1985), 273-76. This and other documented evidence have been cited in Yoshimi, *Jūgun ianfu*, 113-15.

36 The Central Archives of China, Document 119-2-988-1-10, published in Zhongyang et al., *RQHZD*, 2-3.

37 Suzuki Hiraku's confession, kept in the Central Archives of China, Document 119-2-1-1-4, published in Zhongyang et al., *RQHZD*.

38 Chen, *Rijun weianfu zhidu pipan*, 199.

39 He, "Lun Rijun zai Zhongguo Huabei de xingbaoli," in Su et al., *Taotian zuinie*, 260-61.

40 The weights and measures have been converted to those familiar to Western readers. In the document the last of the benefits is written as *mo* (ink), which may have been a misprint of *mei* (coal), for which the pronunciation is similar.

41 "Wenshui hanjian 'Tongling' qiangzheng jinü" [The collaborators in Wenshui County ordered to draft prostitutes by force], in *Wenxian* 5 (February 1939): 57, cited in Su Zhiliang, *Rijun xingnuli* [Japanese military sex slaves] (Beijing: Renming chubanshe, 2000), 87.

42 Xie et al., *RQHZS*, 397-404.

43 Mizobe Kazuto, ed., *Dokusan ni: Mōhitotsu no sensō* [The 2nd Independent Mountain Artillery Regiment: Another war] (Yamaguchi: Privately published, 1983), 58, cited in Yoshimi, *Jūgun ianfu*, 116-17. Cf. O'Brien's translation in Yoshimi, *Comfort Women*, 120.

44 Mizobe, *Dokusan ni*, 55.

45 Hu Jiaren (narrator), Zhuo Shichun and Chen Yunhong (recorders), "Fuli-miao Rijun he ziweituan de judian qingkuang jiqi baoxing" [The strongholds of the Japanese military and self-guard league at Fuli-miao and their atrocities], in Fu, *TXXX*, 308-9.

46 The original text seems to contain a misprint in this sentence. *"Suijing"* should be *"xüjing,"* judging from the context.

47 Wang Bizhen, "Weiansuo li de nütongbao" [Women in the comfort station], *Guangxi funü* 17-18 (1941): 36.

48 Collaboration in occupied China is a complicated issue, and its study has just begun. In his in-depth analysis of the subject, Timothy Brook follows Henrik Dethlefsen in defining collaboration as "the continuing exercise of power under the pressure produced by the presence of an occupying power." See Henrik Dethlefsen, "Denmark and the German Occupation: Cooperation, Negotiation, or Collaboration?" *Scandinavian Journal of History* 15, 3 (1990): 193-206. Cited in Timothy Brook, *Collaboration: Japanese Agents and Local Elites in Wartime China* (Cambridge, MA: Harvard University Press, 2005), 2.

49 Shao Minghuang, "Taiwan in Wartime," in MacKinnon et al., *China at War*, 101.

50 He Shili, "Sanbai 'weianfu' cansi taiban: Shilu tiekuang 'weiansuo' diaocha shikuang" [Over half of the three hundred "comfort women" died: An investigative record of the Shilu iron mine "comfort station"], in *Tietixiade xingfeng xueyu: Rijun qin-Qiong baoxing shilu* [Bloody crimes of the occupation rule: Records of the atrocities committed by the Japanese military in Hainan], comp. Fu Heji (Hainan: Hainan chubanshe, 1995), 748-50. Hereafter Fu, *TXX*.

51 Fu Heji, "Qin-Qiong Rijun 'weianfu' shilu" [The reality of the Japanese military "comfort women" in Hainan], in Su et al., *Taotian zuinie*, 191-96.

52 *Shenbao* (Hong Kong edition), 6 March 1938.

53 Beijing Archives Bureau (Beijingshi dang'anguan), "Rijun qiangzheng 'weianfu' shiliao yijian" [A historical document on the Japanese military's forcible drafting of "comfort women"], in Su et al., *Taotian zuinie*, 623-26. The article includes Zhou Qian's as well as a victim's written testimony as submitted to the court. For more information about the Japanese military's forcing prostitutes in Tianjin to be comfort women, see Lin Boyao, "Tianjin Rijun 'weianfu' zhi gongji xitong" [The Japanese military "comfort women" procurement system in Tianjin.], in Su et al., *Taotian zuinie*, 269-307.

54 The Eighth Route Army was one of the two major Chinese Communist forces during the War of Resistance from 1937 to 1945.
55 Taguchi Shinkichi, "Chūgoku Kahokushō no rikugun jūgun ianfu" [The army's comfort women in Hebei Province of China], in *Shōgen "jūgun ianfu": Daiyaru 110 ban no kiroku* [Military comfort women: Records of the dial-in testimonies], ed. Nitchō kyōkai Saitama-ken rengōkai (Urawa: Nitchō kyōkai Saitama-ken rengōkai, 1995), 45.
56 See, for example, Jiang Hao, *Zhaoshi: Zhongguo weianfu – kuaguo kuashidai diaocha baipishu* [Exposé: Chinese comfort women – An investigation across the boundaries of nations and times] (Xining: Qinghai renmin chubanshe, 1998), 53-97.
57 See, for example, the murder of pregnant comfort woman Li Yaqian, reported by Lin Pagong and recorded by Zhang Yingyong, "Rijun 'Zhandi houqin fuwudui' zhong de Lizu funü" [The Li ethnic women drafted into the Japanese military "Battlefield rear service team"], in Fu, *TXX*, 547-49.
58 Hora Tomio, *Nankin daigyakusatsu* [Nanjing massacre] (Tokyo: Gendaishi shuppankai, 1982), 72.
59 In the 1930s and 1940s, local Chinese people often used the traditional lunar calendar, although the Gregorian calendar had been adopted by the newly formed Republic of China in 1912 for official business and was officially adopted in 1929 after the Nationalist government reconstituted the Republic of China. According to the lunar calendar, each year has twelve regular months and every second or third year has an intercalary month. Each month has twenty-nine or thirty days.
60 Fu, "Qin-Qiong Rijun 'weianfu' shilu," in Su et al., *Taotian zuinie*, 198.
61 Xie et al., *RQHZS*, 419.

Chapter 3: Different Types of Military "Comfort Stations" in China
1 This information is based on Su Zhiliang, *Weianfu yanjiu* [A study of the comfort women] (Shanghai: Shanghai shudian chubanshe, 1999), 275-76; Miki Y. Ishikida, *Toward Peace: War Responsibility, Postwar Compensation, and Peace Movements and Education in Japan* (New York: iUniverse, 2005), 61; and Sarah Soh, *The Comfort Women: Sexual Violence and Postcolonial Memory in Korea and Japan* (Chicago: University of Chicago Press, 2008), 137-38.
2 Su, *Weianfu yanjiu*, 275-76.
3 Chen Lifei, *Rijun weianfu zhidu pipan* [A critical analysis of the Japanese military comfort women system] (Beijing: Zhonghua shuju, 2006), 123-28.
4 Yuki Tanaka writes that a large number of Japanese military documents, including records of military plans and operations and field diaries, are still classified and are not open to public investigation. The Japanese police documents from the time of the Asia-Pacific War are also closed. In addition, documents prepared by the Japanese government ministries that reveal who were responsible for rounding up and trafficking women for the comfort stations are not accessible to researchers. See Yuki Tanaka, *Japan's Comfort Women: Sexual Slavery and Prostitution during World War II and the US Occupation* (New York: Routledge, 2002), 19-20.
5 Hirofumi Hayashi, "Disputes in Japan over the Japanese Military 'Comfort Women' System and Its Perception in History," *Annals of American Academy of Political and Social Science* 617 (2008): 127.
6 Tanaka, *Japan's Comfort Women*, 19-28.
7 The information is from Chen, *Rijun weianfu zhidu pipan*, 180.
8 Nagasawa Ken'ichi, *Kankō ianjo* [Comfort stations in Hankou] (Tokyo: Tosho shuppansha, 1983), 44, cited in Yoshimi Yoshiaki, *Jūgun ianfu* [Military comfort women] (Tokyo: Iwanami shoten, 1995), 131. Translation of this information owes much to Suzanne O'Brien, trans., *Comfort Women*, 132-33.

9 Li Xianheng, "Rijun shezhi weiansuo de baoxing" [Japanese army's violence in setting up comfort stations] in *Qin-Hua Rijun baoxing zonglu* [Collection of investigative records of the atrocities committed by the Japanese forces during Japan's invasion of China], ed. Li Bingxin, Xu Junyuan, and Shi Yuxin (Shijiazhuang: Hebei renmin chubanshe, 1995), 1275. Hereafter Li et al., *QHRBZ*.

10 Asō Tetsuo, *Shanhai yori Shanhai e: Heitan byōyin no sanfujinkai* [From Shanghai to Shanghai: A gynecologist at the commissariat hospital] (Fukuoka: Sekifūsha, 1993), 214-30.

11 Su, *Weianfu yanjiu*, 57-71.

12 Ibid., 59.

13 For earlier researchers' discussions of the varieties of comfort stations, see Yoshimi, *Jūgun ianfu*, 74; Tanaka, *Japan's Comfort Women*, 18-19; and Soh, *Comfort Women*, 117-32.

14 Asō, *Shanhai yori Shanhai e*, 214-30.

15 Chen, *Rijun weianfu zhidu pipan*, 182.

16 Wu Liansheng's testimony, in *Tietixiade xingfeng xueyu: Rijun qin-Qiong baoxing shilu, Xu* [Sequel to Bloody crimes of the occupation rule: Records of the atrocities committed by the Japanese military in Hainan], ed. Fu Heji, 272-79 (Hainan: Hainan chubanshe, 1995). Hereafter Fu, *TXXX*.

17 Li Shi, "Rijun zai Fuyang-xian de baoxing" [Japanese army's atrocities at Fuyang county], in Li et al., *QHRBZ*, 768.

18 Fang Zhiyuan, "Yige xiuru de baogao" [A humiliating report], in Chen Sibai, *Yeshou zai jiangnan* [The monstrous troops in south China] (Shangyao: Qianxian ribaoshe, 1939), 89-92.

19 Kim Il-myon. *Tennō no guntai to Chōsenjin ianfu* [The emperor's forces and the Korean comfort women] (Tokyō: Sanichi shobō, 1976), 124.

20 Chen Liming, "Anhui Bangbu zuihou yichu qin-Hua Rijun weiansuo jiuzhi jiang bei chaiqian" [The last building of the former Japanese military comfort station in Anhui Bangbu will be demolished] *Xin'an wanbao*, 19 September 2005; http://china.com.cn.

21 Wen Yan, "Fengyang 'weiansuo'" [Comfort stations at Fengyang], in Li et al., *QHRBZ*, 734.

22 Tanaka, *Japan's Comfort Women*, 51-52.

23 Yoshimi, *Jūgun ianfu*, 130.

24 Yoshimi Yoshiaki, ed., *Jūgun ianfu shiryōshū* [A collection of documents on military comfort women] (Tokyo: Otsuki shoten, 1992), 285-86.

25 Yamada Seikichi, *Bukan heitan: Shina hakkengun ian kakarichō no shuki* [The Wuhan commissariat: Memoir of the department head of the China detachment army comfort facilities] (Tokyo: Tosho shuppansha, 1978), 86; cited in Yoshimi, *Comfort Women*, 135.

26 He Shili, "Sanbai 'weianfu' cansi taiban-Shilu tiekuang 'weiansuo' diaocha shikuang" [Over half of three hundred "comfort women" died: An investigative record of the Shilu iron mine "comfort station"], in *Tietixiade xingfeng xueyu: Rijun qin-Qiong baoxing shilu* [Bloody crimes of the occupation rule: Records of the atrocities committed by the Japanese military in Hainan], comp. Fu Heji, 748-50 (Hainan: Hainan chubanshe, 1995). Henceforth Fu, *TXX*.

27 Song Fuhai (narrator), and Chen Ziming and Wang Ji (recorders), "Wo qindu de Xinying Rijun 'weiansuo'" [The Japanese military Xinying "comfort station" I witnessed], in Fu, *TXXX*, 188-90.

28 Zhang Lianhong and Li Guanglian, "Nanjing Xiaguan-qu qin-Hua Rijun weiansuo de diaocha baogao" [Investigative report on the Japanese military comfort stations in the Xiaguan District of Nanjing], in *Taotian zuinie: Erzhan shiqi de Rijun weianfu zhidu* [Monstrous atrocities: The Japanese military comfort women System during the Second World War], ed. Su Zhiliang, Rong Weimu, and Chen Lifei (Shanghai: Xuelin chubanshe, 2000), 146.

29   Ibid., 147-48. The Japanese *yen* was divided into 100 *sen* before 1954. The reason for the different fees for soldiers and officers is not clear; perhaps it had to do with the fact that the officers were allowed bigger blocks of time and better time periods than soldiers.

30   Asō, *Shanhai yori Shanhai e*, 42.

31   Yoshimi, *Jūgun ianfu shiryōshū*, 285-87. Partial English translation of the regulations can be found in Suzanne O'Brien's translation of Yoshimi, *Comfort Women*, 136-37.

32   According to Yoshimi Yoshiaki's research, the Construction Section of the Ministry of War's Accounting Bureau and the Military Supply Headquarters worked together to send condoms to Japanese troops in the field. See Yoshimi, *Jūgun ianfu*, 71.

33   Su, *Weianfu yanjiu*, 231.

34   Ibid.

35   Lin Pagong (narrator) and Zhang Yingyong (recorder), "Rijun zhandi houqin fuwudui zhong de Lizu funü" [The Li ethnic women drafted into the Japanese military "Battlefield rear service team"] in Fu, *TXX*, 547-49.

36   Wu Liansheng's testimony, in Fu, *TXXX*, 272-79.

37   Wang Yexin, "Fengyi-lou weiansuo shimo" [The Fengyi-lou comfort station], in Su et al., *Taotian zuinie*, 182.

38   A testimony relating to such cases can be found in Tanaka, *Japan's Comfort Women*, 53. See also George Hicks, *The Comfort Women: Japan's Brutal Regime of Enforced Prostitution in the Second World War* (New York: W.W. Norton, 1994), 93-96.

39   Zhang and Li, "Nanjing Xiaguan-qu qin-Hua Rijun weiansuo de diaocha baogao," in Su et al., *Taotian zuinie*, 151.

40   Naka-Shina haken kempeitai shireibu [Headquarters of military police dispatched to central China], "Rikugun gunjin gunzoku hikōhyō" [A list of misconducts by army personnel and civilian army enployees], entries dated November 1941 and February 1942, *Rikushifu dainikki* 6, 9 (1942), in Bōeichō bōei kenkyūjo toshokan [Japan Defence Agency Defence Library], cited in Yoshimi, *Jūgun ianfu*, 143.

41   Yoshimi, *Jūgun ianfu*, 144.

42   Information in the chart is from Chen, *Rijun weianfu zhidu pipan*, 132.

43   USNA collection, Allied Translation and Interpreter Section Research Report No. 120, *Amenities in the Japanese Armed Forces* (November 1945), 12, cited in Tanaka, *Japan's Comfort Women*, 54.

44   Marai gunseikan, "Ian shisetsu oyobi ryokan eigyō junshu kisoku" [Regulations for the operation of comfort facilities and inns], *Gunsei kiteishū* 3, 11 (1943), cited in Yoshimi, *Jūgun ianfu*, 145.

45   Yoshimi, *Jūgun ianfu*, 145. Translation here and in the following sentences is based on Suzanne O'Brien's translation of Yoshimi, *Comfort Women*, 142.

46   Yoshimi, *Jūgun ianfu*, 145.

47   Ibid., 148.

48   Ibid., 146-48.

49   Much research reveals the brutal exploitation of comfort women drafted from Japan and its colonies. See, for example, Kim, *Tennō no guntai to Chōsenjin ianfu*; Jūgun Ianfu 110-ban Henshū Iinkai, *Jūgun ianfu 110-ban denwa no mukō kara rekishi no koe ga* [Military comfort women hotlines: The voices of history from the other end of the telephone] (Tokyo: Akashi Shoten, 1992); Senda, *Jūgun ianfu*; Yoshimi, *Jūgun ianfu*; Hicks, *Comfort Women*; Tanaka, *Japan's Comfort Women*; Keith Howard, ed., *True Stories of the Korean Comfort Women: Testimonies Compiled by the Korean Council for Women Drafted for Military Sexual Slavery by Japan and the Research Association on the Women Drafted for Military Sexual Slavery by Japan* (London: Cassell, 1995); Dai Sil Kim-Gibson, *Silence Broken: Korean Comfort Women* (Parkersburg: Mid-Prairie Books, 2000.).

50 The Association of Advancement of Unbiased View of History, "Comfort Women," ABC of modern Japanese History. Available at http://www.jiyuushikan.org/ (viewed 13 October 2010).

51 Wang, "Weiansuo li de nütongbao" [Women in the comfort station] *Guangxi funü* 17-18 (1941): 36.

52 Chen, *Rijun weianfu zhidu pipan,* 239-40; cf. Tanaka, *Japan's Comfort Women,* 46-47.

53 Soh, *Comfort Women,* 3.

Chapter 4: Crimes Fostered by the "Comfort Women" System

1 Tang Huayuan, "Rijun zai Yueyang jiansha funü de baoxing" [Raping and killing women: The Japanese army's atrocities in Yueyang], in *Qin-Hua Rijun baoxing zonglu,* ed. Li Bingxin, Xu Junyuan, and Shi Yuxin (Shijiazhuang: Hebei renmin chubanshe, 1995), 1010. Hereafter Li et al., *QHRBZ.*

2 Ibid.

3 Ibid.

4 Zhang Huaiqing, "Fengyang da can'an" [Massacres in Fengyang], in Li et al., *QHRBZ,* 710.

5 One of the two major forces led by the Chinese Communist Party during the War of Resistance.

6 Zhang Huaiqing, "Fengyang da can'an," 710-11.

7 Tang, "Rijun zai Yueyang jiansha funü de baoxing," in Li et al., *QHRBZ,* 1010.

8 Ibid.

9 Wu Liansheng's testimony, in *Tietixiade xingfeng xueyu: Rijun qin-Qiong baoxing shilu, Xu* [Sequel to Bloody crimes of the occupation rule: Records of the atrocities committed by the Japanese military in Hainan], ed. Fu Heji, 272-79 (Hainan: Hainan chubanshe, 1995), 274. Hereafter Fu, *TXXX.*

10 Satō Kanji, *Akai chūrippu no heitai: Aru heishi no ashiato* [Troops of red tulips: A soldier's footprints] (Tokyo: Senshūsha, 1978), 77-78, cited in Yoshimi, *Comfort Women: Sexual Slavery in the Japanese Military during World War II* (New York: Columbia University Press, 2000), 134-35.

11 Chen Lifei, *Rijun weianfu zhidu pipan* [A critical analysis of the Japanese military comfort women system] (Beijing: Zhonghua shuju, 2006), 291.

12 He Shili, "Sanbai 'weianfu' cansi taiban – Shilu tiekuang 'weiansuo' diaocha shikuang" [Over half of the three hundred "comfort women" died: An investigative record of the Shilu iron mine "comfort station"], in *Tietixiade xingfeng xueyu: Rijun qin-Qiong baoxing shilu* [Bloody crimes of the occupation rule: Records of the atrocities committed by the Japanese military in Hainan], comp. Fu Heji (Hainan: Hainan chubanshe, 1995), 748-50. Hereafter Fu, *TXX.*

13 Yoshimi Yoshiaki, *Jūgun ianfu* [Military comfort women] (Tokyo: Iwanami shoten, 1995), 145-46.

14 Wu Liansheng's testimony, in Fu, *TXXX,* 272-79.

15 Ayan's testimony recorded by Li Weilin in Fu, *TXX,* 649-50,

16 Wu Liansheng's testimony, in Fu, *TXXX,* 275.

17 Chen Zuliang, "Qin-Hua Rijun Dianxi weiansuo yu 'weianfu'" [The Japanese military comfort stations and "comfort women" in western Yunnan], in *Taotian zuinie: Erzhan shiqi de Rijun weianfu zhidu* [Monstrous atrocities: The Japanese military comfort women system during the Second World War], ed. Su Zhiliang, Rong Weimu, and Chen Lifei (Shanghai: Xuelin chubanshe, 2000), 315.

18 Song Fuhai, "Wo qindu de Xinying Rijun 'weiansuo'" [The Japanese military Xinying "comfort station" I witnessed], in Fu, *TXXX,* 188-90.

19 In *Jūgun ianfu,* Yoshimi provides evidence of this by citing the military records. See Yoshimi, *Jūgun ianfu,* 154.

20 He, "Sanbai 'weianfu' cansi taiban," in Fu, *TXX*, 748-50.
21 Zhong Qiang, "Wo suo zhidao de Rijun Huangliu jichang de 'weiansuo'" [The Japanese military Huangliu airport comfort station I saw], in Fu, *TXX*, 646-47.
22 Fu Heji, "Qin-Qiong Rijun 'weianfu' shilu" [The reality of the Japanese military "comfort women" in Hainan], in Su et al., *Taotian zuinie*, 198.
23 Ibid., 199.
24 Yoshimi Yoshiaki, ed., *Jūgun ianfu shiryōshū* [A collection of documents on military comfort women] (Tokyo: Otsuki shoten, 1992), 229-32.
25 Inaba Masao, ed. *Okamura Yasuji taishō shiryō: Senjō kaisō hen, jō* [Sources of general Okamura Yasuji: Recollections of the battlefield, vol. 1] (Tokyo: Hara shobō, 1970), 302-3. Translation of this passage is from Suzanne O'Brien's translation in Yoshimi, *Comfort Women*, 66.
26 Rikujō jieitai eisei gakkō, ed., *Daitōa sensō rikugun eiseishi* [A medical history of the army in the great East Asia war] (Tokyo: Rikujō jieitai eisei gakkō, 1971), 1: 605-7, cited in Yoshimi, *Jūgun ianfu*, 51.
27 Cases of mass murder of comfort women at the end of the war have been described in several studies and wartime memoirs. See, for example, Kim Il Myon, *Tennō no guntai to Chōsenjin ianfu* [The emperor's forces and the Korean comfort women] (Tokyō: Sanichi shobō, 1976); George Hicks, *The Comfort Women: Japan's Brutal Regime of Enforced Prostitution in the Second World War* (New York: W.W. Norton, 1994); and Nishino Rumiko, *Senjō no ianfu* [Comfort women in the battlefields] (Tokyo: Akashi shoten, 2003).
28 Chen Zuliang, "Qin-Hua Rijun Dianxi weiansuo yu 'weianfu'" [The Japanese military comfort stations and "comfort women" in western Yunnan], in Su et al., *Taotian zuinie*, 322.
29 "Di suijun yingji diaocha: Tengchong-cheng nei yiqun kelianchong," [An investigative report of the enemy's military prostitutes: A group of poor women at Tengchong], *Saodang bao*, 26 September 1944, cited in Chen, "Qin-Hua Rijun," in Su et al., *Taotian zuinie*, 322.
30 Alice Yun Chai, "Korean Feminist and Human Right Politics: The *Chongshindae/Jugunianfu* ('Comfort Women') Movement," in *Korean American Women: From Tradition to Modern Feminism*, ed. Young In Song and Ailee Moon (Westport: Praeger, 1998), 240.
31 Su Zhiliang, Hou Guifang, and Hu Haiying, *Riben dui Hainan de qinlüe jiqi baoxing* [The Japanese invasion of Hainan and Its atrocities] (Shanghai: Shanghai cishu chubanshe, 2005), 184-86.
32 Ibid., 185-89.
33 Su Zhiliang and Chen Lifei. "Qin-Hua Rijun weianfu zhidu lüelun" [A study of the Japanese military comfort women system in China], in Su et al., *Taotian zuinie*, 29.
34 The interviews were conducted by Su Zhiliang, Chen Lifei, Hou Guifang, and Hu Haiying from 2000 to 2004. Of the forty-two survivors found in the Hainan region, fourteen had already died and eight were not available for interviews.
35 Su et al., *Riben dui Hainan de qinlüe jiqi baoxing*, 284-85.
36 Diana Lary and Stephen MacKinnon, eds. *Scars of War: The Impact of War on Modern China* (Vancouver: UBC Press, 2001).

PART 2: THE SURVIVORS' VOICES

1 Testimonies of Yin Yulin and Wan Aihua, collected by Japanese researchers, are published in Japanese in Ishida Yoneko and Uchida Tomoyuki, eds., *Kōdo no mura no seibōryoku: Dā'nyan tachi no sensō wa owaranai* [Sexual violence in the villages located in the area of the yellow earth: The war is not over to these aged women] (Tokyo: Sōdosha, 2004). Excerpts and testimonies of these women, collected by different researchers, also appear in Chinese journalist reports and scholarly works, but none of them has been published in English.

2 The tribunal was convened on 8 December 2000 and adjourned on 12 December 2000. It was a people's tribunal organized by Asian women and human rights organizations and supported by international NGOs. It was convened to adjudicate Japan's military sexual violence, in particular the enslavement of "comfort women." This information is cited from the website of Violence against Women in War-Network Japan.

Chapter 5: Eastern Coastal Region

1 This was one kind of arranged marriage practised in China before the People's Republic of China was established in 1949: a family in economic hardship would give or sell a young daughter to another family. The girl would be treated as an adopted daughter who would be married to a male member of the adoptive family when grown up – hence, literally, "the child raised to be daughter-in-law" *(tongyangxi)*. In many cases, her in-laws used the child-daughter-in-law as free labour.
2 The Japanese troops invaded the Nanjing area in the winter of 1937. Lei Guiying's description here is consistent with historical fact.
3 Foot-binding was practised on girls and women in China from around the tenth century to the first half of the twentieth century. Binding a girl's feet tightly from a very young age in order to achieve the desired smallness often caused life-long disabilities, particularly for those whose arches or toes were broken.
4 Jiangsu-sheng Rugao-shi difangzhi bianzhuan weiyuanhui, *Rugao xianzhi* [Historical record of Rugao County] (Hong Kong: Xianggang xin Yazhou chubanshe youxiangongsi, 1995), 594-604.
5 The New Fourth Army was a unit of the National Revolutionary Army of the Republic of China established in 1937. Different from most of the National Revolutionary Army units, it was led by the Chinese Communist Party. Beginning in 1938, the New Fourth Army and the Eighth Route Army were the two main communist forces. The New Fourth Army was active south of the Changjiang River, while the Eighth Route Army was based in northern China.
6 Wang Jingwei (1983-44) was a member of the Chinese Nationalist Party, and he held prominent posts in the Nationalist government. A long-time rival of Jiang Jieshi, Wang became the head of the puppet state set up by Imperial Japan during its invasion of China.
7 This information is from the investigative notes of Su Zhiliang and Chen Lifei, which were written in Chinese.
8 According to local history, the company had approximately sixty or seventy soldiers.
9 This building has now been demolished; the Miaozhen Town Hall now stands in its old location.
10 Su Zhiliang and Chen Lifei, investigative notes.

Chapter 6: Warzones in Central and Northern China

1 Hans van de Ven and Edward J. Drea, "Chronology of the Sino-Japanese War," in *The Battle for China: Essays on the Military History of the Sino-Japanese War of 1937-1945*, ed. Mark Peattie, Edward J. Drea, and Hans van de Ven (Stanford: Stanford University Press, 2011), 9.
2 Edward J. Drea and Hans van de Ven, "An Overview of Major Military Campaigns," in Peattie et al., *Battle for China*, 34-35.
3 It is not clear what kind of pills Yuan Zhulin was forced to take. Yuan seemed to suspect that they were some sort of contraceptive drug, but the availability of oral contraceptives at that time is questionable. Some other survivors also mentioned that the comfort stations made them take pills, but the nature and effect of these drugs is unclear.
4 Shihuiyao is today's Huangshi City, Hubei Province.

5   A neighbourhood committee (*Jumin weiyuan hui*, or simply *Juweihui*) is under the administration of each district of a city in the urban areas of China. It is responsible for neighbourhood residential administrative matters.

6   van de Ven and Drea, "Chronology of the Sino-Japanese War," 12.

7   Stephen MacKinnon, "The Defense of the Central Yangtze," in Peattie et al., *Battle for China*, 201-4; Tobe Ryōichi, "The Japanese Eleventh Army in Central China, 1938-1941," in Peattie et al., *Battle for China*, 217-18, 226-27; Wang Qisheng, "The Battle of Hunan and the Chinese Military's Response to Operation Ichigō," in Peattie et al., *Battle for China*, 403-18. See also, Zhang Xianwen, *Zhongguo kang-Ri zhanzheng shi* [A history of China's resistance war against Japan] (Nanjing: Nanjing daxue chubanshe, 2001), 608-28, 815-35, 954-66, 1069-82.

8   A collection of proverbs. The authorship and date of the book are unknown.

9   A four-volume collection of proverbs, which was used for the education of children and was compiled by Cheng Dengji during the late Ming Dynasty (1368-1644).

10   Today's Town of Zhuliang-qiao, Ningxiang County.

11   In ancient China this term was used as an honorific to show respect to someone else's mother but it is not commonly used in modern China. During the war, Chinese people in occupied areas were often forced to call the Japanese military men *taijun*.

12   van de Ven and Drea, "Chronology of the Sino-Japanese War," 8.

13   Xie Zhonghou, Tian Susu, and He Tianyi, eds., *Riben qinlüe Huabei zuixing shi gao* [A history of atrocities: Japan's invasion of northern China]. (Beijing: Shehui kexue wenxian chubanshe, 2005), 41-143. Hereafter Xie et al. *RQHZS*.

14   "Jin Ji nütongbao canzao diren roulin" [Women in Jin and Ji regions are brutally raped], in *Xinhua ribao*, 9 April 1938.

15   Drea and van de Ven, "Overview of Major Military Campaigns," 39.

16   Zhang, *Zhongguo kang-Ri zhanzheng shi*, 733-51.

17   Su Zhiliang and Chen Lifei, investigative notes.

18   Because the written characters for these names were not given, all the personal and place names in this account are transcribed according to the pronunciations recorded during the interview.

19   Same as child-daughter-in-law. A child-bride was raised in her in-laws' family and would then marry their son when she grew up. A child-bride/child-daughter-in-law was at the bottom of the family hierarchy.

20   According to Wan Aihua's recollection, because of her contribution to the anti-Japanese invasion, the local CCP committee made an exception and allowed her to become a CCP member before the age of eighteen.

21   Li Guiming is a villager in Yu County and a supporter of the local surviving comfort women. He helped several survivors in the area, including Wan Aihua, in their lawsuits for redress.

Chapter 7: Southern China Frontlines

1   Hans van de Ven and Edward J. Drea, "Chronology of the Sino-Japanese War," in *The Battle for China: Essays on the Military History of the Sino-Japanese War of 1937-1945*, ed. Mark Peattie, Edward J. Drea, and Hans van de Ven (Stanford: Stanford University Press, 2011), 11.

2   Pan Xian'e, "Rijun qin-Ling shishi gaiyao" [An outline of the history of the Japanese military invasion of Lingshui County], *Tietixiade xingfeng xueyu: Rijun qin-Qiong baoxing shilu* [Bloody crimes of the occupation rule: Records of the atrocities committed by the Japanese military in Hainan], comp. Fu Heji (Hainan: Hainan chubanshe, 1995), 448-62. Hereafter Fu, *TXX*. Also, information from investigative notes of Su Zhiliang and Chen Lifei.

3 According to Chinese tradition, a person is considered one year old at birth and a year is added to one's age each Lunar New Year. Therefore, by Western reckoning, Huang Youliang was actually only fourteen years old at the time.

4 The majority of China's population is composed of Han people.

5 Yang Jiechen, "Rijun qinzhan Yaxian jiqi baoxing jishi" [Historical records of the Japanese military occupation of Ya County and the atrocities they committed], in Fu, *TXX*, 401-13.

6 van de Ven and Drea, "Chronology of the Sino-Japanese War," in Peattie et al., *Battle for China*, 20.

7 Zhang Yingyong, "Rijun ruqin Baoting-xian shimo" [A history of Japanese army's invasion of Baoting County], in Fu, *TXX*, 531-41; Wang Shizhong, Li Zhaochang, and Ji Xuehai, Ji Xuexin (narrators), Zhang Yingyong (recorder), "Rijun zai Nanlin-xiang de zuixing shilu" [A record of the atrocities committed by the Japanese military in Nanlin Township], in Fu, *TXX*, 538-50.

8 Lin Yajin had trouble figuring out the years of some important events in her life according to the Western calendar. Based on her narration, her wedding should have taken place in the late 1940s.

9 "Eating from the same big pot" *(chi da guo fan)* was an extremist practice in China during the failed industrialization campaign known as the "Great Leap Forward" *(dayuejin)* initiated by CCP leader Mao Zedong between 1958 and early 1960. The campaign encouraged rural communities to take unrealistic initiatives, such as the communization of agriculture and the construction of backyard steel furnaces. By the middle of 1958, communes had been created in the countryside and peasants' belongings, even the pigs and fruit trees in their courtyards, had been made communal property. "Eating from the same big pot" became a synonym for the to-each-according-to-his-needs institutions created at the time. The failure of the campaign and a poor harvest in 1959 resulted in mass starvation.

10 In the people's commune system, "work-points" *(gongfen)* were used to measure a member's work. The annual payment of grain to a commune member was based on the number of work-points she or he had earned. Because Lin's husband was labelled as a counter-revolutionary, she was also subjected to persecution and was given fewer points for her work than she deserved.

11 Hagiwara Mitsuru, "The Japanese Air Campaigns in China, 1937-1945," in Peattie et al., *Battle for China*, 250. See also, Asano Toyomi, "Japanese Operations in Yunnan and North Burma," in Peattie et al., *Battle for China*, 361-85.

12 Chen Zuliang, "Qin-Hua Rijun Dianxi weiansuo yu 'weianfu'" [The Japanese military comfort stations and "comfort women" in western Yunnan], in *Taotian zuinie: Erzhan shiqi de Rijun weianfu zhidu* [Monstrous atrocities: The Japanese military comfort women system during the Second World War], ed. Su Zhiliang, Rong Weimu, and Chen Lifei, 308-22 (Shanghai: Xuelin chubanshe, 2000).

13 The east side of the river was under the control of the Chinese Expeditionary Army at the time.

Chapter 8: Wounds That Do Not Heal

1 Yuki Tanaka, *Japan's Comfort Women: Sexual Slavery and Prostitution during World War II and the US Occupation* (New York: Routledge, 2002), 86.

2 On 17 April 2007, Hayashi Hirofumi, Yoshimi Yoshiaki, and a group of historians announced in Tokyo the discovery of seven official interrogation records and statements documenting how the Japanese military coerced women to work at some of their frontline brothels in Indonesia, China, East Timor, and Vietnam. These documents were presented to the International Military Tribunal for the Far East. See Reiji Yoshida, "Evidence Documenting

Sex-Slave Coercion Revealed," *Japan Times,* 18 April 2007. See also, Yuma Totani, *The Tokyo War Crimes Trial: The Pursuit of Justice in the Wake of World War II* (Cambridge: Harvard University Asia Center, 2008), 176-79, 181-82, and 185-86.

3 Totani, *Tokyo War Crimes Trial,* 185.

4 *Tokyo Judgment,* 1:392-93, cited in Totani, *Tokyo War Crimes Trial,* 185.

5 Totani, *Tokyo War Crimes Trial,* 185.

6 Tanaka, *Japan's Comfort Women,* 87.

7 John Dower, *Embracing Defeat: Japan in the Wake of World War II* (New York: W.W. Norton, 1999), 469.

8 Ibid.

9 Dower, *Embracing Defeat,* 632.

10 Ibid., 443-49.

11 Yoshimi Yoshiaki, *Jūgun ianfu* [Military comfort women] (Tokyo: Iwanami shoten, 1995), 175-92. See also Tanaka, *Japan's Comfort Women,* 86; and C. Sarah Soh, *The Comfort Women: Sexual Violence and Postcolonial Memory in Korea and Japan* (Chicago: University of Chicago Press, 2008), 22.

12 Tanaka, *Japan's Comfort Women,* 86. See also Toshiyuki Tanaka, "Naze Beigun wa jūgun ianfu mondai o mushishita no ka" [Why the US forces ignored the military comfort women issue?], *Sekai* 627 (1996): 174-83, and 628 (1996): 270-79.

13 Tanaka, *Japan's Comfort Women,* 87.

14 George Hicks, *The Comfort Women: Japan's Brutal Regime of Enforced Prostitution in the Second World War* (New York: W.W. Norton, 1995), 167; Tanaka, *Japan's Comfort Women,* 110-32.

15 Hicks, *Comfort Women,* 158-62; Tanaka, *Japan's Comfort Women,* 133-66.

16 Takemae Eiji, *The Allied Occupation of Japan,* trans. Robert Ricketts and Sebastian Swann (New York: Continuum, 2002), 67-71.

17 *Yomiuri Shimbun,* 3 September 1945, morning edition.

18 Totani, *Tokyo War Crimes Trial,* 185-89.

19 Ibid., 151.

20 Ibid., 152-55.

21 Nicola Henry, *War and Rape: Law, Memory and Justice* (New York: Routledge, 2011), 40.

22 Ibid., 28-60.

23 Pilip R. Piccigallo, *The Japanese on Trial: Allied War Crimes Operations in the East, 1945-1951* (Austin: University of Texas Press, 1979), 158-73.

24 Ishida Yoneko and Uchida Tomoyuki, *Kōdo no mura no seibōryoku: Dā'nyan tachi no sensō wa owaranai* [Sexual violence in the villages located in the area of the yellow earth: The war is not over to these aged women] (Tokyo: Sōdosha, 2004), 225-28.

25 Ibid.

26 Ibid.

27 Ibid., 377.

28 Ibid., 363.

29 Ibid., 49-56.

30 The pension is based on the work Wang Gaihe did as a Resistance Movement member before she was captured by the Japanese army; it is not compensation for her forced sexual slavery as a comfort woman.

31 Ishida and Uchida, *Kōdo no mura no seibōryoku,* 114-17.

32 Ibid. 76-79.

33 Su Zhiliang and Chen Lifei's investigative notes.

34 Chen Lifei, *Rijun weianfu zhidu pipan* [A critical analysis of the Japanese military comfort women system] (Beijing: Zhonghua shuju, 2006), 325-26.

35 Ibid.
36 Ibid., 398-99. Also, Su Zhiliang and Chen Lifei, interview notes.
37 Han Wenning and Feng Chunlong. *Riben zhanfan shenpan* [Trials of the Japanese war criminals] (Nanjing: Nanjing Chubanshe, 2005), 91.
38 For a more detailed discussion of the investigation, see Ishida and Uchida, *Kōdo no mura no seibōryoku*, 225-28.

Chapter 9: The Redress Movement

1 Senda Kakō, *Jūgun ianfu* [Military comfort women] (Tokyo: Kōdansha, 1984); and Kim Il-myon, *Tennō no guntai to Chōsenjin ianfu* [The emperor's forces and the Korean comfort women] (Tokyō: Sanichi shobō, 1976).
2 For detailed information about the contents and circumstances of the publications, see Sarah Soh, *The Comfort Women: Sexual Violence and Postcolonial Memory in Korea and Japan* (Chicago: University of Chicago Press, 2008), 146-48.
3 For example, Yoshida Seiji, *Chōsenjin ianfu to Nihonjin: Moto Shimonoseki rōhō dōin buchō no shuki* [Korean comfort women and Japanese people: Memoir of the former mobilization department head] (Tokyo: Shinjinbutsu ōraisha, 1977); and Yamada Seikichi, *Bukan heitan: Shina hakkengun ian kakarichō no shuki* [The Wuhan commissariat: Memoir of the department head of the China detachment army comfort facilities] (Tokyo: Tosho shuppansha, 1978). Since 1992, Yoshida's book has been discredited by some historians. See Soh, *Comfort Women*, 152-55.
4 Research has been published in English on the activities of the Korean and Japanese women's groups. See, for example, Keith Howard, ed., *True Stories of the Korean Comfort Women* (London: Cassell, 1995), v-viii; Watanabe Kazuko, "Militarism, Colonialism, and the Trafficking of Women: 'Comfort Women' Forced into Sexual Labour for Japanese Soldiers," *Bulletin of Concerned Asian Scholars* 26, 4 (1994): 3-17; George Hicks, *The Comfort Women: Japan's Brutal Regime of Enforced Prostitution in the Second World War* (New York: W.W. Norton, 1994), 195-219; and Alice Yun Chai, "Korean Feminist and Human Rights Politics: The *Chongshindae/Juguianfu* ('Comfort Women') Movement," in *Korean American Women: From Tradition to Modern Feminism*, ed. Young I. Song and Ailee Moon (Westport: Praeger, 1998), 237-54.
5 Bonnie B.C. Oh, "The Japanese Imperial System and the Korean 'Comfort Women,'" in *Legacies of the Comfort Women of World War II*, ed. Margaret Stetz and Bonnie B.C. Oh, 3-25 (Armonk, NY: M.E. Sharpe, 2001), 14.
6 The investigative report can be found in Josei no tame no Ajia heiwa kokumin kikin, comp., *Seifu chōsa "jūgun ianfu" kankei shiryō shūsei* [Governmental investigations: Documents concerning the military "comfort women"] (Tokyo: Ryūkei Shosha, 1999), 1:7-10. See also "Statement by Chief Cabinet Secretary Kato Regarding the So-Called Problem of Korean Comfort Women," Ministry of Foreign Affairs, Japan, 6 July 1992. Available at http://www.mofa.go.jp/ (viewed on 15 October, 2010).
7 Hicks, *Comfort Women*, 220-28.
8 Ibid.
9 Researchers such as Yoshimi Yoshiaki and women activists in both Korea and Japan were particularly critical.
10 *Asahi Shimbun*, 4 August 1993. The report can be viewed at Ministry of Foreign Affairs, Japan, "Iwayuru jūgun ianfu mondai ni tsuite" [On the so-called "comfort women" issue], 4 August 1993. http://www.mofa.go.jp/ (viewed 15 October 2010).
11 Yoshimi Yoshiaki, *Jūgun ianfu* [Military comfort women] (Tokyo: Iwanami shoten, 1995), 6-8. A discussion of the Kōno statement and its criticism can be found in Yoshiko Nozaki, "Feminism, Nationalism, and the Japanese Textbook Controversy over 'Comfort Women,'"

in *Feminism and Antiracism: International Struggle for Justice,* ed. France Winddance Twine and Kathleen M. Blee, 173-74 (New York: New York University Press, 2001).

12 See Norma Field, "War and Apology: Japan, Asia, the Fiftieth, and After," *positions* 5, 1 (1997): 1-51.

13 Philip A. Seaton, *Japan's Contested War Memories* (London: Routledge, 2007), 95.

14 See the AWF website at http://www.awf.or.jp/ (viewed 3 March, 2013). Japan's minister of foreign affairs estimated the total donations to be about 600 million yen. See http://www. mofa.go.jp/.

15 Nozaki, "Feminism, Nationalism, and the Japanese Textbook Controversy," 175.

16 *The Allied Occupation of Japan,* 557.

17 Ibid., 673.

18 For a discussion of the establishment of the Citizens' Asian Peace Fund for Women and its criticism, see C. Sarah Soh, "Japan's Responsibility toward Comfort Women Survivors," Japan Policy Research Institute, University of San Francisco Center for the Pacific Rim, *JPRI Working Paper* 77 (May 2001), available at http://www.jpri.org/.

19 Chuang Kuo-ming, "Rang zhengyi suxing: Taiwan 'weianfu' jishi" [Restore justice: Notes on Taiwanese "comfort women"], in *Taotian zuinie: Erzhan shiqi de Rijun weianfu zhidu* [Monstrous atrocities: The Japanese military comfort women system during the Second World War], ed. Su Zhiliang, Rong Weimu, and Chen Lifei (Shanghai: Xuelin chubanshe, 2000), 378-82; Wang Ching-feng, "Tamen de shangkou shangwei yuhe" [Their wounds have not healed], in Su et al., *Taotian zuinie,* 384.

20 "Statement of Jan Ruff O'Herne, Surviving Comfort Woman, Friends of Comfort Women in Australia," hearing before the Subcommittee on Asia, the Pacific, and the Global Environment of the Committee on Foreign Affairs House of Representatives, 110th Congress, 1st Session, 15 February 2007.

21 Cited from appendix to *Contemporary Forms of Slavery: Systematic Rape, Sexual Slavery and Slavery-Like Practices during Armed Conflict,* final report submitted by Special Rapporteur Gay J. McDougall to United Nations Commission on Human Rights, Sub-Commission on Prevention of Discrimination and Protection of Minorities, 50th Session, UN Doc. E/CN.4/Sub.2/1998/13, 22 June 1998, 39, para. 4.

22 Ibid., 38-55, para 14-30. This is a summary of the relevant points from the appendix of the report.

23 Ibid., 46, para. 31.

24 See also Yoshiaki Yoshimi, *Comfort Women: Sexual Slavery in the Japanese Military during World War II,* trans. Suzanne O'Brien (New York: Columbia University Press, 2000), 153-76, for a detailed discussion of how Japan's setting up of the comfort women system violated international law.

25 The full text of Tong Zeng's memorandum can be found in Gao Fanfu, "Zhuisuo zhengyi yu zunyan de jiannan suqiu" [The difficult road of seeking justice and dignity]. (PhD diss., Shanghai Normal University, 2006), 229-40. The text is also posted on the website of Zhongguo minjian dui-Ri suopei lianhehui (Association of Chinese civilian war victims seeking compensations from Japan), available at http://www.cfdc.org.cn/ (viewed 6 June 2012).

26 Li Guping contends that the Chinese government neither informed the Chinese citizens nor consulted with the National People's Congress – the highest organ of state power, according to the Chinese Constitution – before including in the 1972 Sino-Japanese Joint Communiqué its statement regarding the abandoning of its right to claim war reparations. This occurred in the middle of the infamous Cultural Revolution. See Li Guping's open letter to the National People's Congress, "Yige putong gongmin jiu Riben qin-Hua zhanzheng peichang wenti gei Quanguo Renmin Daibiao Dahui de yifeng gong kaixin" [An

ordinary citizen's open letter to the National People's Congress regarding the reparation issues of Japan's aggressive war in China], in Gao, "Zhuisuo zhengyi yu zunyan de jiannan suqiu," 217-24.

27 Ibid.

28 Chūgokujin sensō higai baishō seikyū jiken bengodan, *Sajō no shōheki: Chūgokujin sengo hoshō saiban 10 nen no kiseki* [Walls on sands: Tracing the ten years of trials regarding postwar compensation to Chinese people] (Tokyo: Nihon hyōronsha, 2005), 6-7.

29 Wang Lusheng, "Minjian dui-Ri suopei: Tong Zeng de wenzhang yinchu renda daibiao shi ge ti'an" [Citizens demand compensation from Japan: Tong Zeng's article inspired ten proposals from the representatives of the National People's Congress], posted on *China. com* on 18 August 2005. Available at http://news.china.com/ (viewed 5 April 2009). See also Li Xiuping, *Shiwan weianfu* [One hundred thousand comfort women] (Beijing: Renmin Zhongguo chubanshe, 1993), 190-205.

30 Li, *Shiwan weianfu,* 190-93.

31 "Zhonghua renmin gongheguo zhengfu he Ribenguo zhengfu lianhe shengming" [Sino-Japanese Joint Communiqué], 29 September 1972, posted on Ministry of Foreign Affairs, People's Republic of China, website. Available at http://www.fmprc.gov.cn/ (viewed 5 April 2009).

32 *Cankao xiaoxi,* 25 February 1992.

33 Chūgokujin sensō higai baishō seikyū jiken bengodan, *Sajō no shōheki,* 22.

34 Ōmori Noriko, *Rekishi no jijitsu to mukiatte: Chūgokujin "ianfu" higaisha to tomo ni* [Facing the truth of history: Together with the Chinese "comfort women" victims] (Tokyo: Shin Nihon shuppansha, 2008), 29-33.

35 For detailed information on the event, see Hicks, *Comfort Women,* 254-66.

36 Yuki Terazawa, "The Transnational Campaign for Redress for Wartime Rape by the Japanese Military: Cases for Survivors in Shanxi Province," *National Women's Studies Association Journal* 18, 3 (2006): 136.

37 Cai Pa, "Fu Heji: Tansuo lishi zhenxiang de ren" [Fu Heji: A man devoted to seeking historical truth], in *Hainan ribao,* 8 May 2005, posted on *Hainanwang.* Available at http://www.hinews.cn, (viewed 21 May 2009).

38 "Tamen wei 'weianfu' benbo caolao" [They work hard for the "comfort women"], in *Haikou wanbao,* 15 August 2005.

39 Su Shi, "Riben qinlüezhe qiangpo Zhongguo funü zuo Rijun 'weianfu' shilu" [Japanese invaders forced Chinese women to be Japanese military "comfort women"], *Kang-Ri zhanzheng yanjiu* 1992 (4): 14-23. Gao Xingzu, "Rijun Nanjing qiangjian shijian yu weiansuo de chuxian" [The rapes committed by Japanese forces in Nanjing and the establishment of the comfort stations], *Minguo chunqiu* 3 (1993), reprinted in Su Zhiliang, et al, *Taotian zuinie,* 123-26; Guan Ning, "Weianfu wenti yu Riben de guojihua" [The "comfort women" issue and its impact on Japan's relationship with the international community], *Shijieshi yanjiu dongtai* 9 (1993): 27-39; and He Ji, "Rijun qiangbi Zhongguo funü wei 'weianfu' ziliao zhaibian" [Selected documents concerning the Japanese military forcing Chinese women to be "comfort women"], *Kangri zhanzhen yanjiu* 4 (1993): 37-51. For more studies in Chinese on the comfort women issue that have come out since 1993, see the bibliography.

Chapter 10: Litigation on the Part of Chinese Survivors

1 Onodera Toshitaka, "Sengo rokujūnen sasaeru kai jisshūnen: Koremade no ayumi to korekara" [Sixty years after the war and the tenth anniversary of the association for supporting the claims by Chinese war victims: What we have done and what we shall do], posted on the homepage of Chūgokujin sensō higaisha no yōkyū o sasaeru kai [Association

for supporting the claims by Chinese war victims], available at http://www.suopei.jp (viewed 5 April 2009).

2 Ibid.

3 Cao Pengcheng, "Zi tao yaobao daili suopei: Ri lüshi bang Zhongguo yuangao daguansi" [Paying out of his own pocket to represent the war victims' cases: The Japanese lawyer who has helped Chinese plaintiffs with their lawsuits], *Huanqiu shibao*, 24 August 2005.

4 Li Gongjian, "Wei Shanhong: Yi zhengyi gandong Zhongguo" [Oyama Hiroshi: His great sense of justice moved China], *China Reports*, 24 February 2004.

5 Phone interview with Attorney Kang Jian, 7 July 2009.

6 Ōmori Noriko, *Rekishi no jijitsu to mukiatte: Chūgokujin "ianfu" higaisha to tomo ni* [Facing the truth of history: Together with the Chinese "comfort women" victims] (Tokyo: Shin Nihon shuppansha, 2008), 15.

7 He Degong, "Wo weihe ti Zhongguo shouhaizhe bianhu: Fang Ri lüshi Xiaoyesi Lixiao" [Why I have represented Chinese victims: An interview with Japanese attorney Onodera Toshitaka], *Cankao xiaoxi tekan*, posted on www.news.cn, 4 August 2005. Available at http://news.xinhuanet.com/ (viewed 5 April 2009).

8 Yuki Terazawa, "The Transnational Campaign for Redress for Wartime Rape by the Japanese Military: Cases for Survivors in Shanxi Province," *National Women's Studies Association Journal* 18, 3 (2006): 137.

9 Chen Lifei, *Rijun weianfu zhidu pipan* [A critical analysis of the Japanese military comfort women system] (Beijing: Zhonghua shuju, 2006), 365.

10 Chen, *Rijun weianfu zhidu pipan*, 355. Masami Ito's 2004 report indicates that the amount of compensation demanded is 23 million *yen*. See "High court convenes, snubs sex slave appeal, calls it a day," *The Japan Times*, December 16, 2004. http://www.japantimes.co.jp. According to the Board of Governors of the Federal Reserve System, on 1 August 1995, the exchange rate of the Japanese *yen* to one US dollar was 94.7383. See http://research.stlouisfed.org (viewed 8 June 2012).

11 Chūgokujin sensō higaisha no yōkyū o sasaeru kai, "Ikiteiru kagiri tatakai tsuzukemasu" [We will continue fighting as long as we live], *web-suopei*, 29 April 2004, available at http://www.suopei.jp (viewed 15 October 2010).

12 Phone interview with Attorney Kang Jian, 7 July 2009. See also Chūgokujin sensō higaisha no yōkyū o sasaeru kai, "Chūgokujin ianfu daiichiji soshô saikô hanketsu" [The Supreme Court judgment on the first Chinese comfort women lawsuit], *web-suopei*, 27 April 2007, available at http://www.suopei.jp (viewed 15 October 2010).

13 Dwight Daniels, "'Comfort Women' Deserve Justice," *China Daily*, 28 March 2005. http://www.chinadaily.com.cn (viewed 8 April, 2009). *The Kyodo News* reports that the plaintiffs sought a combined 46 million *yen* in redress. See "Top Court: No War Redress for Chinese; Rights Void but Abuses Admitted – Suits to Fail," *Japan Times* online, 28 April 2007, available at http://search.japantimes.co.jp (viewed 8 April 2009). According to the Board of Governors of the Federal Reserve System, on 1 February 1996, the exchange rate of the Japanese *yen* to one US dollar was 105.7880. See http://research.stlouisfed.org (viewed 8 June 2012).

14 *Kyodo News*, "Top Court."

15 Dwight Daniels, "'Comfort Women' Deserve Justice."

16 "Japan Rejects Comfort Women Claims," *China View*, 19 March 2005, available at http://news.xinhuanet.com (viewed 8 April 2009).

17 Masami Ito, "High Court Rejects Sex-Slave Suit: Judge Trots Out Treaty with Nationalists, Statute of Limitations," *Japan Times* online, 19 March 2005, available at http://search.japantimes.co.jp (viewed 8 April 2009).

18 *Kyodo News*, "Top Court."

19 Ibid.
20 "China Blasts Japan Court's Rejection on WW2 Suits," *China Daily* online, 28 April 2007, available at http://www.chinadaily.com.cn (viewed 8 April 2009).
21 Chen, *Rijun weianfu zhidu pipan*, 362.
22 "Court rejects lawsuit on wartime rape," *Japan Times*, April 25, 2003. Retrieved from http://www.japantimes.co.jp (viewed 8 April 2009).
23 "Zhongguo weianfu yaoqiu Riben zhengfu xiezui susong qingqiu zai zao bohui" [Chinese comfort women's demand for an apology and compensation from Japanese government is denied again], *Xinhuanet*, 31 March 2005, available at http://news.xinhuanet.com (viewed 9 April 2009).
24 Interview with Kang Jian, 8 July 2009.
25 According to the Board of Governors of the Federal Reserve System, on 1 July 2001, the exchange rate of the Japanese *yen* to one US dollar was 124.4981. See http://research.stlouisfed.org (viewed 8 June 2012).
26 Chūgokujin sensō higai baishō seikyū jiken bengodan, *Sajō no shōheki-Chūgokujin sengo hoshō saiban 10 nen no kiseki* [Walls on sands: Tracing the ten years of trials regarding postwar compensation to Chinese people] (Tokyo: Nihon hyōronsha, 2005), 62-63. In *China View's* article, "Tokyo Court Rejects Damages Suit Filed by WWII Chinese Sex Slaves," posted on *China View*, 2 March 2009, the plaintiffs' demand for compensation is reported as 23 million *yen*. See http://news.xinhuanet.com.
27 "Litigation on Comfort Women Wins Support," *China Daily*, 20 March 2006, available at http://www.chinadaily.com.cn (viewed 6 April 2009).
28 "Tokyo Court Rejects Damages Suit Filed by WWII Chinese Sex Slaves," *China View*, 27 March 2009.
29 Permanent Mission of People's Republic of China to the UN, available at http://www.china-un.org (viewed 24 October 2010).
30 Wang Chingfeng, "Tamen de shangkou shangwei yuhe—Taiwan 'weianfu' wenti de jinzhan" [Their wounds have not healed: The development of "comfort women" issue in Taiwan], in *Taotian zuinie: Erzhan shiqi de Rijun weianfu zhidu* [Monstrous atrocities: The Japanese military comfort women system during the Second World War], ed. Su Zhiliang, Rong Weimu, and Chen Lifei (Shanghai: Xuelin chubanshe, 2000), 383-89. See also, Mo Yan-chih, "Comfort Women Still Fighting," *Taipei Times* online, 27 December 2010, available at http://www.taipeitimes.com (viewed 15 July 2012).
31 "Taiwanese Comfort Women," filed with *Memory and Reconciliation in the Asia-Pacific*, a Research and Policy Program at the George Washington University, Washington, DC, available at http://www.gwu.edu/~memory/data/judicial/comfortwomen_japan/Taiwanese.html (viewed 15 July 2012).
32 According to Taipei Women's Rescue Foundation, Taiwanese victims numbered 2,000 or more. See "Comfort Women" at www.twrf.org.
33 "Comfort Women," www.twrf.org.tw.
34 "Qi ming beipo zuo weianfu de Taiwan funü zhuanggao Riben zhengfu baisu" [Seven Taiwanese women who had been forced to become comfort women lost their lawsuit against Japanese Government], *Xinhuanet*, 10 February 2004, available at http://news.xinhuanet.com/ (viewed 9 April 2009).
35 "Taiwanese Comfort Women," filed with *Memory and Reconciliation in the Asia-Pacific*.
36 See "Claim for Compensation of Pusan Comfort Women and Women's Voluntary Labour Corps and Demand for Official Apology to the Women's Voluntary Labour Corps and to the Comfort Women," Decision of 27 April 1998 (following oral arguments of 29 September 1997), Shimonoseki Branch, Yamaguchi District Court. Translation is from Appendix to *Contemporary Forms of Slavery: Systematic Rape, Sexual Slavery and Slavery-Like Practices during Armed Conflict*, final report submitted by Special Rapporteur Gay J. McDougall to

United Nations Commission on Human Rights, Sub-Commission on Prevention of Discrimination and Protection of Minorities, 50th Session, UN Doc. E/CN.4/Sub.2/1998/13, 22 June 1998, 51, para. 50.

37 McDougall, *Contemporary Forms of Slavery*, Appendix, 39, para. 6.

38 Special Rapporteur Theo van Boven's statement on the right to restitution (E/CN.4/Sub. 2/1993/8. p. 56, para. 2), cited in paragraph 124 of "Report of the Special Rapporteur on violence against women, its causes and consequences, Ms. Radhika Coomaraswamy, in accordance with Commission on Human Rights resolution, 1994/45; Report on the mission to the Democratic People's Republic of Korea, the Republic of Korea and Japan on the issue of military sexual slavery in wartime," UN Doc., E/CN.4/1996/53/Add.1, 4 January 1996.

39 McDougall, *Contemporary Forms of Slavery*, 49, para. 44.

40 Japanese courts also rejected the Japanese government's defences with regard to certain cases filed by Chinese forced labourers. On 12 July 2001, for example, the Tokyo District Court rejected the defence of "time limitation" put forward by the Japanese government and recognized the claim made by the Chinese forced labour victim Liu Lianren. Thereafter, Japanese courts applied the basic legal principle of equity and justice and rejected the "time limitation" defence. In another case of Chinese forced labour victims versus the Japanese government and Nippon Yakin Kogyo Corp. (decided on 15 January 2003), the Kyoto District Court rejected the defence of "state immunity," although its decision did not support the claim by Chinese plaintiffs. Later, in cases decided by the Tokyo High Court, the Fukuoka High Court, and the Niigata District Court, the Japanese government's claim of "state immunity" was also rejected. See William Underwood and Kang Jian, "Japan's Top Court Poised to Kill Lawsuits by Chinese War Victims," posted on *Asia-Pacific Journal Japan Focus*, 2 March 2007, available at http://japanfocus.org (viewed 20 March 2009).

41 John Price points out that China's exclusion from the treaty talk might be attributable to the fact that the United States and others were fighting Chinese troops in the Korean War. The US government considered South Korean participation to be risky as Koreans who were critical of the Japanese government might have upset US plans to push through the treaty. The Japanese leader Yoshida Shigeru also wanted to exclude Koreans as signatories, otherwise Korean nationals in Japan might have been eligible for treaty benefits. See John Price, "Fifty Years Later, It's Time to Right the Wrongs of the San Francisco Peace Treaty," in *Japan Times* online, 6 September 2001. Available at http://www.japantimes.co.jp/ (viewed on 2 December 2012).

42 For the positions of the Democratic People's Republic of Korea, the Republic of Korea, and Japan on the issue, see sections 5, 6, and 7 of Radhika Coomaraswamy's report.

43 William Underwood and Kang Jiang, "Japan's Top Court Poised to Kill Lawsuits by Chinese War Victims."

44 McDougall, *Contemporary Forms of Slavery*, app., 53, para. 61.

45 Underwood and Kang, "Japan's Top Court Poised to Kill Lawsuits by Chinese War Victims."

46 McDougall, *Contemporary Forms of Slavery*, 52, para. 55.

47 Underwood and Kang, "Japan's Top Court Poised to Kill Lawsuits by Chinese War Victims."

48 For a discussion in English of the Japanese government's interpretation of the waiver section of the San Francisco Peace Treaty, see Kinue Tokudome, "POW Forced Labor Lawsuits against Japanese Companies," *JPRI Working Paper* (Japan Policy Research Institute at the University of San Francisco for the Pacific Rim), no. 82, November 2001, available at http://www.jpri.org.

49 John Price, "Fifty Years Later, It's Time to Right the Wrongs of the San Francisco Peace Treaty," *Japan Times* online, 6 September 2001.

50 Ibid.

51 Carol Gluck, "Operations of Memory: 'Comfort Women' and the World," in *Ruptured Histories: War, Memory, and the Post-Cold War in Asia*, ed. Sheila Miyoshi Jager and Rana Mitter (Cambridge: Harvard University Press, 2007), 48.

52 "Japan Rejects Lawsuit by WWII Sex Slaves," *People's Daily* online, 20 September 2000, available at http://english.peopledaily.com.cn (viewed 11 April 2009).

53 Kinue Tokudome, "POW Forced Labor Lawsuits against Japanese Companies," *JPRI Working Paper* No. 82, November 2001.

54 They are Fritz Kalshoven (honorary professor, Leiden University), Lepa Mladjenovic (Autonomous Women's Centre against Sexual Violence, Serbia), Yamada Akira (associate professor, Meiji University), Hayashi Hirofumi (professor, Kanto Gakuin University), Yoshimi Yoshiaki (professor, Chuo University), and Fujime Yuki (associate professor, Osaka University of Foreign Studies). Information is taken from "The Women's International War Crimes Tribunal on Japan's Military Sexual Slavery," Violence against Women in War Network Japan, available at http://www1.jca.apc.org/vaww-net-japan/english/womens tribunal2000/whatstribunal.html.

55 The VAWW-NET (Violence against Women in War Network) Japan listed the following participating Chinese survivors, Yang Ming-zhen, Yuan Zhu-lin, Wan Ai-hua, Li Xiu-mei,* Guo Xi-cui, Chen Ya-bian,* Huang You-liang,* and Liu Mian-huan* (asterisks indicate video testimony). See http://www1.jca.apc.org.

56 Chen, *Rijun weianfu zhidu pipan*, 378.

57 Rumi Sakamoto notes that, among Japanese and Korean researchers and activists, the comfort women issue emerged in the context of postcolonial discourse. Feminists, concerned that the issue might become subsumed within the rhetoric of nationalism, tried to extend the debate by linking the comfort women issue to contemporary international human rights issues. The tribunal, in this sense, is part of their efforts to view the issue from an international perspective. See Rumi Sakamoto, "The Women's International War Crimes Tribunal on Japan's Military Sexual Slavery: A Legal and Feminist Approach to the 'Comfort Women' Issue," *New Zealand Journal of Asian Studies* 3, 1 (2001): 49-58.

58 McDougall, *Contemporary Forms of Slavery*, 23-31.

59 Sakamoto, "Women's International War Crimes Tribunal," 54-55.

Chapter 11: International Support

1 Hirofumi Hayashi, "Disputes in Japan over the Japanese Military "Comfort Women" System and Its Perception in History," *Annals of the American Academy of Political and Social Science* 617 (2008): 123-24.

2 Tessa Morris-Suzuki, "Japan's 'Comfort Women:' It's Time for the Truth (in the Ordinary, Everyday Sense of the Word)," *Asia-Pacific e-Journal: Japan Focus*, 8 March 2007. Available at http://www.japanfocus.org.

3 Dongwoo Lee Hahm, "Urgent Matters: Redress for Surviving 'Comfort Women,'" in *Legacies of the Comfort Women of World War II*, ed. Margaret Stetz and Bonnie B.C. Oh (Armonk, NY: M.E. Sharpe, 2001), 128.

4 Founded in 1992 to promote research and education pertaining to crimes against comfort women during the Second World War, it is an independent, non-profit, non-partisan educational organization.

5 It was founded in 1994 for the preservation of the historical truth of the Asia-Pacific War (1931-45). The organization is also involved in activities such as supporting comfort station survivors and organizing the Peace and Reconciliation Tour of China.

6 Commenced in Shanghai in September 2003, the International Solidarity Council Demanding Settlement of Japan's Past has subcommittees in China, Japan, South Korea, North Korea, the Philippines, Indonesia, Taiwan, and the Netherlands. The coordinators

of the subcommittees meet annually to discuss the plans for activities in various countries as well as the movement of the council as a whole.

7 Resolution of the International Solidarity Council Demanding Settlement of Japan's Past, 5th Conference, The Hague, Netherlands, in commemoration of the 101st anniversary of the 1907 Hague Convention, 4 October 2008.

8 The proposed bill can be found in the appendix to an article by Totsuka Etsurō, "Shimin ga kimeru 'ianfu' mondai no rippō kaiketsu: Senji seiteki kyōsei higaisha mondai kaiketsu sokushin hōan no jitsugen o motomete" [The legislative resolution of the "comfort woman" issue is in the hands of citizens: Seeking legislative resolution of the issues concerning victims of wartime sexual violence]. *Kokusai jinkenhō seisaku kenkyū*, vols. 3 and 4 (2008): 59-62.

9 Ibid., 30.

10 According to a 2009 statistic, about half of the women had already died by that year. See "'Ianfu' mondai no rippō kaikatsu o motomeru kai" [Association for legislative resolution of the comfort women issue] and "Senji seiteki kyōsei higaisha mondai kaiketsu sokushin hōan no rippō o motomeru renraku kaigi" [Coalition for seeking legislation of the bill on issues concerning wartime sexual violence victims], "*Ianfu" mondai no sōki rippō kaiketsu no tameni* [For the timely resolution of the "comfort women" issue through legislation] (January 2009), 1.

11 Hahm, "Urgent Matters," 128.

12 Unpublished report from Taipei Women's Rescue Foundation.

13 In December 1997 the Taiwanese government provided 2 million *yen* as temporary payment to the forty-two former comfort women who came forth to testify in support of their litigation against the Japanese government. In April 1998, the Government of South Korea paid about 3 million *yen* to the former comfort women who had refused to accept the payment from the AWA. See "*Ianfu" mondai no sōki rippō kaiketsu no tameni*, 2.

14 The findings are published on the All China Lawyers Association's website, http://www. acla.org.cn/ (viewed 2 January 2009).

15 Zhongguo yuan "weianfu" shouhai shishi diaocha weiyuanhui, "Zhongguo yuan 'weianfu' shouhai shishi diaocha weiyuanhui fabu diyi jieduan diaocha jieguo" [The results of the first phase of the investigation published by the committee for the victimization of former Chinese comfort women], post on www.ACLA.org.cn (viewed 2 January 2009).

16 Ibid.

17 One of the eight political parties in China. The members of the Zhi Gong Party are mainly overseas Chinese who have returned and relatives of overseas Chinese.

18 Ge Shuya, "Dongjia-gou weiansuo de xinfaxian" [New discovery at the Dongjia-gou comfort station], *Minzhu yu fazhi shibao*, 1 November 2010.

19 Chen Zuliang, "Qin-Hua Rijun Dianxi weiansuo yu 'weianfu'" [The Japanese military comfort stations and "comfort women" in western Yunnan], in *Taotian zuinie: Erzhan shiqi de Rijun weianfu zhidu*, ed. Su Zhiliang, Rong Weimu, and Chen Lifei (Shanghai: Xuelin chubanshe, 2000), 308-22.

20 Ibid., 313-22.

21 Retrieved from the Women's Active Museum website, http://www.wam-peace.org/.

Epilogue

1 Wang, Yufeng, "Scholars propose memorializing 'comfort stations': The Ravages of Time," *Global Times*, September 22, 2011.

2 Ibid.

3 Zhuang Qinghong, "Riben nüxing jishu de Zhongguo 'weianfu' lishi" [The history of Chinese "comfort women" documented by Japanese women], *Zhongguo qingnianbao*, 5 April 2010.

4 Ōmori Noriko, *Rekishi no jijitsu to mukiatte: Chūgokujin "ianfu" higaisha to tomo ni* [Facing the truth of history: Together with the Chinese "comfort women" victims] (Tokyo: Shin Nihon shuppansha, 2008), 111.

5 Ikeda Eriko, "Tamura Taijirō ga egaita senjō no sei: Sanseishō Nihongun shihaika no baishun to kyōkan" [Tamura Taijirō's portrayal of sex in the battlefields: Prostitution and rape under the Japanese military occupation in Shanxi Province], in *Kōdo no mura no seibōryoku: Dā'nyan tachi no sensō wa owaranai* [Sexual violence in the villages located in the area of the yellow earth: The war is not over to these aged women], ed. Ishida Yoneko and Uchida Tomoyuki (Tokyo: Sōdosha, 2004), 320. Kondō's recollections are also recorded by Ōmori in *Rekishi no jijitsu to mukiatte*, 112.

6 Ibid.

7 This discussion is inspired by the observation Timothy Brook made in *Collaboration: Japanese Agents and Local Elites in Wartime China* (Cambridge, MA: Harvard University Press, 2005), 23-24.

8 Nicola Henry, *War and Rape: Law, Memory and Justice* (London: Routledge, 2011), 52.

Bibliography

Newspapers
Asahi Shimbun
Cankao xiaoxi
China Daily
Dadi zhoubao
Dagong bao
Global Times
Hainan ribao
Huanqiu shibao
Minzhu yu fazhi shibao
People's Daily
Renmin ribao
Renmin ribao haiwaiban
Shen bao
Japan Times
Yomiuri Shimbun
Zhongguo qingnian bao

Internet Resources
All China Lawyers Association. www.ACLA.org.cn.
China View. www.chinaview.cn.
Chinese "Comfort Women" Research Center. http://cms.shnu.edu.cn/.
Chūgoku Kainantō senji seibōryoku higaisha e no shazai to baishō o motomeru nettowāku (Hainan NET). http://hainannet.org/.
Chūgokujin sensō higaisha no yōkyū o sasaeru kai [Association supporting claims by Chinese war victims]. http://www.suopei.jp.
House of Sharing. http://nanum.org.
Josei no tame no Ajia heiwa kokumin kikin [Citizens' Asia peace fund for women], often referred to as the Asian Women's Fund, or AWF. http://www.awf.or.jp.
Korean Council for Women Drafted for Military Sexual Slavery by Japan. http://saynoto violence.org.
Ministry of Foreign Affairs, Japan. http://www.mofa.go.jp.
Ministry of Foreign Affairs, People's Republic of China. http://www.fmprc.gov.cn.
Renminwang (People). http://www.people.com.cn.
Taipei Women's Rescue Foundation. http://www.twrf.org.tw.
United Nations documents. http://www.unhchr.ch.
Violence Against Women in War – Network Japan (VAWW-NET Japan). http://www1. jca.apc.org/vaww-net-japan/.

Women's Active Museum on War and Peace. http://www.wam-peace.org/.

Xinhuawang (Xinhuanet). http://news.xinhuanet.com.

Zhongguo minjian dui-Ri suopei lianhehui [Association of Chinese civilian war victims seeking compensations from Japan], http://www.cfdc.org.cn.

Books and Articles

An Ming. *Weianfu de xuelei qing* [Sorrow of the comfort women]. Beijing: Junshi yiwen chubanshe, 1999.

Asian Women's Fund. *"Ianfu" kankei bunken mokuroku* [A bibliography of publications on the "comfort women" issue]. Tokyo: Gyōsei, 1997.

Asō Tetsuo. *Shanhai yori Shanhai e: Heitan byōin no sanfujinkai* [From Shanghai to Shanghai: A gynecologist at the commissariat hospital]. Fukuoka: Sekifūsha, 1993.

Ban Zhongyi. *Xuelei "Gai Shanxi": Rijun Shanxi xingbaoli shinian diaocha* [The sufferings of "The Number One Beauty in Shanxi": Ten years of investigation of the Japanese military sexual violence in Shanxi]. Beijing: Zhongguo wenlian chubanshe, 2006.

Beijingshi dang'anguan. "Rijun qiangzheng 'weianfu' shiliao yijian" [A historical document on the Japanese military's forcible drafting of "comfort women." In *Taotian zuinie: Erzhan shiqi de Rijun weianfu zhidu*, ed. Su Zhiliang, Rong Weimu, and Chen Lifei, 623-26. Shanghai: Xuelin Chubanshe, 2000.

Bian Xiuyue. "Weianfu wenti yu Riben zhanzheng zuize" [The comfort women issue and Japan's responsibility for its war crimes]. *Kang-Ri zhanzheng yanjiu* 1999 (2): 159-73.

Brook, Timothy. *Collaboration: Japanese Agents and Local Elites in Wartime China.* Cambridge, MA: Harvard University Press, 2005.

Brownmiller, Susan. *Against Our Will: Men, Women, and Rape.* New York: Simon and Schuster, 1975.

Bu Ping. "Weianfu wenti yu Riben de zhanzheng zeren renshi" [The comfort women issue and Japan's attitude toward its responsibility for war crimes]. *Kang-Ri zhanzheng yanjiu* 2000 (2): 162-80.

Cao Baoming. *Weianfu kaocha shouji* [Investigative notes: The comfort women]. Changchun: Jilin wenshi chubanshe, 2007.

Chai, Alice Yun. "Asian-Pacific Feminist Coalition Politics: The Chengshindae/Jugunianfu ('Comfort Women') Movement, *Korean Studies* 1993 (17): 67-91.

—. "Korean Feminist and Human Rights Politics: The Chongshindae/ Jugun ianfu ('Comfort Women') Movement." In *Korean American Women: From Tradition to Modern Feminism*, ed. Young I. Song and Ailee Moon, 237-54. Westport: Praeger, 1998.

Chang, Iris. *The Rape of Nanking: The Forgotten Holocaust of World War II.* New York: Penguin, 1998.

Chavez, Linda. "Contemporary Forms of Slavery." Working paper on the situation of systematic rape, sexual slavery, and slavery-like practices during wartime, including internal armed conflict, submitted in accordance with subcommission decision 1994/109, UN Doc. E/CN.4/Sub.2/1995/38.1995.

Chen Jingyan. "Riben qin-Hua qijian qiangzheng Zhongguo weianfu wenti" [Issues concerning Japan's forcing Chinese women to be comfort women during its invasion of China]. *Dongbeiya luntan* 2001 (3): 60-64.

Chen Juan. "Nanjing Rijun 'weianfu' zhidu de shishi" [The implementation of the Japanese military "comfort women" system in Nanjing]. In *Taotian zuinie: Erzhan shiqi de Rijun weianfu zhidu*, ed. Su Zhiliang, Rong Weimu, and Chen Lifei, 152-60. Shanghai: Xuelin chubanshe, 2000.

Chen Lifei. *Rijun weianfu zhidu pipan* [A critical analysis of the Japanese military comfort women system]. Beijing: Zhonghua shuju, 2006.

Chen Lifei and Su Zhiliang. *Zhuisuo: Chaoxian weianfu Piao Yongxin he tade jiemeimen* [Tracing the history: Korean comfort woman Pahk Young-sim and her sisters-in-suffering]. Guangzhou: Guangdong renmin chubanshe, 2005.

Chen Qinggang, ed. *Xue tong: Ershiliu ge weianfu de kongsu* [Bleeding wounds: The testimonies of twenty-six comfort women]. Beijing: Beijing chubanshe, 2005.

Chen Shurong. "Guojifa toushi xia de Rijun 'weianfu' wenti" [Examining the issue of Japanese military "comfort women" through international law]. *Shijiazhuang xueyuan xuebao* 2005 (4): 35-38.

Chen Sibai. *Yeshou zai jiangnan* [The monstrous troops in south China]. Shangyao: Qianxian ribaoshe, 1939.

Chen Zhengqin. "Qin-Hua Rijun Huazhong 'weianfu' zuixing xinzheng" [New evidence of the crimes committed by the invading Japanese army against "comfort women" in central China]. *Dang'an yu shixue* 2003 (1): 39-46.

Chen Zhengqin, and Zhuang Zhiling. "Dang'an zhong faxian de youguan Shanghai Rijun weianfu wenti" [Newly discovered archival evidence of the Japanese military comfort women in Shanghai]. *Dang'an yu shixue* 2000 (2): 47-51.

Chen Zuliang. "Qin-Hua Rijun Dianxi weiansuo yu 'weianfu'" [The Japanese military comfort stations and "comfort women" in western Yunnan]. In *Taotian zuinie: Erzhan shiqi de Rijun weianfu zhidu,* ed. Su Zhiliang, Rong Weimu, and Chen Lifei, 308-22. Shanghai: Xuelin Chubanshe, 2000.

Choi, Chungmoo. *The Comfort Women: Colonialism, War, and Sex* (*positions: east asia cultures critique* 5, 1 [1997], special issue). Durham: Duke University Press, 1997.

Chuang Kuo-ming. "Rang zhengyi suxing: Taiwan 'weianfu' jishi" [Restore justice: Notes on Taiwanese "comfort women"]. In *Taotian zuinie: Erzhan shiqi de Rijun weianfu zhidu,* ed. Su Zhiliang, Rong Weimu, and Chen Lifei, 378-82. Shanghai: Xuelin Chubanshe, 2000.

Chūgoku kikansha renrakukai, ed. *Kanzenban Sankō* [The three alls: A complete collection]. Tokyo: Banseisha, 1984.

Chūgokujin sensō higai baishō seikyū jiken bengodan. *Sajō no shōheki-Chūgokujin sengo hoshō saiban 10 nen no kiseki* [Walls on sands: Tracing the ten years of trials regarding postwar compensation to Chinese people]. Tokyo: Nihon hyōronsha, 2005.

Chung, Chin Sung. "Korean Women Drafted for Military Sexual Slavery by Japan." In *True Stories of the Korean Comfort Women: Testimonies Compiled by the Korean Council for Women Drafted for Military Sexual Slavery by Japan and the Research Association on the Women Drafted for Military Sexual Slavery by Japan,* ed. Keith Howard, trans. Young Joo Lee, 11-30. London: Cassell, 1995.

Chung, Chin-sung. "Wartime State Violence against Women of Weak Nations; Military Sexual Slavery Enforced by Japan during World War II." *Korean and Korean American Studies Bulletin* 5 (2-3) (1994): 15-27.

Coomaraswamy, Radhika. *Report of the Special Rapporteur on Violence against Women, Its Causes and Consequences, Ms. Radhika Coomaraswamy, in Accordance with Commission on Human Rights Resolution, 1994/45. Report on the Mission to the Democratic People's Republic of Korea, the Republic of Korea and Japan on the Issue of Military Sexual Slavery in Wartime.* UN Doc. E/CN.4/1996/53/Add.1, 4 January 1996.

Dethlefsen, Henrik. "Denmark and the German Occupation: Cooperation, Negotiation, or Collaboration?" *Scandinavian Journal of History* 15, 3 (1990): 193-206.

Dolgopol, Ustinia, and Snehal Paranjape. *Comfort Women: An Unfinished Ordeal.* Report of a Mission. Geneva, CH: International Commission of Jurists, 1994.

Dower, John. *Embracing Defeat: Japan in the Wake of World War II.* New York: W.W. Norton, 1999.

Drea, Edward J., and Hans van de Ven. "An Overview of Major Military Campaigns during the Sino-Japanese War, 1937-1945." In *The Battle for China: Essays on the Military History of the Sino-Japanese War of 1937-1945*, ed. Mark Peattie, Edward J. Drea, and Hans van de Ven, 27-47. Stanford: Stanford University Press, 2011.

Egami, Sachiko. "Rijun funü baoxing he zhanshi Zhongguo funü zazhi" [Japanese military's violence against women and wartime Chinese women's magazines]. In *Taotian zuinie: Erzhan shiqi de Rijun weianfu zhidu*, ed. Su Zhiliang, Rong Weimu, and Chen Lifei, 56-70. Shanghai: Xuelin Chubanshe, 2000.

Eguchi Keiichi. *Jūgonen sensō shōshi* [A history of the fifteen-year war]. Tokyo: Aoki shoten, 1986.

Fang Jianchang. "Rikou tietixia Hankou de Riben lujun weiansuo" [The Japanese army's comfort station in Hankou during the Japanese occupation]. *Wuhan wenshi ziliao* 2000 (4): 37-41.

Fang Zhiyuan. "Yige xiuru de baogao" [A humiliating report]. In *Yeshou zai jiangnan* [The monstrous troops in south China], ed. Chen Sibai, 89-90. Shangyao: Qianxian ribaoshe, 1939.

Field, Norma. "War and Apology: Japan, Asia, the Fiftieth, and After." *positions* 5 (1) (1997): 1-49.

Flath, James, and Norman Smith. *Beyond Suffering: Recounting War in Modern China*. Vancouver: UBC Press, 2011.

Fogel, Joshua A. ed., and Charles S. Maier, foreword. *The Nanjing Massacre in History and Historiography*. Berkeley: University of California Press, 2000.

Fu Heji. "Qin-Qiong Rijun 'weianfu' shilu" [The reality of the Japanese military "comfort women" in Hainan]. *Kang-Ri zhanzheng yanjiu* 4 (1996): 34-50.

–, comp. *Tietixiade xingfeng xueyu: Rijun qin-Qiong baoxing shilu* [Bloody crimes of the occupation rule: Records of the atrocities committed by the Japanese military in Hainan]. Hainan: Hainan chubanshe, 1995.

–, ed. *Tietixiade xingfeng xueyu: Rijun qin-Qiong baoxing shilu, Xu* [Sequel to Bloody crimes of the occupation rule: Records of the atrocities committed by the Japanese military in Hainan]. Hainan: Hainan chubanshe, 1996.

Fujioka Nobukatsu. *Jigyaku shikan no byōri* [An analysis of the masochistic views of history]. Tokyo: Bungeishunjū, 1997.

Gao Fanfu. "Riben shehui chuantong yu Rijun weianfu zhidu" [The tradition of Japanese society and the Japanese military comfort women system]. *Xuehai* 2005 (3): 59-61.

–. "Zhuisuo zhengyi yu zunyan de jiannan suqiu" [The difficult road of seeking justice and dignity]. PhD diss., Shanghai Normal University, 2006.

Gao Xingzu. "Nanjing datusha qijian Rijun weiansuo cankuang" [The horrors in the comfort stations during the Nanjing Massacre]. In *Taotian zuinie: Erzhan shiqi de Rijun weianfu zhidu*, ed. Su Zhiliang, Rong Weimu, and Chen Lifei, 137-43. Shanghai: Xuelin Chubanshe, 2000.

–. "Rijun Nanjing qiangjian shijian yu weiansuo de chuxian [The rapes committed by Japanese forces in Nanjing and the establishment of the confort stations]." In *Taotian zuinie: Erzhan shiqi de Rijun weianfu zhidu*, ed. Su Zhiliang, Rong Weimu, and Chen Lifei, 123-26. Shanghai: Xuelin Chubanshe, 2000.

Ge Shuya, "Dongjia-gou weiansuo de xinfaxian" [New discovery at the Dongjia-gou comfort station]. In *Minzhu yu fazhi shibao*, 1 November 2010.

Gluck, Carol. "Operations of Memory: 'Comfort Women' and the World." In *Ruptured Histories: War, Memory, and the Post-Cold War in Asia*, ed. Sheila Miyoshi Jager and Rana Mitter, 47-77. Cambridge, MA: Harvard University Press, 2007.

–. "Sekinin/Responsibility in Modern Japan." In *Word in Motion,* ed. Carol Gluck and Anna Lowenhaupt Tsing, 83-106. Durham: Duke University Press, 2009.

Guan Jianqiang. "Cong guojifa kan Ribenguo qin-Hua zhanzheng de minjian peichang wenti" [Compensations to civilian victims of Japan's war crimes during its invasion of China: A study from the perspective of international law]. *Faxue* 2000 (3): 49-52.

Guan Ning. "Weianfu wenti yu Riben de guojihua" [The comfort women issue and its impact on Japan's relationship with the international community]. *Shijieshi yanjiu dongtai* 1993 (9): 27-39.

Guan Wenhua. "Rijun dui Beipiao funü de lingru" [Japanese troops' sexual violence against women in Beipiao]. In *Qin-Hua Rijun baoxing zonglu,* ed. Li Bingxin, Xu Junyuan, and Shi Yuxin, 69. Shijiazhuang: Hebei renmin chubanshe, 1995.

Guo Rugui, Huang Yuzhang, and Tian Zhaolin. *Zhongguo kang-Ri zhanzheng zhengmian zhanchang zuozhan ji* [Major battles during China's Resistance War]. Nanjing: Jiangsu renmin chubanshe, 2002.

Hahm, Dongwoo Lee. "Urgent Matters: Redress for Surviving 'Comfort Women.'" In *Legacies of the Comfort Women of World War II,* ed. Margaret Stetz and Bonnie B.C. Oh, 128-41. Armonk, NY: M.E. Sharpe, 2001.

Han Wenning and Feng Chunlong. *Riben zhanfan shenpan* [Trials of the Japanese war criminals]. Nanjing: Nanjing Chubanshe, 2005.

Hata Ikuhiko. *Ianfu to senjō no sei* [Comfort women and sex in the battlefield]. Tokyo: Shinchōsha, 1999.

–. "The Nanking Atrocities: Fact and Fable." In *Japan Echo* 25 (4) (1998): 47-57.

Hayashi, Hirofumi. "Disputes in Japan over the Japanese Military 'Comfort Women' System and Its Perception in History." *Annals of the American Academy of Political and Social Science* 617 (2008): 123-32.

–. "Rikugun no ianjo kanri no ichisokumen" [One aspect of the management of the army comfort stations]. *Sensō sekinin kenkyū* 1 (1993): 16-17.

He Degong, "Wo weihe ti Zhongguo shouhaizhe bianhu: Fang Ri lüshi Xiaoyesi Lixiao" [Why I have represented Chinese victims: An interview with Japanese attorney Onodera Toshitaka]. *Cankao xiaoxi tekan,* posted on www.news.cn, 4 August 2005.

He Ji, ed. "Rijun qiangbi Zhongguo funü wei 'weianfu' ziliao zhaibian" [Selected documents concerning the Japanese military's forcing Chinese women to be "comfort women"]. *Kang-Ri zhanzheng yanjiu* 1993 (4): 37-51.

He Shili. "Sanbai 'weianfu' cansi taiban: Shilu tiekuang 'weiansuo' diaocha shikuang" [Over half of three hundred "comfort women" died: An investigative record of the Shilu iron mine "comfort station"]. In *Tietixiade xingfeng xueyu: Rijun qin-Qiong baoxing shilu,* ed. Fu Heji, 748-50. Hainan: Hainan chubanshe, 1995.

He Tianyi. "Lun Rijun zai Zhongguo Huabei de xingbaoli" [The Japanese military's sexual violence in northern China]. In *Taotian zuinie: Erzhan shiqi de Rijun weianfu zhidu,* ed. Su Zhiliang, Rong Weimu, and Chen Lifei, 254-68. Shanghai: Xuelin Chubanshe, 2000.

Hein, Laura. "Savage Irony: The Imaginative Power of the 'Military Comfort Women' in the 1990s." *Gender and History* 11(2) (1999): 336-72.

Henry, Nicola. *War and Rape: Law, Memory and Justice.* London: Routledge, 2011.

Henson, Maria Rosa. *Comfort Woman: A Filipina's Story of Prostitution and Slavery under the Japanese Military.* Lanham, MD.: Rowman and Littlefield, 1999.

Hicks, George. *The Comfort Women: Japan's Brutal Regime of Enforced Prostitution in the Second World War.* New York: W.W. Norton, 1995.

Hirabayashi Hisae. *Kyōsei renkō to Jūgun Ianfu* [Draft by force and military comfort women]. Tokyo: Nihon Tosho Sentā, 1992.

Hirota Kazuko. *Shōgen kiroku jūgun ianfu/kangofu: Senjō ni ikita onna no dōkoku* [Records of testimonies by military comfort women/nurses: Lamentations of women who lived in the battlefield]. Tokyo: Shinjinbutsuōraisha, 1975.

Hite, Katherine. *Politics and the Art of Commemoration: Memorials to Struggle in Latin America and Spain.* London: Routledge, 2011.

Honda, Katsuichi. *The Nanjing Massacre: A Japanese Journalist Confronts Japan's National Shame.* London: M.E. Sharpe, 1999.

Hora Tomio. *Nankin daigyakusatsu: Ketteihan* [Nanjing massacre: an authoritative edition]. Tokyo: Gendaishi shuppankai, 1982.

Howard, Keith, ed. *True Stories of the Korean Comfort Women.* London: Cassell, 1995.

Hu Jiaren (narrator), Zhuo Shichun and Chen Yunhong (recorders). "Fuli-miao Rijun he zijingtuan de judian qingkuang jiqi baoxing" [The strongholds of the Japanese military and self-guard league at Fuli-miao and their atrocities.' In *Tietixiade xingfeng xueyu: Rijun qin-Qiong baoxing shilu, Xu,* ed. Fu Heji, 308-9. Haikou: Hainan chubanshe, 1996.

"Ianfu" mondai no rippō kaikatsu o motomeru kai [Association seeking legislative resolution of the "comfort women" issue] and Senji seiteki kyōsei higaisha mondai kaiketsu sokushin hōan no rippō o motomeru renraku kaigi [Coalition for seeking legislation of the bill on issues concerning wartime sexual violence victims]. *"Ianfu" mondai no sōki rippō kaiketsu no tameni* [For the timely resolution of the "comfort women" issue through legislation]. January 2009.

Ienaga Saburō. *The Pacific War: World War II and the Japanese, 1931-1945.* New York: Pantheon Books, 1978.

Ikeda Eriko. "Tamura Taijirō ga egaita senjō no sei-Sanseishō: Nihongun shihaika no baishun to gōkan" [Tamura Taijirō's portrayal of sex in the battlefields: Prostitution and rape under the Japanese military occupation in Shanxi Province]. In *Kōdo no mura no seibōryoku: Dā'nyan tachi no sensō wa owaranai* [Sexual violence in the villages located in the area of the yellow earth: The war is not over to these aged women], ed. Ishida Yoneko and Uchida Tomoyuki, 296-325. Tokyo: Sōdosha, 2004.

Inaba Masao, ed. *Okamura Yasuji taishō shiryō: Senjō kaisō hen, jō* [Sources of General Okamura Yasuji: Recollections of the battlefield, vol. 1]. Tokyo: Hara shobō, 1970.

Ishida Yoneko and Uchida Tomoyuki. *Kōdo no mura no seibōryoku: Dā'nyan tachi no sensō wa owaranai* [Sexual violence in the villages located in the area of the yellow earth: The war is not over to these aged women]. Tokyo: Sōdosha, 2004.

Ishikida, Miki Y. *Toward Peace: War Responsibility, Postwar Compensation, and Peace Movements and Education in Japan.* New York: iUniverse, 2005.

Jager, Sheila Miyoshi, and Rana Mitter, eds. *Ruptured Histories: War, Memory, and the Post-Cold War in Asia.* Cambridge, MA: Harvard University Press, 2007.

Japanese Delegation to the Photo Exhibitions of War Atrocities Committed by Japanese Army. *The Asian Holocaust 1931-1945: Hidden Holocaust in World War II by the Japanese Army-Unit 731, BCW, Nanjing Massacre, Comfort Women.* Tokyo, 1998.

Jiang Gonggu. *Xian jing sanyue ji* [The fall of the capital: A journal of the three months]. Nanjing: Nanjing chubanshe, 2006. (Reprint of the 1938 edition.)

Jiang Hao. *Zhaoshi: Zhongguo weianfu – kuaguo kuashidai diaocha baipishu* [Exposé: Chinese comfort women – An investigation across the boundaries of nations and times]. Xining: Qinghai renmin chubanshe, 1998.

Jiang Weijiu. "Lun Erzhan pingmin shouhai peichang zeren" [On the responsibilities for compensation to individual victims of the Second World War]. *Shehui kexue zhanxian* 2000 (1): 238-43.

Jiangsu-sheng Rugao-shi difangzhi bianzhuan weiyuanhui. *Rugao xianzhi* [Historical record of Rugao County]. Hongkong: Xianggang xin Yazhou chubanshe youxiangongsi, 1995.

Jindaishi ziliao bianjibu, Zhongguo renmin kang-Ri zhanzheng jinianguan, ed. *Rijun qin-Hua baoxin shilu* [The atrocities committed by Japanese military during its invasion of China]. Beijing: Beijing chubanshe, 1996.

Jing Shenghong. "Nanjing de weianfu yu weiansuo" [The comfort stations and comfort women in Nanjing]. *Kang-Ri zhanzheng yanjiu* 1999 (2): 191-99.

—. "Qinhua Rijun zai Nanjing shishi 'weianfu' zhidu shimo" [The Japanese invaders' establishment of the "comfort women" system in Nanjing]. In *Taotian zuinie: Erzhan shiqi de Rijun weianfu zhidu*, eds. Su Zhiliang, Rong Weimu, and Chen Lifei, 161-73. Shanghai: Xuelin Chubanshe, 2000.

Josei no tame no Ajia heiwa kokumin kikin, ed. *Seifu chōsa "jūgun ianfu" kankei shiryō shūsei* [Governmental investigations: Documents concerning the military "comfort women"], 5 vols. Tokyo: Ryūkei shosha, 1997-98.

Jūgun ianfu 110-ban henshū iinkai. *Jūgun ianfu 110 ban-Denwa no mukō kara rekishi no koe ga* [Military comfort women hotlines: The voices of history from the other end of the telephone]. Tokyo: Akashi shoten, 1992.

Kasahara Tokushi. *Nankin jiken* [The Nanjing incident]. Tokyo: Iwanami shoten, 1997.

—. *Nankin jiken to sankō sakusen: Mirai ni ikasu sensō no kioku* [The Nanjing incident and the war of "burn all, kill all, loot all": War memories to be kept alive for the future]. Tokyo: Otsuki shoten, 1999.

—. "Chūgoku sensen ni okeru Nihongun no seihanzai: Kahokushō, Sanseishō no jirei" [The Japanese army's sexual crimes at the frontlines in China: The cases of Hebei and Shanxi Provinces]. In *Sensō sekinin kenkyū* [Studies of war responsibilities] 13 (1996): 2-11

Kawada Fumiko. *Sensō to sei* [War and sex]. Tokyo: Akashi shoten, 1995.

Kim, Il-myon. *Tennō no guntai to Chōsenjin ianfu* [The emperor's forces and the Korean comfort women]. Tokyō: Sanichi shobō, 1976.

—. *Yūjo, karayuki, ianfu no keifu* [The genealogy of prostitutes, overseas prostitutes, and comfort women]. Tokyo: Yūzankaku shuppan, 1997.

Kim-Gibson, Dai Sil. *Silence Broken: Korean Comfort Women.* Parkersburg: Mid-Prairie Books, 2000.

Korean Council for the Women Drafted for Military Sexual Slavery by Japan. Ed. Keith Howard, trans. Young Joo Lee. *True Stories of the Korean Comfort Women.* London: Cassell, 1995.

Lary, Diana, and Stephen MacKinnon, eds. *Scars of War: The Impact of Warfare on Modern China.* Vancouver: UBC Press, 2001.

Li, Danke. *Echoes of Chongqing: Women in Wartime China.* Urbana: University of Illinois Press, 2010.

Li Bihua. *Yanhua sanyue* [Misty spring]. Guangzhou: Huacheng chubanshe, 2005.

Li Bingxin, Xu Junyuan, and Shi Yuxin, eds. *Qin-Hua Rijun baoxing zonglu* [Collection of investigative records of the atrocities committed by the Japanese forces during Japan's invasion of China]. Shijiazhuang: Hebei renmin chubanshe, 1995.

Li Jinlian. "Kangzhan shiqi Rijun dui Dianxi funü de xingbaoxing chutan" [An examination of the sexual violence committed by the Japanese military against women in western Yunnan Province during the Resistance War]. *Chuxiong shifan xueyuan xuebao* 2003 (1): 65-68.

Li Qin. "Xin faxian de Rijun qiangzheng Tianjin funü chongdang 'weianfu' shiliao xi" [An analysis of the newly discovered historical documents relating to the Japanese military forcing Tianjin women to be "comfort women"]. In *Taotian zuinie: Erzhan shiqi de Rijun weianfu zhidu*, ed. Su Zhiliang, Rong Weimu, and Chen Lifei, 638-45. Shanghai: Xuelin Chubanshe, 2000.

Li Shimin, "Qiao Hongnian choushe weiansuo" [Qiao Hongnian prepared and set up comfort stations]. *Dadi zhoubao*, 31 (1946): 2.

Li Shitian and Li Zhizhong. "Zhanhou Riben dui-Hua peichang wenti" [Issues regarding Japan's postwar compensation to China]. *Kang Ri zhanzheng yanjiu* 3 (1997): 187-200.

Li Xiaofang. *Shiji nahan: 67-wei xingcun weianfu shilu* [Cries of the century: Testimonies of 67 surviving comfort women]. Beijing: Zhonggong dangshi chubanshe, 2008.

Li Xiaojiang. comp. *Rang nüren ziji shuohua: Qinli zhanzheng* [Let women tell their own stories: The wartime experiences]. Sanlian shudian, 2003.

Li Xiuping. *Shiwan weianfu* [One hundred thousand comfort women]. Beijing: Renmin Zhongguo chubanshe, 1993.

Lin Boyao. "Tianjin Rijun 'weianfu' zhi gongji xitong" [The Japanese military "comfort women" procurement system in Tianjin]. In *Taotian zuinie: Erzhan shiqi de Rijun weianfu zhidu*, ed. Su Zhiliang, Rong Weimu, and Chen Lifei, 269-307. Shanghai: Xuelin Chubanshe, 2000.

Ling Yian. "Huzhou de Rijun weiansuo" [Japanese military comfort station in Huzhou]. *Gujin tan* 4 (2001): 21-27.

Liu Ping. "Guanyu Rijun qiangzheng Shanxi 'weianfu' de diaocha baogao" [Investigative report on the Japanese army's abduction of "comfort women" in Shanxi]. *Kang-Ri zhanzheng yanjiu* 2 (1999): 181-90.

Lu, Suping. *They Were in Nanjing: The Nanjing Massacre Witnessed by American and British Nationals.* Hong Kong: Hong Kong University Press, 2004.

MacKinnon, Stephen R., Diana Lary, and Ezra Vogel, eds. *China at War: Regions of China, 1937-1945.* Stanford: Stanford University Press, 2007.

McDougall, Gay J. *Contemporary Forms of Slavery: Systematic Rape, Sexual Slavery and Slavery-Like Practices during Armed Conflict.* Final report submitted to United Nations Commission on Human Rights, Sub-Commission on Prevention of Discrimination and Protection of Minorities, fiftieth session. UN Doc. E/CN.4/Sub.2/1998/13, 22 June 1998. Appendix: "An Analysis of the Legal Liability of the Government of Japan for 'Comfort Women Stations' Established during the Second World War."

Matsui, Yayori. "Women's International War Crimes Tribunal on Japan's Military Sexual Slavery: Memory, Identity, and Society." In *East Asia: An International Quarterly* 19, no. 4 (Winter 2001): 119-42.

Matsusaka, Yoshihisa Tak. *The Making of Japanese Manchuria, 1904-1932.* Cambridge: Harvard University Asia Center, 2001.

Mayo, Marlene J., and J. Thomas Rimer with H. Eleanor Kerkham, eds. *War, Occupation, and Creativity: Japan and East Asia, 1920-1960.* Honolulu: University of Hawai'i Press, 2001.

Morisaki Kazue. *Karayuki san* [Overseas prostitutes]. Tokyo: Asahi shimbunsha, 1976.

Morris-Suzuki, Tessa. "Japan's 'Comfort Women:' It's Time for the Truth (in the Ordinary, Everyday Sense of the Word)." *Asia-Pacific e-Journal: Japan Focus,* 8 March 2007.

Nankin jiken chōsa kenkyūkai, ed. *Nankin jiken shiryōshū* [Documents on the Nanjing incident]. Tokyo: Aoki shoten, 1992.

Nihon bengoshi rengokai. *Investigative Report in Relation to Cases of Japan's Imperial Military "Comfort Women" of Taiwanese Descent.* Tokyo: Japan Federation of Bar Associations, 1997.

Nishino Rumiko, Hayashi Hirofumi, and VAWW-NET Japan, comp. *"Ianfu:" Senji seibō-ryoku no juttai (2) Chūgoku, Tōnanajia, Taiheiyō hen* ["Comfort women": The reality of sexual violence during the war (2) China, Southeast Asia, and the Pacific]. *Nihongun seidoreisei o sabaku: 2000 Josei kokusai senpan hōtei no kiroku* [Judging the Japanese military sexual slavery system: 2000 Women's International War Criminal Tribunal records], 4. Tokyo: Ryokufūsha, 2000.

Nishino Rumiko. *Jūgun ianfu: Moto heishi tachi no shōgen* [Military comfort women: Testimonies of former soldiers]. Tokyo: Akashi shoten, 1992.

–. *Senjō no ianfu* [Comfort women in the battlefields]. Tokyo: Akashi shoten, 2003.

Nitchō kyōkai Saitama-ken rengōkai, ed. *Shōgen "jūgun ianfu": Daiyaru 110 ban no kiroku* [Military comfort women: Records of the dial-in testimonies]. Urawa: Nitchō kyōkai Saitama-ken rengōkai, 1995.

Nozaki, Yoshiko. "Feminism, Nationalism, and the Japanese Textbook Controversy over 'Comfort Women.'" In *Feminism and Antiracism: International Struggles for Justice*, ed. France Winddance Twine and Kathleen M. Blee, 170-89. New York: New York University Press, 2001.

–. "The Comfort Women Controversy: History and Testimony." In *Asia-Pacific Journal: Japan Focus*. Available at www.japanfocus.org.

–. *War Memory, Nationalism and Education in Postwar Japan, 1945-2007: The Japanese History Textbook Controversy and Ienaga Saburo's Court Challenges*. New York: Routledge, 2008.

Okabe Naosaburō. *Okabe Naosaburō taishō no nikki* [General Okabe Naozaburō diary]. Tokyo: Fuyō shobō, 1982.

Ōmori Noriko. *Rekishi no jijitsu to mukiatte: Chūgokujin "ianfu" higaisha to tomo ni* [Facing the truth of history: Together with the Chinese "comfort women" victims]. Tokyo: Shin Nihon shuppansha, 2008.

Ōmori Noriko, and Kawata Fumiko. *Ianfu mondai ga toutekita koto* [Questions raised by the comfort women issue]. Tokyo: Iwanami shoten, 2012.

Pan Xian'e. "Rijun qin-Ling shishi gaiyao" [An outline of the history of the Japanese military invasion of Lingshui County]. In *Tietixiade xingfeng xueyu: Rijun qin-Qiong baoxing shilu, Xu*, ed. Fu Heji, 448-62. Haikou: Hainan chubanshe, 1995.

Peattie, Mark, Edward J. Drea, and Hans van de Ven, eds. *The Battle for China: Essays on the Military History of the Sino-Japanese War of 1937-1945*. Stanford: Stanford University Press, 2011.

Piccigallo, Philip R. *The Japanese on Trial: Allied War Crimes Operations in the East, 1945-1951*. Austin: University of Texas Press, 1979.

Price, John. "Fifty Years Later, It's Time to Right the Wrongs of the San Francisco Peace Treaty." *Japan Times* online, 6 September 2001.

Rabe, John. *The Good Man of Nanking: The Diaries of John Rabe*. New York: Vintage Books, 1998.

Ruff-O'Herne, Jan. *50 Years of Silence*. Sydney, AU: ETT Imprint, 1994.

Roberts, J.A.G. *A Concise History of China*. Cambridge: Harvard University Press, 1999.

Saaler, Sven, and Wolfgang Schwentker, ed. *The Power of Memory in Modern Japan*. Folkestone, UK: Global Oriental, 2008.

Sakamoto, Rumi. "The Women's International War Crimes Tribunal on Japan's Military Sexual Slavery: A Legal and Feminist Approach to the 'Comfort Women' Issue." *New Zealand Journal of Asian Studies* 3, 1 (2001): 49-58.

Sakurada Takeshi, and Shikanai Nobutaka. *Ima akasu sengo hishi* [A secret postwar history now revealed], vol. 1. Tokyo: Sankei shuppan, 1983.

Sancho, Nelia, ed. *War Crimes on Asian Women: Military Sexual Slavery by Japan during World War II; The Case of the Filipino Comfort Women*. Manila: Asian Women Human Rights Council, 1998.

Satō Kanji. *Akai chūrippu no heitai: Aru heishi no ashiato* [Troops of red tulips: A soldier's footprints]. Tokyo: Senshūsha, 1978.

Schellstede, Sangmie Choi, ed. *Comfort Women Speak: Testimony by Sex Slaves of the Japanese Military*. New York: Holmes and Meier, 2000.

Schmidt, David A. *Ianfu: The Comfort Women of the Japanese Imperial Army of the Pacific War – Broken Silence*. Lewiston: Edwin Mellon Press, 2000.

Seaton, Philip A. *Japan's Contested War Memories*. London: Routledge, 2007.

Senda Kakō. *Jūgun ianfu* [Military comfort women]. Tokyo: Kōdansha, 1984.

–. *Jūgun ianfu Keiko: Shisen o samayotta onna no shōgen* [Military comfort woman Keiko: The testimony of a woman who had been to hell]. Tokyo: Tsunetomo shuppan, 1995.

Soh, C. Sarah. *The Comfort Women: Sexual Violence and Postcolonial Memory in Korea and Japan.* Chicago: University of Chicago Press, 2008.

–. "Japan's Responsibility toward Comfort Women Survivors." *Japan Policy Research Institute Working Paper* 77 (2001). Available at http://www.jpri.org/.

Song Fuhai (narrator), Chen Ziming and Wang Ji (recorders). "Wo qindu de Rijun Xinying 'weiansuo'" [The Japanese military Xinying "comfort station" I witnessed]. In *Tietixiade xingfeng xueyu: Rijun qin-Qiong baoxing shilu, (Xu)*, ed. Fu Heji, 188-90. Hainan: Hainan chubanshe, 1995.

–. "Xinying weiansuo" [Xinying comfort station]. In *Xue tong: Ershiliu ge weianfu de kongsu*, ed. Chen Qinggang, 18-19. Beijing: Beijing chubanshe, 2005.

Song, Young I., and Ailee Moon, ed. *Korean American Women: From Tradition to Modern Feminism.* Westport: Praeger, 1998.

Stetz, Margaret, and Bonnie B.C. Oh, eds. *Legacies of the Comfort Women of World War II.* Armonk, NY: M.E. Sharpe, 2001.

Su Shi. "Riben qinlüezhe qiangpo Zhongguo funü zuo Rijun 'weianfu' shilu" [Japanese invaders forced Chinese women to be Japanese military "comfort women"]. *Kang-Ri zhanzheng yanjiu* 1992 (4): 14-23.

Su Zhiliang. "Guanyu Rijun weianfu zhidu de jidian bianxi" [An examination of the Japanese military comfort women system]. *Kang-Ri zhanzheng yanjiu* 1997 (3): 166-80.

–. "Shi lun zhanhou Riben dui weianfu wenti de taidu" [A discussion of Japan's attitude towards the comfort women issue after the Second World War]. *Riben yanjiu* 1999 (3): 26-32.

–. *Rijun xingnuli* [Japanese military's sex slaves]. Beijing: Renming chubanshe, 2000.

–. *Weianfu yanjiu* [A study of the comfort women]. Shanghai: Shanghai shudian chubanshe, 1999.

–. "Xianggang Rijun weiansuo diaocha ji" [Investigative record of the Japanese military comfort stations in Hong Kong]. *Tansuo yu zhengming* 2000 (2): 44-48.

Su Zhiliang, and Chen Lifei. "Qin-Hua Rijun weianfu zhidu lüelun" [A study of the Japanese military comfort women system in China]. *Lishi yanjiu* 1998 (4): 89-104.

Su Zhiliang, Chen Lifei, and Yao Fei. *Shanghai Rijun weiansuo shilu* [Investigative records of Japanese military comfort stations in Shanghai]. Shanghai: Shanghai sanlian shudian, 1995.

Su Zhiliang, Hou Guifang, and Hu Haiying. *Riben dui Hainan de qinlüe jiqi baoxing* [The Japanese invasion of Hainan and its atrocities]. Shanghai: Shanghai cishu chubanshe, 2005.

Su Zhiliang, Rong Weimu, and Chen Lifei, ed. *Taotian zuinie: Erzhan shiqi de Rijun weianfu zhidu* [Monstrous atrocities: The Japanese military comfort women system during the Second World War]. Shanghai: Xuelin chubanshe, 2000.

Sun, Youli. *China and the Origins of the Pacific War, 1931-1941.* New York: St. Martin's Press, 1993.

Sun Xun. *Weianfu xuelei* [Blood and tears of the comfort women]. Xi'an: Taibai wenyi chubanshe, 2001.

Sun Zhaiwei. "Lun Nanjing datusha zhong de xingbaoli wenti" [Sexual violence during the Nanjing Massacre]. *Minguo dang'an* 4 (2000): 91-96.

Suzuki Yūko. *Feminizumu to sensō* [Feminism and war]. Tokyo: Marujusha, 1986.

–. *"Jūgun ianfu" mondai to seibōryoku* ["Military comfort women" issue and sexual violence]. Tokyo: Miraisha, 1993.

Taibeishi funü jiuyuan shehui fuli shiye jijinhui. *Taiwan "weianfu" baogao* [Reports on the comfort women in Taiwan]. Taibei: Shangwu yinshuguan, 1999.

Takagi Ken'ichi. *Jūgun ianfu to sengo hoshō: Nihon no sengo sekinin* [Military comfort women and postwar compensation: Japan's responsibility after the war]. Tokyo: Sanichi shobō, 1992.

Takemae Eiji. *The Allied Occupation of Japan.* Trans. Robert Ricketts and Sebastian Swann. New York: Continuum, 2002.

Tanaka, Yuki. *Japan's Comfort Women: Sexual Slavery and Prostitution during World War II and the US Occupation.* New York: Routledge, 2002.

Tanaka Toshiyuki. "Naze Beigun wa jūgun ianfu mondai o mushishita no ka" [Why the US forces ignored the problem of the military comfort women]. *Sekai* 627 (1996): 174-83; and 628 (1996): 270-79.

Tang Huayuan. "Rijun zai Yueyang jiansha funü de baoxing" [Raping and killing women: The Japanese army's atrocities in Yueyang]. In *Qin-Hua Rijun baoxing zonglu,* ed. Li Bingxin, Xu Junyuan, and Shi Yuxin, 1010. Shijiazhuang: Hebei renmin chubanshe, 1995.

Terazawa, Yuki. "The Transnational Campaign for Redress for Wartime Rape by the Japanese Military: Cases for Survivors in Shanxi Province." *National Women's Studies Association Journal* 18, 3 (2006): 133-45.

Tian Susu. "Rijun weianfu zhengce zai Huabei diqu de shishi" [The implementation of the Japanese military comfort woman policy in northern China]. *Kang-Ri zhanzheng yanju* 2005 (2): 166-88.

—. "Xin faxian de Rijun zai Huabei shezhi weiansuo de zuizheng" [Newly discovered evidence of the comfort stations established by the Japanese military in northern China]. *Dang'an tiandi* 1 (2005): 14-17.

Tokudome, Kinue. "POW Forced Labor Lawsuits against Japanese Companies," *Japan Policy Research Institute Working Paper* 82 (2001). Available at http://www.jpri.org/.

Tomishima Kenji. Inu [Dog]. In *Sankō: Kanzenban* [The three alls: A complete collection]. Comp. Chūgoku kikansha renrakukai, 101-9. Tokyo: Banseisha, 1984.

Tong Zeng. "Zhongguo yaoqiu Riben shouhai peichang keburonghuan" [Demanding war indemnity from Japan is of great urgency to China]. Memorandum submitted to the Administrative Office of National People's Congress, 1991. In Gao Fanfu, "Zhuisuo zhengyi yu zunyan de jiannan suqiu" [The difficult road of seeking justice and dignity], 229-40. PhD diss., Shanghai Normal University, 2006.

Totani, Yuma. *The Tokyo War Crimes Trial: The Pursuit of Justice in the Wake of World War II.* Cambridge: Harvard University Asia Center, 2008.

Totsuka Etsurō. "Commentary on a Victory for 'Comfort Women': Japan's Judicial Recognition of Military Sexual Slavery." In *Pacific Rim Law and Policy Journal* 8 (161) (1999): 47-61.

—. "Shimin ga kimeru 'ianfu' mondai no rippō kaiketsu: Senji seiteki kyōsei higaisha mondai kaiketsu sokushin hōan no jitsugen o motomete" [The legislative resolution of the "comfort woman" issue is in the hands of citizens: Seeking legislative resolution of the issues concerning victims of wartime sexual violence]. *Kokusai jinkenhō seisaku kenkyū,* vols. 3 and 4 (2008): 16-65.

Ueno, Chizuko. *Nationalism and Gender.* Trans. Beverley Yamamoto. Melbourne: Trans Pacific Press, 2004.

Underwood, William, and Kang Jian. "Japan's Top Court Poised to Kill Lawsuits by Chinese War Victims." *Asia-Pacific Journal Japan Focus,* 2 March 2007. Available at http://www.japanfocus.org/.

Utsumi, Aiko. "How the Violence against Women Were Dealt with in War Crime Trials." In *Common Grounds: Violence against Women in War and Armed Conflict Situations.* Quezon: Asian Center for Women's Human Rights, 1998.

Utsumi Aiko, Ishida Yoneko, and Katō Nobuhiro. *Aru Nihonhei no futatsu no senjō: Kondō Hajime no owaranai sensō* [A Japanese soldier's two battlefields: The unending war of Kondō Hajime]. Tokyo: Shakai hyōronsha, 2005.

Wang Bizhen. "Weiansuo li de nütongbao" [Women in the comfort station] *Guangxi funü* 17-18 (1941): 36.

Wang Ching-feng. "Tamen de shangkou shangwei yuhe" [Their wounds have not healed]. In *Taotian zuinie*, ed. Su, Zhiliang, Rong Weimu, and Chen Lifei, 383-89. Shanghai: Xuelin Chubanshe, 2000.

Wang Shizhong, Li Zhaochang, Ji Xuehai, and Ji Xuexin (narrators), Zhang Yingyong (recorder). "Rijun zai Nanlin-xiang de zuixing shilu" [A record of the atrocities committed by the Japanese military in Nanlin Township]. In *Tietixiade xingfeng xueyu*, comp. Fu Heji, 538-50. Hainan: Hainan chubanshe, 1995.

Wang Yanhua. "Guanyu Rijun de 'weianfu' zhidu" [The Japanese military 'comfort woman' system]. *Qiqihaer daxue xuebao* 5 (1995): 125-28.

Wang Yexin. "Fengyi-lou weiansuo shimo" [The Fengyi-lou comfort station]. *Wuhu wenshi ziliao* 3: 17-23.

Wang, Yufeng. "Scholars propose memorializing 'comfort stations': The Ravages of Time." *Global Times*, 22 September 2011.

Wang Zhonglu and Liu Taiheng. *Guoren yifa qisu qin-Hua Rijun* [Chinese people's lawsuits against the Japanese military invaders]. Haikou: Hainan chubanshe, 1993.

Watanabe Kazuko. "Militarism, Colonialism, and the Trafficking of Women: 'Comfort Women' Forced into Sexual Labour for Japanese Soldiers." *Bulletin of Concerned Asian Scholars* 26, 4 (1994): 3-17.

Wen Yan. "Fengyang 'weiansuo'" [Fengyang comfort stations], and "Anhui Rijun 'weiansuo'" [Japanese military "comfort stations" in Anhui Province]. In *Qin-Hua Rijun baoxing zonglu*, comp. Li Bingxin, Xu Junyuan, and Shi Yuxin, 734 and 742-43. Shijiazhuang: Hebei renmin chubanshe, 1995.

Women's Active Museum on War and Peace. *Aruhi Nihongun ga yattekita: Chūgoku – Senjō de no kyōkan to ianjo* [One day the Japanese army came: China – rape and comfort stations at the battlefield], WAM catalog 6. Tokyo: Women's Active Museum on War and Peace, 2008.

Wood, Nancy. *Vectors of Memory: Legacies of Trauma in Postwar Europe*. Oxford: Berg, 1999.

Wu Guangyi. *Qin-Hua Rijun Nanjing datusha rizhi* [Chronology of Nanjin massacre committed by the Japanese army]. Beijing: Shehui kexue wenxian chubanshe, 2005.

Wu Liansheng (narrator), Lin Liangcai, Liang Chuntian, and Fu Heji (recorders). "Chuguan beige hongyan xuelei: Rijun Nada weiansuo qindu ji" [Tragic stories of the suffering women: The Japanese military Nada Comfort Station I witnessed], in *Tietixiade xingfeng xueyu: Rijun qin-Qiong baoxing shilu, Xu*, ed. Fu Heji, 272-79. Hainan: Hainan chubanshe, 1995.

Xiaosu. "'Weianfu' zhe yiye quru hei'an de lishi: Rijun zai Huabei shishi 'weianfu' zhidu zuixing shizheng" ("Comfort Women," a dark phase of history: Historical evidence of the Japanese military "comfort women" system in north China). *Dang'an tiandi* 4 (2004): 4-9.

Xie Zhonghou, Tian Susu, and He Tianyi, eds. *Riben qinlüe Huabei zuixing shigao* [A history of atrocities: Japan's invasion of northern China]. Beijing: Shehui kexue wenxian chubanshe, 2005.

Yamada Sadamu. *Kempei nikki* [A military policeman's diary]. Tokyo: Surugadai shobō, 1985.

Yamada Seikichi. *Bukan heitan: Shina hakkengun ian kakarichō no shuki* [The Wuhan commissariat: Memoir of the department head of the China detachment army comfort facilities]. Tokyo: Tosho shuppansha, 1978.

Yamashita Akiko. *Senso to onna no jinken* [War and women's human rights]. Tokyo: Akashi shoten, 1997.

Yang, Daqing. "Atrocities in Nanjing: Searching for Explanations." In *Scars of War: The Impact of Warfare on Modern China*, ed. Diana Lary and Stephen MacKinnon, 76-96. Vancouver: UBC Press, 2001.

Yang Jiechen "Rijun qinzhan Yaxian jiqi baoxing jishi" [Historical records of the Japanese military occupation of Ya County and the atrocities they committed]. In *Tietixiade xingfeng xueyu*, comp. Fu Heji, 401-13. Hainan: Hainan chubanshe, 1995.

Yoshida, Takashi. *The Making of the "Rape of Nanking:" History and Memory in Japan, China, and the United States*. Oxford: Oxford University Press, 2006.

Yoshida Seiji. *Chosenjin ianfu to Nihonjin: Moto Shimonoseki roho doin bucho no shuki* [Korean comfort women and Japanese people: Memoir of the former mobilization Department head]. Tokyo: Shinjinbutsu Oraisha, 1977.

Yoshimi Yoshiaki. *Comfort Women: Sexual Slavery in the Japanese Military during World War II*. Trans. Suzanne O'Brien. New York: Columbia University Press, 2000.

—. *Jugun ianfu* [Military comfort women]. Tokyo: Iwanami Shoten, 1995.

—, comp. *Jugun ianfu shiryoshu* [A collection of documents on military comfort women]. Tokyo: Otsuki Shoten, 1992.

Yoshimi Yoshiaki and Hayashi Hirofumi. *Kyodo kenkyu Nihongun ianfu* [A joint study: The Japanese forces' comfort women]. Tokyo: Otsuki shoten, 1995.

Yoshimi Yoshiaki (editor-in-chief), Utsumi Aiko, Udagawa Kota, Takahashi Shigehito, and Tsuchino Mizuho, eds. *Tokyo saiban: Seiboryoku kankei shiryo* [Tokyo trial: Documents regarding sexual violence]. Tokyo: Gendai shiryo shuppan, 2011.

Yun Chong-ok. *Chosenjin josei ga mita "ianfu mondai": Asu o tomo ni tsukuru tame ni* [The "comfort woman" issue from the perspective of Korean women: Creating tomorrow together]. Tokyo: Sanichi shobo, 1992.

Zhang Bofeng and Zhuang Jianping, comps., *Kang-Ri zhanzheng* [The Anti-Japanese War], 7 vols. Chengdu: Sichuan daxue chubanshe, 1997.

Zhang Huaiqing. "Fengyang da can'an" [Massacres in Fengyang]. In *Qin-Huan Rijun baoxing zonglu*, comp. Li Bingxin, Xu Junyuan, and Shi Yuxin, 710-11. Shijiazhuang: Hebei renmin chubanshe, 1995.

Zhang Lianhong and Li Guanglian. "Nanjing Xiaguan-qu qin-Hua Rijun weiansuo de diaocha baogao" [Investigative report on the Japanese military comfort stations in the Xiaguan District of Nanjing]. In *Taotian zuinie*, ed. Su Zhiliang, Rong Weimu, and Chen Lifei, 144-51. Shanghai: Xuelin chubanshe, 2000.

Zhang Xianwen, chief compiler. *Zhongguo kang-Ri zhanzheng shi* [A history of China's Resistance War against Japan]. Nanjing: Nanjing daxue chubanshe, 2001.

Zhang Yingyong. "Rijun ruqin Baoting-xian shimo" [The Japanese invasion of Baoting County]. In *Tietixiade xingfeng xueyu: Rijun qin-Qiong baoxing shilu*, comp. Fu Heji, 531-41. Hainan: Hainan chubanshe, 1995.

—. "Rijun 'Zhandi houqin fuwu dui' zhong de Lizu funü" [The Li ethnic women drafted into the Japanese military "Battlefield rear service team"]. *Baoting wenshi* 9 (1995): 17-21.

Zhong Qiang. "Wo suo zhidao de Rijun Huangliu jichang weiansuo" [The Japanese military Huangliu airport comfort station I saw]. In *Tietixiade xingfeng xueyu: Rijun qin-Qiong baoxing shilu*, comp. Fu Heji, 646-47. Hainan: Hainan chubanshe, 1995.

Zhongguo kang-Ri zhanzhengshi xüehui and Zhongguo renmin kang-Ri zhanzheng ji'nianguan. *Rijun qin-Hua baoxing shilu* [Records of atrocities committed by Japanese forces during their invasion of China]. Beijing: Beijing chubanshe, 1995.

Zhongyang Danganguan, Zhongguo Dier Lishi Danganguan, Hebei-sheng Shehui Kexueyang, comps., Tian Susu, ed. *Riben qinlüe Huabei zuixing dangan 9: Xingbaoli* [Documented war crimes during Japan's invasion of north China, volume 9: Sexual violence]. Shijiazhuang: Hebeirenming shubanshe, 2005.

Zhu Telan. "Taiwan 'weianfu' dang'an diaocha yu lishi zhenxiang yanjiu" [Archival investigations and the studies of the historical truth of the 'comfort women' in Taiwan]. *Yazhou zhoukan* 7 (1999): 19-25.

Index

Note: "(f)" following a page number indicates a figure; "(t)" following a page number indicates a table

users' military rank, 57; "entertainment"
facilities approved by military, 55-56;
established by Chinese collaborators,
56-57; formal comfort stations, 31, 42,
50, 54-55; improvised comfort stations,
10-11, 50, 54-55; locations, 52-53; management by civilian proprietors, under
military supervision, 55; mobile and
temporary, 50, 54; secret stations under
direct military control, 33-34. *See also*
comfort stations, management by
Japanese military
Comfort Woman: Slave of Destiny
(Henson), 2
comfort women: "comfort objects" and
"military supplies" according to military,
36, 45, 64-65; condom regulation and
usage, 60, 128, 132, 137; English publications of their narratives, 1-3; estimated number of victims in military system,
4, 6, 37-40; illegal drugs supplied by military or station proprietors, 71; Japanese
euphemism *ianfu*, 1; murdered at end
of war to destroy "evidence," 73-74, 190;
ransom paid by families or friends, xviii
11, 65, 73, 74, 92, 112; ratio of comfort
women to soldiers, 32, 37-38; "replacement rate" for comfort women, 37-38;
sexually transmitted diseases, infections,
61, 70; shame and silence about being
comfort women (until 1990s), xix, 5,
158; source materials for current book,
13-18; term specific to Japanese military's system of sexual slavery, 1; trans-
port to different locations, 36-37; true
number of deaths almost impossible to
determine, 40, 48. *See also* survivors'
narratives; *entries beginning with* comfort women
*The Comfort Women: Colonialism, War,
and Sex* (Choi), 2
*The Comfort Women: Sexual Violence
and Postcolonial Memory in Korea and
Japan* (Soh), 4, 9-10
Comfort Women: An Unfinished Ordeal
(International Commission of Jurists), 2
comfort women, drafted from Japan and
Korea, brutal treatment of, 44-45, 64-65,
190; death rate, 73; estimated number,
37-38; false job offers used to "recruit"
comfort women, 7; payments to and ex-

ploitation of, 63-65; registration of comfort women, 58; South Korean victims'
testimony about abuse, xxx, 2-3; trafficked to Chinese mainland, 31-32, 157-
58, 204n56; treatment of pregnant
Japanese woman, 60. *See also* redress
movements in South Korea for comfort
women; South Korea, postwar environment for comfort women
comfort women, drafted from Mainland
China: abuse of women considered a
"sport," 8-9, 70-71; brutal treatment, 4-5,
6, 12, 49, 69, 194-95; closely guarded as
"enemies" of Japan, 58, 61, 71, 92, 111,
128, 137, 143; Confucian social conventions and, 5; death rate, 40, 46, 48-49,
71-74; discrimination, ostracism, and
poverty of comfort women postwar,
5, 13, 77, 154-56, xix; distress recalling
trauma, 77-78, 88, 96, 101, 107, 117-18,
132-33, 137, 193; drug addiction (drugs
supplied by military or management),
69, 71; escapes from comfort stations,
71, 73, 74, 78, 100-1, 121-22, 138, 143-
44; female POWs, treatment, 47-48, 121;
grassroots movement in China to shed
light on issue, 6; Hou Dong'e and beginning of grassroots redress movement,
168; murder of comfort women with
forces' withdrawal from area, 73-74, 190,
212n27; number of deaths almost impossible to determine, 40, 48; number of victims, 4, 6, 37-40; payments to and money
owed by, 62-65, 129, 132; pregnant
women, murder and beating of, 48, 60,
105; prostitutes forced to become comfort women, 47; ransom paid for freedom, xviii, 11, 65, 73, 74, 92, 112; ratio of
comfort women to soldiers, 32, 37-38;
rescued by families or local people, 73,
74, 112, 123, 129, 132-33, 138, 143;
shame and silence about being comfort
women (until 1990s), xix, 5, 158; source
materials for current book, 13-18; suicide, 55, 57, 64, 68, 69, 71-72, 128; treatment under Cultural Revolution, 5, 129,
133, 140. *See also* Chen Yabian; Huang
Youliang; Lei Guiying; Li Lianchun; Lin
Yajin; Lu Xiuzhen; survivors' narratives;
Tan Yuhua; Wan Aihua; Yin Yulin; Yuan
Zhulin; Zhou Fenying; Zhu Qiaomei

Wuhan and Guangzhou (1938), 35, 102; Chinese casualties, 35, 204n2; Chinese forced labour, 16, 35, 110, 135, 142, 166, 204n3; Chinese Hundred Regiments Offensive, 114; Chinese resistance, 21-22, 27, 35, 40, 102, 108, 114, 141; comfort station system expanded after Nanjing (1937), 10, 29-33; comfort station system started in Shanghai (1932), 22; invasion of Yunnan Province (1942), 141; Japanese occupation in Manchuria (1932), 13, 21; Lugou-qiao (Marco Polo Bridge) incident (1937), 27; makeshift comfort stations, 10-11; Mukden (or Manchurian) Incident (1931), 21; Nanjing Massacre (Rape of Nanjing) (1937), 13, 27-28; Operation Destroy All (Japanese), 35, 154; random rapes and murder of civilians by soldiers rarely punished, 29; Sino-Japanese Joint Communiqué (1972) and war compensation, 166-68, 175, 180-81; Sino-Japanese Peace Treaty (1952, with Taiwan), 175, 179-81; soldiers permitted to rape and then kill Chinese women, 48-49; source documents, 14; treatment of female Chinese POWs, 47-48, 121; US air force assistance to Chinese military operations, 141. *See also* Chinese forces; Japanese military
Self-Guard Corps, 116, 126, 132
Senda Kakō, 17, 37, 160
Shanghai: abduction of women for comfort stations, 47; army comfort stations, 25-26; battles at Shanghai, 21-22, 27; comfort station infrastructure provided by the Japanese *kashizashiki* (brothel), 23-24; early naval comfort stations, 22-23; the first formal comfort station in China, 22; Japanese prostitutes pre-1932, 23-24; Military Entertainment Facility, 37; number and size of comfort stations, 11, 25, 25(f), 33; occupation by Japanese (1932), 22, 27
Shanghai Normal University: Chinese Comfort Women Archives, 135(f), 156, 188-89. *See also* Research Centre for Chinese "Comfort Women" (Shanghai Normal University)
Shanxi Province: comfort women system perpetuated after end of war, 188; estab-lishment of Hejia-xiang Brothel, 42-43; first lawsuit against Japanese government by Shanxi residents, 174; formation of transnational support groups for redress movement, 168; international groups' investigations into comfort women issue, 172-73; occupation by Japanese (1937), 114. *See also* Yu County, Shanxi Province
Shen Fugen, 53-54
Shen Panwen, 167
Shen Xiaomei, 53-54
Shen Yuexian, 53-54
Shi Liuliu, 53-54
Shikanai Nobutaka, 36
Shimizu Yukiko, 173
Silence Broken: Korean Comfort Women (Kim-Gibson), 2
Sino-Japanese Joint Communiqué (1972): debate over right of individual Chinese to claim war compensation, 166-68, 175, 180-81; defence in second lawsuit by Chinese survivors, 175; nullification of Sino-Japanese Peace Treaty (1952), 180
Sino-Japanese Peace and Friendship Treaty (1978), 166
Sino-Japanese Peace Treaty (1952, with Taiwan), 175, 179-81
Soh, C. Sarah, 4, 9-10
Song Fuhai, 58-59
South Korea, postwar environment for comfort women: apology by Japanese prime minister (1992), 161; financial aid for former comfort women, 187, 224n13; Korean Council for the Women Drafted for Military Sexual Slavery by Japan, 2; Museum of Sexual Slavery by Japanese Military, 188; recommendation urging Japan to accept responsibility for comfort women system, 184; Research Association on the Women Drafted for Military Sexual Slavery by Japan, 2, 13-14, 36-37; *Silence Broken: Korean Comfort Women* (Kim-Gibson), 2; South Korean Church Women's Alliance, 160; *True Stories of Korean Comfort Women* (Howard), 2; War and Women's Human Rights Museum, Seoul, 190; Yun Chong-ok, 160. *See also* comfort women, draft-ed from Japan and Korea; redress

movements in South Korea for comfort women

South Korean Church Women's Alliance, 160

Su Guangming, 133, 169

Su Shi, 169

Su Zhiliang: on brutalization of Chinese civilians in "recruiting" comfort women, 8; estimated number of comfort women and "replacement" rate, 6, 38; financial aid for comfort station survivors, 187; financial contribution to cost of investigation, 170; investigation of comfort women system on Hainan Island, 173; leader in researching comfort women in China, 13-14, 169; on location of Yangjiazhai Entertainment Centre, 53; photograph, 173(f); prosecutor at Women's International War Crimes Tribunal, 182; response to AWF inquiry, 163-64; on scope of victimization, 11; verification of survivors' stories, 78, 144, 194

Sugino Shigeru, 31

survivors' narratives: contribution to current knowledge of comfort women, 6-12; interview process, 77-78; Liu Mianhuan, xvii-xix; reason for telling these stories, xx; testimonies largely unavailable to non-Chinese-speaking audiences, 6; testimonies notarized, 77, 101; verification of oral accounts, 78-79, 194. *See also* Chen Yabian; Huang Youliang; Lei Guiying; Li Lianchun; Lin Yajin; Lu Xiuzhen; Tan Yuhua; Wan Aihua; Yin Yulin; Yuan Zhulin; Zhou Fenying; Zhu Qiaomei

Suzuki Hiraku, 42

Suzuki Yūko, 17

Taguchi Shinkichi, 47-48

Taipei Women's Rescue Foundation, 163, 186

Taiwan, postwar environment for comfort women: "comfort women's" museum, 186; financial aid for former comfort women, 187, 224n13; lawsuit on behalf of survivors against Japanese government, 177-78; recommendation urging Japan to accept responsibility for comfort women system, 184; Taipei Women's Rescue Foundation to aid comfort

women, 163, 186; Taiwanese women trafficked by Japanese as comfort women, 31-32, 189. *See also* comfort women, drafted from Taiwan

Takagi Ken'ichi, 17

Takemae Eiji, 152, 163

Takizawa Takaomi, 176

Tan Guifu, 112

Tan Yadong, 176-77

Tan Yaluan, 136

Tan Yayou, 136

Tan Yuhua: bailed out by Yao Jufeng, 112; deteriorating health, 113, 197; early life, 109-10; kidnapped and enslavement as comfort woman, 110-12; life and marriages after enslavement, 112-13; photograph, 108; talk in 2008 about experiences, 187(f)

Tan Yulian, 176-77

Tanaka, Yuki, 9, 51

Tanaka Toshiyuki, 17

Taotian zuinie: Erzhan shiqi de Rijun weianfu zhidu (Monstrous atrocities: The Japanese military comfort women system during the Second World War), 16-17

three alls (kill all, loot all, burn all; *sanguang*), 35, 154

Tietixiade xingfeng xueyu: Rijun qin-Qiong baoxing shilu (Bloody crimes of the occupation rule: Records of the atrocities committed by the Japanese military in Hainan), 16

Tokyo War Crimes Tribunal, 29

Tomishima Kenji, 8-9

Tong Zeng, 165-66, 167, 218n25

Tongcheng, Hubei Province, comfort station, 44-45, 64-65

Totsuka Etsurō, 17

True Stories of Korean Comfort Women (Howard), 2

Tsen, Shui Fang, Mrs., 30

Tsuchiya Kōken, 173, 185

Uchida Tomoyuki, 17, 154

Ueno Chizuko, 17

United Kingdom, on Japan's responsibility for comfort women system, 184

United Nations, reports on Japan's legal liability for sex slavery (1996, 1998), 164-65, 179-80

THE OXFORD ORAL HISTORY SERIES

J. TODD MOYE (University of North Texas),
KATHRYN NASSTROM (University of San Francisco), and
ROBERT PERKS (The British Library), *Series Editors*
DONALD A. RITCHIE, *Senior Advisor*